Sacred Secrets

Sacred Secrets

Prison Empire Publishing books may be ordered through the author, booksellers or by contacting:

PrisonEmpirePublishing@protonmail.com

Cover Art was designed by Kenya K.

ISBN: *979-8-2956-3209-9*

Printed in the United States of America

Dedication

For those who have carried unbearable truths in silence.

For anyone who has ever wondered, "Am I still worthy of love after everything?"

For those learning that healing is not perfection, but permission.

Prologue

Secrets.
Everyone has a secret. Some have more than one.

Secrets of the heart.
Secrets of the soul.
Childhood secrets.
Financial secrets.
Adult secrets.

Some are small. Some are devastating. Some never change shape, no matter how long we carry them.

Dark secrets.
Sweet secrets.
Secrets built around a lie.

Secrets.

Those hidden areas of one's life. Those concealed thoughts and intentions. Those masked feelings or private identities. They do not arrive all at once. They accumulate.

Secrets that carry weight. Burdens often too heavy to carry alone, yet impossible to release. Secrets that hold dire consequences. And still, we keep them.

Secrets that make you smile when no one is looking.

Naughty secrets.

Embarrassing secrets.

Devastating secrets.

Some are held so tightly that they become sacred. Secrets do not only live inside people. They live inside places.

Cities hold secrets the way bodies do, quietly and without apology. They absorb them through brick and pavement, through whispers exchanged on sidewalks, through confessions uttered behind closed doors and promises made under dim lights. A city remembers everything, even when the people inside it try to forget.

Washington, DC is a city built on secrets.

Behind its monuments and museums, behind the polished facades and carefully measured power, there are truths buried beneath marble and concrete. There are stories never written down. Decisions never spoken aloud. Lives shaped in silence. The city breathes secrecy into those who walk its streets, teaching them how to compartmentalize, how to perform, how to survive.

Homes hold secrets too.

Every house has a memory embedded in its walls. Every doorway remembers who crossed its threshold and what they carried with them. Laughter lingers. Pain echoes. The past settles into corners and closets, unseen but present. Some homes feel warm because they have learned how to hold joy. Others feel heavy because they have learned how to hold grief.

And some homes, no matter how beautiful, hold truths that were never meant to be spoken.

But the most dangerous secrets do not live in cities or houses. They live in people. They live in the places we refuse to look.

In the memories we rename. In the moments we justify. In the wounds we normalize.

They hide in the body, long after the mind has learned how to move on. They lodge themselves in desire, in fear, in longing, in habit. They shape the way we love, the way we touch, the way we pull away.

Some secrets are born in innocence and carried into adulthood like unfinished sentences. Others are forged in moments of confusion, when right and wrong blur, and the body learns lessons the heart cannot explain. Some secrets arrive suddenly. Others grow slowly, fed by silence and survival.

There are secrets that protect us. And secrets that destroy us. There are secrets we keep because we are ashamed. And secrets we keep because telling them would fracture everything we have built. There are secrets that ask to be healed. And secrets that demand to be honored, even when they hurt.

And then there are sacred secrets. The ones wrapped in ritual and routine. The ones justified by faith, by love, by loyalty, by fear. The ones we kneel beside. The ones we pray over. The ones we swear will never be spoken.

Sacred secrets are the most dangerous of all. Because they convince us we are doing the right thing, even as they slowly undo us.

This is a story about those secrets. The ones whispered in quiet rooms. The ones hidden behind professional titles and polished smiles. The ones buried beneath devotion and desire. The ones passed down through memory, culture, and silence. The ones that refuse to stay buried.

This is a story about what happens when secrets collide. When the past reaches forward. When the sacred and the forbidden blur. When a life built on strength begins to fracture under the weight of what was never healed.

Some secrets survive the dark.

Others demand the light.

And some, once revealed, change everything.

Chapter One

Tuesday. A blustery late winter, early spring morning. Too early to be unpacking feelings. That was certain.

Dr. Zora Holley stood at the bottom of the cement steps, staring up at the building in front of her. Twelve steps. She counted them automatically, the way she always did. Twelve steps between avoidance and effort. Twelve steps between control and vulnerability.

She did not move.

Her shoulders were squared, posture polished, coat buttoned neatly, the picture of composure. Anyone passing by would have seen a confident woman, professionally dressed, unbothered. No one would have guessed that she was frozen, locked in a silent negotiation with herself.

"Probably another unproductive session," she thought.

Another hour of circling. Another hour of intellectualizing pain instead of touching it.

She knew better. She knew all the language. She taught this language. She had lectured on it. Written about it. Spoken about it on stages in rooms full of strangers who trusted her with their stories.

Even therapists need therapists.

She believed that. She told her clients that.

What she did not believe was that she was doing this well.

In fact, she was certain she was the worst client imaginable.

She exhaled slowly. Drew in a breath that felt shallow no matter how hard she tried to deepen it. Her chest was already tight, already buzzing with anticipation and resistance.

One step.

Then another.

By the time she reached the entrance, her palms were damp.

The lobby greeted her with quiet grandeur. Polished marble floors reflected the muted morning light. Tall columns rose toward a ceiling that carried decades of whispered intentions. The air smelled old and clean at the same time, like history that had learned how to polish itself.

Framed portraits lined the walls. Black historians. Philanthropists. Civil rights crusaders. Faces that had endured, survived, and carried burdens larger than themselves. Their eyes followed her as she walked, steady and unblinking.

This building had once been a landmark. Now it housed organizations devoted to healing, advocacy, and inner-city causes. Two therapy practices occupied different floors, as if the building itself understood that one kind of healing was never enough.

Her footsteps echoed as she moved toward the elevator. Too loud. Too present. She hated that sound. It made her feel seen.

Her fingers trembled slightly as she pressed the call button.

Third floor.

Her breathing was shallow now, her thoughts racing ahead of her body.

You can do this, Zora.

She considered turning around. Considered leaving. Considered pretending she had an emergency, a meeting, a class, anything.

But the elevator doors opened before she could decide.

The ride up felt longer than it was. Her reflection in the mirrored panel looked calm. Controlled. Unbothered. The image felt dishonest.

When the doors slid open, Libby was already standing at the desk, smiling brightly as if she had been waiting for her.

"Good morning, Ms. Holley. Great to see you again. Let me check you in."

Libby's energy was relentless in the best way. Cheerful. Efficient. Warm. The kind of person who made optimism feel effortless.

Zora managed a polite smile.

"Good morning."

Libby clicked her mouse, eyes scanning the screen. "All checked in. Dr. Hanson will be with you shortly."

Zora nodded. "Thank you, Libby."

The smile she gave this time was thinner. More practiced. She did not want conversation. Did not want warmth. Did not want to be cracked open by kindness before she was ready.

She sat, clasping her hands together, staring at a framed poster about self-awareness and emotional safety. Words she knew by heart. Words she had said to others a thousand times.

Libby's voice cut through her thoughts.

"Dr. Hanson is ready to see you now."

Zora stood, her legs feeling slightly heavier than they should have. She walked down the hall slowly, the carpet muting her steps. The last door on the left bore a placard that read:

Dr. Gemini "Gemi" Hanson

Zora paused before knocking. Just for a second.

Then she tapped lightly.

"Come on in."

Dr. Gemi Hanson's office was a sanctuary. Warm without being sleepy. Calm without being sterile. Green plants filled the room, perched on shelves, windowsills, and corners like quiet sentinels. The air carried a gentle blend of sage and lilac, grounding without being overwhelming.

The walls held images of Black people from all walks of life. Faces that had known struggle and survived it. African prints and pieces of mud cloth hung thoughtfully, draped from preserved wood rods. Nothing felt accidental. Nothing felt performative.

Dr. Hanson sat in a leather club chair, her posture relaxed, her presence steady. Sister locs framed her face beneath a vibrant headwrap. Her clothing spoke of heritage and authority, softness and strength.

She did not conduct sessions from behind a desk. Zora appreciated that. Barriers mattered.

Zora lowered herself into the chair across from her, smoothing her skirt automatically.

"Zora," Dr. Hanson said gently. "How have you been? It's been about a month since you last came in. Tell me what your month has been like."

Zora shrugged slightly. "It's been okay. Busy. Nothing much to report. Things are as well as can be."

Dr. Hanson did not respond immediately. She studied Zora with the practiced calm of someone who had learned how to listen beneath words.

"Zora," she said, "generic responses are not a pathway to healing. You know that. Therapy requires more than showing up to get past the deeper things. You've been seeing me for over six months now. What do you think has been accomplished?"

Zora rolled her eyes internally. Externally, she smiled faintly.

"This space isn't comfortable for me," she admitted. "Talking about my issues. I can help others. Helping myself feels… different. Harder. I know it's fear. I just can't seem to reach those places that keep haunting me. Sometimes I feel like I'm wasting your time."

Dr. Hanson nodded once.

"Only you can breach that fear," she said. "I can't do it for you. You show up physically, but you don't engage mentally or emotionally. Healing doesn't come from facades, platitudes, or reasoning your way around your truth."

Zora's hands twisted together in her lap. Her eyes dropped to the floor. Her shoulders curved inward, her body shrinking in a way she hated but could not stop.

"I want to try something today," Dr. Hanson continued. "I need you to trust me and the process."

Zora let out a short breath. "Trust is not a word I respond to easily."

"I'm not here to harm you," Dr. Hanson said calmly. "You need movement. This technique may open that door. May I try it?"

Zora closed her eyes. Tilted her head back. Breathed in. Breathed out.

"Sure."

"I'd like to introduce EMDR," Dr. Hanson said. "Guided eye movements to help the brain reprocess distressing memories. We're just introducing it today. All you need to do is follow along."

"I guess I'm as ready as I'll ever be," Zora said, her sarcasm thin and brittle.

Dr. Hanson began the process, guiding her gently toward relaxation. Zora resisted. Her mind fought. Her body tightened. She made excuses internally, questioned the technique, clung to control.

Then, without warning, it happened.

A flash.

A memory.

Sharp. Intrusive. Uninvited.

Her body reacted before her mind could make sense of it. Her breath hitched. Her heart began to race. Tears flooded her eyes as panic surged through her chest.

"No," she whispered, though she did not know who she was speaking to.

"Zora," Dr. Hanson said softly. "Breathe. Can you hear me?"

Zora could not.

She was already standing, already grabbing her coat and purse, already running.

"Zora, wait," Dr. Hanson said, rising. "Ground yourself. Stay with me."

But Zora was gone.

She bolted down the hallway, past the reception desk.

"Ms. Holley, we need to schedule your next appoint…"

The words blurred as Zora flew past, pamphlets scattering in her wake. Libby gasped, rushing to gather them as Zora slammed her hand against the elevator button.

"Come on. Come on. Hurry up."

When the doors finally opened, she nearly collided with a woman and a small boy exiting. She barely registered their startled faces as she pressed herself into the corner.

Her skin was slick with sweat. Her hair clung damply to her neck. Her hands shook as she jabbed at the lobby button.

"Hurry. Hurry."

When the doors opened again, she burst out, nearly tripping down the cement steps, cursing her shoes, tears burning hot and unstoppable.

She staggered to the back of the building and collapsed against the brick wall, hands braced on her knees, gasping for air.

Her chest tightened painfully.

Am I having a heart attack?

Rain began to fall, soaking her tan and brown houndstooth trench coat. She did not care. Her body shook violently as the world spun.

Oh God. I'm dying.

Her heartbeat thundered in her ears, loud and relentless.

Focus.

Her eyes locked onto a stop sign at the corner.

Red. White letters.

Inhale.

Exhale.

Again.

She was not dying.

She was having an anxiety attack.

And she had a class to teach in an hour.

She had to breathe.

Chapter Two

Dr. Zora Leigh Holley is twenty-eight years old. An only child. Named after her father's favorite writer, Zora Neale Hurston.

Black. Korean. Born in Texas during her father's military assignment at Wright-Patterson Air Force Base.

Her childhood unfolded in transit.

Different states.

Different schools.

Different climates.

Different accents.

Different rules.

Home was not a place so much as a rhythm she learned to carry inside herself. Pack quickly. Adapt faster. Read the room. Perform competence. Do not complain.

By the time the family settled in Washington, DC during her middle school years, Zora had already mastered the art of becoming whoever a space required her to be.

She learned to bow respectfully during Korean holidays, hands folded, eyes lowered, honoring ancestry and tradition. She learned to stand firm in Black military family culture, spine straight, voice steady, excellence expected and demanded. She learned how to move between worlds without drawing attention to the seams.

Strength was not optional. It was expected.

Even when she felt fractured.

Now, as an adult, she lived in Shaw, in a renovated three-level brownstone that looked like stability incarnate. Her therapy practice occupied the ground floor. Upstairs, her personal life was quiet, curated, controlled.

Zora was a woman made of contradictions.

Emotionally warm yet internally numb.

Brilliant yet unraveling.

Deeply compassionate yet unable to extend that compassion to herself.

She was nurturing, hyper-competent, creative, intuitive.

She was also haunted, clinging, and quietly self-destructive.

On paper, her life was impeccable.

Bachelor of Arts in Psychology from Spelman College.

Master's degree in Mental Health Counseling from Georgia University.

PhD in Counseling and Psychological Studies from Regent University.

She was a licensed counselor with a thriving private practice. A national speaker on trauma and mental health. An adjunct professor at Howard University. An advocate serving marginalized communities. A familiar face at annual mental health fundraisers and donor events.

Applause followed her often.

And still, beneath the titles and recognition, beneath the packed calendar and polished smile, Zora battled a compulsive pattern of seeking. Searching. Digging beneath a truth she refused to name out loud.

A secret that gnawed at her from the inside.

***

Her 11:35 a.m. PSYC 101 class ended in controlled chaos.

The undergraduate students were loud, opinionated, curious, and alive in that way only people just beginning adulthood could be. They asked questions that spiraled. They debated theories with half-formed certainty. They challenged ideas with confidence that had not yet been bruised by experience.

After the morning she'd had with Dr. Hanson, they were a welcome distraction.

As the last student exited the classroom, Zora leaned against her desk and exhaled. 1:15 p.m.

When did I last eat?

She frowned slightly, scrolling through her memory. Breakfast felt distant. Maybe nonexistent.

Did I even eat today?

She reached into the desk drawer and pulled out her phone, thumb hovering for a moment before opening her messages. Without thinking too hard about it, she texted Lai.

***

Lai Timmons was twenty-eight years old.

Chinese American.

Adopted by a Black family at ten months old.

She grew up in Maryland before finishing middle and high school in DC. Like Zora, Lai learned early how to navigate layered identities. She was an Asian face in a Black household. A daughter in a family rooted in love, rhythm, and resilience.

Her parents anchored her in warmth, stability, music, and tradition. R&B slow jams hummed through her childhood. Saturday mornings meant cleaning the house together, gospel music playing in the background. Chinese New Year celebrations were honored alongside summer cookouts and open mic nights.

Her upbringing was multicultural, intentional, and full. Still, there were quiet questions she carried about belonging. Gratitude and curiosity coexisted in her heart.

Lai's voice was a gift. The kind that settled into your bones and stayed there. She earned her Bachelor's degree in Music with a focus on vocal studies and went on to complete a Master's in Business Entrepreneurship at UNC Chapel Hill.

She lived in Dupont Circle and owned Jazz-n-Gems, an intimate jazz spot tucked near the U Street and Adams Morgan border. It was her masterpiece. Her sanctuary. Her offering to the city.

Dim lighting greeted guests at the door. Velvet seating invited conversation. Polished wood floors reflected chandeliers that glowed like melted gold. The stage washed performers in soft blues and purples.

Live jazz.

Open mic poetry.

Spoken word salons.

Curated cocktails.

Chef-designed small plates.

Jazz-n-Gems was where people came to breathe.

Zora often said exactly that.

Lai was the friend everyone leaned on. Calm voice. Open heart. Wise counsel delivered without judgment. She read rooms effortlessly, sensed shifts before words caught up.

In their friend group, Lai was the emotional thermostat. The mediator. The balance keeper. The one who noticed when Zora tilted, even if she did not know why. First to comfort. Last to judge.

***

Zora scrolls to a previous text from Lai.

Zora: Lai, you up for a late lunch?

A few seconds passed.

Lai: Heeey, Z! What you thinkin? I gotta be back at Jazz-n-Gems by 3. Order coming in and my stock clerk is out sick. Inventory waits for no one.

Zora smiled faintly.

Zora: Something quick. Can't remember if I ate today or not. LOL.

Lai: You that busy you forgot to eat? That would never be me. Meet me at Ben's Chili Bowl. I gotta stay close so I can dodge this DC traffic.

Zora: I'll be there in thirty. Just leaving HU. Had a great class.

They met, ate quickly, laughed about nothing and everything. Lai shared updates about upcoming artists scheduled to perform at Jazz-n-Gems, promising to drop details in the group chat later. Zora listened, nodded, smiled.

Her mind drifted.

I'm not going back, she thought briefly. *I can't.*

She did not say it out loud.

She mentioned an upcoming conference in two weeks, spoke about how ready she was for a change of scenery. Lai nodded, unaware of how deeply that escape was already being romanticized in Zora's mind.

Lunch ended with a hug.

"National Harbor, Friday," Lai reminded her. "The Felt. Seven sharp."

"Yeah," Zora replied, her voice a half-beat behind. *Shake it off, Z. Shake it off.*

Chapter Three

Outside, the air had chilled again. Typical early spring in DC. Zora walked to the next block where her Lexus sat parked at a meter blinking dangerously close to expiration.

Relief washed over her as she slid into the driver's seat.

I do not need another parking ticket.

She buckled in and pushed the start button, shivering.

I should have remote-started this car. It's cold.

The engine hummed to life just as her Bluetooth chimed.

Rayven.

***

Rayven Allen was twenty-eight years old. Black. A daughter of DC, raised in Brookland near the arts corridor. She met Zora in the eleventh grade.

Rayven was earth in human form.

She was soulful, intuitive, deeply connected to her body and spirit. An old soul wrapped in youthful grace. She grounded spaces simply by existing in them.

A graduate of Duke Ellington School of the Arts, she earned a full scholarship to Fordham University and the Alvin Ailey School. Ballet. Modern. West African. Jazz. Contemporary. Somatic movement.

Dance was not something Rayven did. It was how she breathed.

She returned home to build Steps Urban Dance Studio near the Rhode Island Avenue Arts District. Brick walls. Hardwood floors. Mirrors wrapped in vines. Incense and essential oils lingering in the air. Afrocentric artwork. Warm lighting. A space that felt alive.

She also founded Keeping Step, a nonprofit program serving underserved youth. Through movement, she taught discipline, expression, breath, and emotional regulation. Her kids adored her.

Rayven noticed everything.

***

Zora answered the call.

"What's up, Ray? What you doing?"

"Trying to stay warm," Rayven laughed. "My joints are stiff from this winter. Cold weather is a dancer's enemy. What you up to?"

"Just had a quick lunch with Lai. Heading home for tea, a book on my lap."

That's not true, Zora thought. *Not even close.*

"Girl," Rayven laughed, "you need more than tea and a juicy book. You need a man."

"No, I do not," Zora replied quickly. "I am good. My life is full. Work, family, travel, y'all. I'm satisfied."

Too satisfied, her mind whispered.

Rayven chuckled. "Okay, okay. I just wanted to check in. You went ghost on me."

"I'm good," Zora said. "Just a lot going on."

Rayven did not press. She rarely did. "Love you, Z."

"Love you too."

As the call was ending, another came through.

Her mother.

Before Zora clicks over to her mother's call, she takes a deep, cleansing breath. Her fingers rest on the steering wheel for a moment longer than necessary. Middle-of-the-day calls from her mother are rarely casual.

What does she want right now?

She exhales slowly, then taps the accept button.

"Annyeong, Eomma!" she says warmly, Korean for *Hi, Momma.*

"Jigeum bappeuseyo? Hoksi gwaenchanheuseyo?" her mother asks. *Are you busy? Did I catch you at a good time?*

Zora smiles despite herself. "English, Mommy," she says, laughing lightly.

Her mother chuckles. "I know, my Zora. I just don't want you to forget the language of your heritage. Knowing Korean is important to your history. It is our responsibility to pass the language and traditions to each generation so they do not get lost in our American lives."

Oh God... is she about to ask me about children and my 'old' age?

"I get it, Mommy. I do," Zora says quickly, her tone softening. "No disrespect meant. I love our language and our heritage. Sometimes I get so comfortable with English that I forget to switch when we talk. I'll do better, I promise. Now tell me what's going on. You okay? Daddy okay?"

"Daddy is doing fine," her mother replies. "Just wearing himself out trying to climb to the next rank. You know how he gets when he is focused. He loves you, Zora. He is just consumed with his military career."

Zora goes quiet, absorbing the familiar explanation.

He loves you, Zora. He's just consumed with his military career.

She stares straight ahead through the windshield, that sentence settling heavily in her chest. She wonders, not for the first time, where that left her when she was growing up. Where it leaves her now, when she still longs for her father's tenderness outside of structure, rank, rules, and expectations.

Her mother continues, unaware of the silence on the other end. "Anyway, I was reaching out to remind you about family dinner on Sunday. I know you remember, but it is your turn to bring the appetizers. I have a taste for Tteokbokki, those little spicy rice cakes, or Mandu, the Korean dumplings. Surprise me," she says, laughing.

Zora smiles, grateful for the shift. "Yes, Mommy," she replies. "I'll surprise you. Four o'clock, right?"

"Yes, my daughter. Four o'clock."

"See you then. I love you. Saranghaeyo, Eomma."

"Nado saranghaeyo, Zora," her mother replies warmly. "Annyeong. I love you too, Zora. Bye-bye."

"Najung-e yaegihaja, Eomma," Zora says softly. *Talk to you later, Mommy.*

The call ends, leaving the car quiet again.

Zora rests her head briefly against the headrest. She has beautiful friends who ground her. Parents who love her, even if her father's love feels distant and duty-bound. She tells herself it is the military training, the discipline, the lifelong conditioning.

Still, the ache remains.

If he had only been more present... would I be so damaged?

The question lingers, unanswered.

Chapter Four

Whew.

The end of another week.

Work stacked on work. Hours of lecturing as a professor, standing in front of eager students who looked at her like she had already figured life out. Six hours of mentoring inner-city youth at the community recreation center off Martin Luther King Jr. Avenue SE, where laughter, pain, bravado, and survival instincts lived side by side. Writing drafts and rewriting drafts of her next keynote for a three-day conference in Georgia, trying to distill trauma into something digestible for an audience that wanted insight without discomfort.

All of it pressing against her at once.

The internal tension never let up. It pulled at her constantly, quietly at first, then louder when she tried to ignore it. A low hum beneath everything she did. Trying to derail what she had worked so hard to become. What she was working even harder to forget.

A constant battle.

She felt the draw growing stronger. More insistent. Less patient.

The tilt.

She could feel it hovering at the edge of her awareness, waiting for her guard to drop. Waiting for exhaustion to win. Waiting for her to slip.

Not this time, she told herself. *I have to win this time.*

It was imperative.

***

Friday evening arrived with the illusion of relief. The temperature had crept up just enough to take the bite out of the air, hovering around fifty degrees as the sun dipped lower in the sky. The city buzzed with weekend anticipation.

Zora, Rayven, Lai, and Nico made their way toward their bi-monthly besties gathering, each in their own rhythm.

Zora drove her Lexus, hands steady on the wheel, grateful for the familiarity of leather seats and climate control. She rarely took public transportation. Too many people. Too many variables. Too much time to think.

Rayven maneuvered her Jeep through traffic, windows cracked slightly, music low, heading to pick Lai up at Jazz-n-Gems before they made their way south.

Nico rode in an Uber, already texting in all caps. He knew himself well enough not to drive tonight. He planned to turn up. Better safe than sorry.

Their destination was **The Felt Bar and Lounge**, tucked inside the MGM National Harbor Casino in Oxon Hill, Maryland. Lai had made the reservation a full month in advance. That was how coveted the spot was. Reservations only. No walk-ins. No exceptions.

Their routine was intentional. Every other besties gathering was upscale. The ones in between were casual, low-pressure, neighborhood vibes. Twice a month, they relaxed, related, and released. It was ritual. It was maintenance. It was survival.

***

As expected, Friday traffic was unforgiving.

Nico arrived first.

Within seconds, all three women felt their phones buzz.

Nico: I'm here. Just got our table. Table 20. Left side. Fourth booth near the center bar. Get your asses in here. NOW. This place is like THAT and I'm ready to parrrrrrrtaaaaaaay!!

In three different parts of the city, three identical eye rolls happened.

That's Nico, Zora thought, despite herself.

Nico Givens rounded out their besties group with unapologetic volume and presence. Twenty-nine years old. Afro-Latino. Raised in Adams Morgan back when it still felt like a neighborhood before gentrification pushed out half the community and renamed the rest.

He met Zora in the tenth grade when she was running late and nearly ran him over racing to her literature class.

"Where's the fire, girl?" he had called out.

They laughed then. They never stopped. They've been attached at the hip ever since. Their history? Complex, but steady.

Nico was vibration in human form. Loud. Bright. Spicy. Emotional. Deeply loyal. Always two seconds away from saying something that made everyone groan and ask why.

But they loved him.

He was charismatic and fiercely protective, especially when it came to Zora. Opinionated, intuitive with people, and terrible at introspection. The friend who would fight for you at three in the morning without hesitation. The one who texted in all caps when excited. The one who side-eyed anyone who looked at Zora too long.

Absurdly gifted, Nico could pick up anything with strings, keys, or sticks and make it sing. Saxophone was his first love. His baby. But he also played drums, classical and electric guitar, piano. He composed, wrote music, and sang quietly when he thought no one was listening.

His sound came from lineage. Go-Go rhythms. Peruvian percussion from his mother's side. Church music. Freestyle sessions in neighborhood alleys. Jazz influences from U Street. Latin beats from family cookouts.

Music was his sanctuary. His therapy. His language. His way of staying alive.

By day, he worked as a social worker, devoted to Black and Brown boys navigating trauma, anger, and instability.

He let them talk while tapping drumsticks on desks. He met them where they were. He remembered what it felt like to be them.

On the side, he taught music. Sax lessons. Drum technique. Beginner piano. Songwriting. Rhythm therapy. Weekend workshops at community centers in Columbia Heights, Brightwood, and Petworth.

A hood griot. A storyteller through sound.

Within the group, Nico was the protector. The stop-doing-dumb-shit truth-teller. The loud laugher. The one who cussed the most. The one who threatened to check Zora's situationships. The one who hugged Lai the longest, danced with Rayven without making it weird, and always paid the check when he felt emotional.

His bond with Zora ran deepest. He saw through her. Called out what he called her "shadow bullshit." Never let her hide behind intelligence or credentials. He was terrified of losing her to the tilt he could feel creeping closer.

And he would fight the entire city for her if it came to that.

Their bond was familial. Intense. Sacred.

***

The elevator doors slide shut behind them, the three women instantly filling the small, mirrored space with perfume, laughter, and energy.

Rayven tilts her head, inspecting Zora from head to toe.

"Mmm. Okay, Doctor Holley," she says slowly. "I see you. Very 'I counsel by day, ruin lives by night.'"

Zora laughs, smoothing the front of her dress. "Please. This is conservative for National Harbor."

Lai chuckles, adjusting her jacket. "Says the woman whose hemline keeps creeping north every time we go somewhere with a view."

Rayven snaps her fingers. "Clocked."

Zora rolls her eyes. "Y'all are ridiculous."

"Ridiculous and correct," Lai replies calmly. "Now Ray, turn around. Let me see the back."

Rayven pivots. Lai nods approvingly.

"Yeah. That's the one. That outfit says, 'I'm grounded, but I can still take your man.'"

The elevator dings.

As the doors open, sound spills in immediately. Music. Laughter. The low hum of money, indulgence, and anticipation. The casino floor glows, lights bouncing off polished surfaces, slot machines chiming in rhythmic chaos.

Zora feels it instantly.

The charge.

The hum beneath her skin.

Stay present, she tells herself. *Just enjoy the night.*

They step off together, heels clicking in unison as they follow the signage toward The Felt Bar & Lounge.

Chapter Five

The entrance to The Felt opens into sultry elegance. Curved couches wrap around low tables. Clusters of people lean close, voices low and intimate. The center bar glows softly, encircled by booths like a crown. Glasses clink. Laughter rises and falls. A live band hums through the space, smooth and unhurried.

"This place is sexy," Rayven murmurs.

Lai smiles. "That's why you dress with intention."

Zora scans the room, absorbing it all.

Too much stimulation, a quiet voice warns.

She pushes it away.

Then she sees him.

Nico, already half out of his seat, arm waving wildly.

"There they are!" he shouts. "The reason this place just got hotter!"

They weave through the crowd and slide into the booth.

Nico grins, drink in hand. "What's up, my chicas? 'Bout damn time you huzzies arrived."

Rayven gasps dramatically. "Huzzies? Did he just call us huzzies?"

She leans forward. "I got your huzzie right here. That's the last one for the night, bruh."

Nico laughs hard. "All love. All love. Y'all know I don't mean nothing by it."

"Too much love in that sentence," Lai says calmly, lifting the menu. "We can do without."

Zora laughs, easing into the booth. For a moment, she feels normal.

***

The waiter approaches, smiling politely. "What can I get you ladies for starters?"

Lai doesn't hesitate. "Mango Mornings. Sounds like sunshine in a glass."

Rayven nods. "Wine spritzer and water. I'm driving."

Zora glances at the menu, indecisive.

Don't overthink it.

"La Blanc," she says finally. "And water."

They lean back as the drinks arrive, clinking glasses softly.

"To making it through another week," Nico declares.

"To surviving ourselves," Rayven adds.

Lai smiles. "To breathing."

They sip.

"So," Nico says, already leaning in. "Who's going first?"

Lai clears her throat. "Jazz-n-Gems is officially at capacity on live nights. We turned people away last weekend."

Zora's eyes widen. "That's huge."

Rayven claps. "Look at you!"

"I'm thinking about doing a set once a week," Lai admits. "Lowkey. Nothing flashy."

Nico nearly chokes on his drink. "Excuse me? The city is not ready."

Zora smiles brightly. "Do it."

"I'm just not sure about expanding yet," Lai says thoughtfully. "Timing matters."

Rayven nods. "Trust yourself."

Rayven shares next. "Keeping Step is thriving. Grades are up. Confidence is up. One of the kids told me dance makes their chest feel calm."

Zora's eyes soften. "That's everything."

"Oh," Rayven adds casually, "and Duke Ellington asked me to teach a master class."

Nico whistles. "Legend behavior."

Zora beams. "I'm so proud of you."

When it's Zora's turn, she straightens. "My practice is growing. Referrals are steady. I might have to cut back on mentoring hours."

Rayven frowns. "You okay with that?"

"I don't know," Zora admits. "I want to be everywhere."

Nico watches her closely.

She mentions the conference in Georgia. Nico's jaw tightens briefly.

Family dinner. Her father. Wanting more from him.

Advice flows gently. Loving. Unforced.

As the drinks continue, Nico grows louder, more animated.

"I'm thinking about going full time with music," he says. "Teaching. Youth programs. But funding…"

Rayven nods. "You'll figure it out."

Zora feels it then.

The fog.

The pull.

Shake it off.

Rayven suggests dancing.

Silence.

Then Nico squeezes Zora's knee under the table. Firm. Grounding.

She blinks, pinches him back.

You're not my father.

His eyes meet hers.

I know you.

She exhales slowly.

"Let's dance," she says lightly.

***

As they walk towards elevator to The Pose Rooftop Club, Nico lags behind, pulling Zora gently back.

"Not tonight," he whispers. "Stay present."

She nods. Barely.

Rayven glances back. "What are y'all whispering about?"

"Nothing," Zora says too quickly.

They laugh it off.

"Later" Zora mutters back to Nico through a clinched smile.

***

They reach the parking garage and get in the car. Zora pushes the start button and the engine purrs to life, low and smooth, filling the silence. The dashboard lights up softly. The garage hums around them. She keeps her eyes straight ahead, hands gripping the steering wheel a little tighter than necessary.

She is distinctly quiet, hoping Nico will take the hint.

He does not.

"Zora…"

Her jaw tightens.

"Nico, not now," she says flatly. "I don't have the energy for this right now."

He exhales sharply, leaning back against the seat. "But you had the energy to tilt," he says, turning toward her. "I felt it. I saw it. I can't keep covering for you, Zora. You need to get control."

Her knuckles whiten.

"How is therapy going?" he asks, softer now but still pressing.

"I have control," she snaps. "Therapy is therapy. Stop fathering me. You're only one year older than I am. I don't need another father."

That lands hard.

Nico's face shifts, hurt flashing before concern takes over again. "I'm not trying to be your father. I'm trying to be your friend," he says. "And I'm concerned about you. You've been glossing over too much lately. Smiling. Deflecting. Redirecting. I think you need to talk about it before it becomes an animal you can't tame."

He pauses. "I see you, Z."

She swallows.

"Nico," she says more quietly now, "thank you for your concern. I mean that. I promise I'll put in the work at therapy. I will. But tonight, I just do not want to talk about it."

His voice rises despite himself. "Z, what would have happened if I weren't there tonight? What the hell, Zora? You want me to just sit back and watch you spiral out of control?"

She flinches.

"What kind of friend would that make me?" he continues. "You want Rayven and Lai to start asking questions you are clearly not ready to answer? Because they will. They already feel it."

He leans closer. "Talk to me."

She shakes her head. "It's late, Nico. I'm not up to talking about it."

"When will you be ready?" he asks, frustration creeping in. "When Zora? This is crazy. I'm afraid for you."

"Don't be afraid for me," she says quickly. "I'm working it out. My own way."

He lets out a short, humorless laugh. "Your way hasn't worked," he says. "Not all this time. And it's getting worse. I'm not always around to put guard rails up for you. Does that even matter to you? That I care? That I'm trying to protect you?"

Silence floods the car.

Zora shifts the gear into drive and pulls out of the parking space, tires humming softly against the concrete as they head toward the exit.

She does not respond.

She does not look at him.

"Zora," Nico says again, incredulous now. "So, you're just going to ignore me? Seriously?"

She reaches over and turns on the radio. Music fills the car, low at first, then louder. A clear signal.

Conversation over.

Nico drops his head back against the seat and bangs it three times against the headrest, controlled but furious. He says nothing else.

The radio plays, but the silence between them screams louder.

They pull up in front of his condo. Zora slows, stops, but keeps her foot on the brake. She keeps her hands on the wheel.

No words.

Nico opens the door, then pauses. He looks back at her, his expression softening despite everything.

"I love you, Z," he says quietly. "Always know that."

She nods once. Barely.

He closes the door.

Car in drive, Zora pulls away, the taillights disappearing into the dark streets as Nico stands on the sidewalk watching her go.

She drives deeper into the city, alone now, surrounded by moving lights and empty lanes, sitting with the darkness pressing against her chest.

And the darkness inside her answers back. She needs to respond.

Chapter Six

Sunday morning arrives quietly.

Zora wakes slowly, groggy, suspended somewhere between sleep and obligation. Pale sunlight slips through the soft gold drapes, casting warm streaks across the walls of her bedroom. The city hums faintly below, but up here, on the third floor of her brownstone, there is stillness.

This is her oasis.

Her sanctuary.

Her secret keeper.

Her bedroom suite stretches wide, airy, intentionally uncluttered. Neutral tones. Plush textures. A private sitting room just beyond the doorway where a chaise lounge waits beside tall windows. This entire floor belongs to her alone. No clients. No expectations. No witnesses.

Downstairs, on the ground floor, her private practice sits behind a separate entrance. Professional. Polished. Contained. No overlap between who she helps and who she hides.

Zora exhales slowly and rolls onto her back, staring at the ceiling.

Family dinner, she reminds herself.

Her mother's voice echoes faintly in her mind, cheerful and insistent. Appetizers. Tradition. Togetherness.

She swings her legs over the side of the bed, running a hand through her hair, already feeling the familiar tension begin to coil low in her body. A quiet warning. A subtle pull.

Focus, she tells herself. *Just get through today.*

***

Even with the chill in the air, the market is busy with late-morning shoppers. Families. Couples. Elderly neighbors moving at an unhurried pace. Zora moves through the aisles wrapped in a mid-length wool trench coat, a basket on her arm, scanning shelves, mentally checking off items her mother requested.

Rice cakes. Dumpling wrappers. Gochujang.

And then it hits her.

The tightening low in her abdomen sharpens, sudden and insistent. Her breath catches. Her body responds before her mind can intervene.

The hunger is rising.

Not food.

Something else.

She pauses near the produce section, fingers tightening around the basket handle. She tries to breathe through it. Tries to redirect.

You are here for groceries, she tells herself. *Nothing more.*

But her eyes betray her.

They search.

She notices him near the refrigerated cases. A stranger. Brown. Tall. Clean-cut. Distracted. Unaware. She knows nothing about him. Not his name. Not his life. Not whether he is married or lonely or simply passing time.

None of that matters.

The pull surges. Unbearable.

Her heart pounds as she steps closer, brushing against him as if by accident. Her arm lingers. Too long. He looks down, surprised at first, then curious.

She smiles. Soft. Inviting. Dangerous.

"Sorry," she murmurs. "Didn't mean to bump into you."

"No problem," he says, still watching her.

She looks around. "Are you in a rush?" she asks, voice low. Casual. Her body leans in closely before her mind can stop it.

He hesitates. He's curious. He grins widely. Then shakes his head, *no*.

Without a word, Zora is pulling him away from the market into a nearby alley.

The alley is narrow. Dim. Private enough to disappear into without being seen in broad daylight. She leads. Intrigued. He follows.

The world cuts away.

Before he can say anything, Zora puts her basket on the ground and then his. Zora is tearing at his clothes. She begins kissing him hungrily, almost to the point of drawing blood, but certainly enough to bruise both of their mouths. He is confused and aroused at the same time. He is looking around unable to comprehend what is happening, but she pulls him into her, frantically rubbing her body against his. At this point, the bite of the chill is an afterthought. Zora is panting wildly. Her eyes intense. Almost animalistic. She is yanking his belt away, snatching his zipper down and flipping his penis from his pants. He has never seen such instinct like this in his life, but he goes with it. She turns herself around and pulls her dress up with one hand and tugging her panties down with the other. In one motion, she shoves herself onto his awaiting penis and allows him to take her right there. Behind a group of garbage dumpsters. He is leaning against the brick wall, and she is thrusting on him with all the power she can muster. She is trying to muffle her own sounds. Her hair is flying wildly in her face as she is bent over as far as she can, while taking all of him in. He obliged her commands and thrusts her deeper. She is grunting for more. She is hungry. Savagely hungry. He is trying to keep up. She is going wild, biting her own lip and drawing blood. The climax is nearing. By this time, she's growling. He is so aroused by this impromptu encounter that he releases with a surge that nearly forces Zora to her knees.

When they both had climaxed and released, Zora just hung there, nearly upside down, hair hanging wildly in her face. He patted her exposed ass, and she came to life again. She pulled away from him, dislodging his penis from her pulsating vagina, in a daze as if she was unaware what had happened. He was clearly pleased and wanted more and offered to give her more. She acknowledged his kindness as if he had just paid her the biggest compliment. She said no words. Just gave him a deep look. He asked for her name and number, but she just adjusted her clothes, grabbed her basket and disappeared into the crowd, leaving him standing there with his pants at his knees, penis still exposed to the elements. All he could think was *"What the hell was that?"* Zora came through that alley like a monsoon and left just as quickly, unassuming, incognito…satisfied. At least for now.

***

Zora stands back in the market minutes later, basket now heavier, her hands slightly unsteady. Her hair is out of place. A faint sheen of perspiration clings to her skin. Her lipstick is smudged. Her breathing shallow. Her vagina still vibrating.

She scans the room quickly, heart racing, half-expecting someone to be staring.

No one is.

She exhales.

Her legs feel weak. Heavy. But her chest feels lighter. The pressure eased. The craving silenced, at least temporarily.

Pull it together, she scolds herself. *You cannot unravel in public spaces ever again.*

She adjusts her coat, wipes her mouth discreetly, and moves toward the checkout line, forcing herself back into the task she came to complete. She feels the chill now. Back to reality.

Appetizers secured. Purpose restored. Mask back in place.

Chapter Seven

She's on her way to her parents' house. Alexandria welcomes her with charm and order.

Tree-lined streets. Manicured lawns. Wrought iron gates. Flags perched proudly on porches, many of them military, their presence unspoken but unmistakable. Duke Street curves gently through the neighborhood, historic and pristine. Main Street hums with quiet affluence.

Zora slows as she pulls into the gated community where her parents live. Their home stands proudly among the others, elegant and warm. Brick facade. Tall windows. Impeccably kept.

She sits in the car for a moment, engine idling.

Game face, she tells herself.

She smooths her dress, demure and understated. Respectable. Appropriate. Beneath it, lace presses against her skin, hidden and aching. A reminder of what no one here knows.

This house was never hers. Her parents bought it after she left for college. Still, it holds expectations. Legacy. Love.

She steps out of the car and stares at it briefly, taking in the life her parents built.

Then she walks inside.

***

The Holley household is built on intention.

Seth and Nun-Nari Holley met through proximity and purpose. Military life has a way of shrinking the world, pulling people together through shared routines, relocations, and unspoken understanding. Seth was already deep into his Air Force career when they met, disciplined and focused, moving with the quiet confidence of a man who knew where he was going. Nun was vibrant and expressive, a creative force with an eye for design and a soul anchored in heritage.

Her parents met at 23 and 21 respectively; and married in Texas at 25 and 23 respectively after 1 1/2 year courtship. Seth Holley had just been promoted to Second Lieutenant (O-1) after completing OCS (Officer Candidate School). Nun was studying fashion design but was working on base as a seamstress to pay her college tuition. Seth came into the base cleaners to have his rank insignia sewn onto three new ABU (Airman Battle Uniform) shirts. He was kind to her and smiled. She had a twinkle in her eye and smiled back. The rest was history.

Where he was structure, she was warmth. Where he saw missions, she saw meaning.

Their marriage worked because they respected what the other brought to the table. Seth grounded her. Nun softened him. Together, they built a life that climbed steadily from modest beginnings into stability, comfort, and influence. They did not always speak the same emotional language, but they were united in love for their daughter and in the belief that hard work and integrity would protect her from the world.

Seth Holley grew up in Danville, Virginia, the youngest of three and the only son in a lower-middle-class household. He watched too many boys he knew settle into narrow lives shaped by circumstance and limitation. He wanted more. The Air Force offered him escape, education, leadership, and the chance to see beyond the two-stoplight radius of his hometown. He never regretted joining. Over decades of service, he built a decorated career, rising to the rank of Colonel, now pushing for the coveted General slot. He is steady, commanding, thoughtful, and unshakeable. As a father, he loves Zora fiercely, but his love often shows up as structure, expectations, and concern disguised as advice. He does not know how to soften without feeling unmoored.

Nun-Nari Holley carries a different history. Born in California to immigrant parents who came to the United States after the Korean War, she was raised with a deep respect for sacrifice, culture, and family pride. Heritage, in her world, is sacred. It must be honored, practiced, and passed down. Failure is not an option. Dishonor is unthinkable. She built Nu-Na Interiors from that foundation, blending modern design with Korean influences, creating spaces that feel both elevated and rooted. Nun is the creative visionary of the firm. Her best friend and business partner, Chae-Yin Lu, runs the operations, budgets, and strategy. They call each other sisters, bound not by blood but by shared history and trust.

Nun is expressive in ways Seth is not. She laughs loudly. Fussing is her love language. She cooks with emotion and believes food heals. She corrects posture, adjusts sleeves, and insists Zora participate in Korean holidays not out of control, but out of protection. To Nun, tradition is armor.

Marcus Stith knows Seth behind the armor.

They met in elementary school, long before ranks and titles. Where Seth is serious, Marcus is witty and disarming, quick with a story and sharp with insight. He is a successful entrepreneur and consultant, though he rarely leads with that. What defines Marcus is his ability to listen, to see all sides without judgment, and to say the thing that needs to be said without wounding. He is Seth's sounding board and Zora's unofficial uncle, the bridge between command and compassion.

Amri Stith complements that balance. Elegant but grounded, she brings warmth and clarity into every room. A thoughtful professional with a polished presence, Amri has a way of sitting with discomfort without trying to fix it. She sees Zora's fragmentation long before it is named. She offers perspective without pressure, and her presence allows conversations to go deeper without becoming heavy.

Chae-Yin Lu is quieter, but no less perceptive. Strategic, protective, and deeply loyal, she sees everything even when she says little. If Nun is the artist, Chae is the architect. She reads energy the way others read spreadsheets. She notices Zora's withdrawal. She clocks the tension in rooms before it surfaces. To Zora, she is family. A watchful aunt figure who understands both cultural expectation and emotional cost.

Together, these five adults form the scaffolding of Zora's world. They are love. They are expectation. They are history and legacy and unspoken pressure. They are the people who shaped her and the people she hides from most.

***

Inside the house, the smell of food settles into the walls like memory. Garlic, sesame oil, slow-simmered sauces. Laughter moves easily from the kitchen to the dining room, warm and unforced.

"Zora!" Nun calls out before she even fully steps inside. "You made it."

Zora slips off her coat and smiles, her posture instinctively straightening as she crosses the threshold. "Of course I did, Mommy." She puts the promised appetizers on the kitchen island.

Nun pulls her into a hug, pressing a kiss against her cheek, hands already adjusting Zora's sleeve. "You look tired. Are you eating enough?"

Zora laughs softly. "I eat. I promise."

Seth stands a few steps back, hands clasped loosely in front of him. “Good to see you,” he says, voice steady, familiar. He leans in, gives her a brief hug, a firm pat on the back.

It is enough for him.

It is not enough for her.

She feels it immediately, the small ache she always has to swallow. *Just once,* she thinks, *hold me like I’m still your little girl.* She lets the thought pass before it can harden.

Marcus steps in seamlessly, as if he felt the shift before she did. “There she is,” he says warmly, opening his arms. His hug is full and grounding, the kind that lingers just long enough to say, I see you.

Zora exhales without realizing she was holding her breath.

Amri smiles from beside him. “You look beautiful, Zora.”

“Thank you,” Zora replies, meaning more than just the compliment.

Chae offers a quiet nod, eyes sharp and observant. “Good to see you.”

They move toward the dining room together. Nun acknowledges that Zora brought *both* of her favorite appetizers. She smiles brilliantly at her daughter, “Thank you, Zora!”

“You’re very welcome, Mommy!” It’s the least Zora could do after her indiscretion at the market. *Unbelievable. I can’t believe I did that without a condom. Careless. I hope I didn’t catch anything. Worse yet. I better not be pregnant.*

The long mahogany table is already set, polished and glowing under soft lighting. Plates are passed. Dishes are served. Wine glasses clink gently.

Conversation begins easily.

"So," Seth says after a few bites, clearing his throat, "the board met again last week."

Marcus leans back slightly. "That sounds like a story already."

Seth shakes his head with a small smile. "They're still evaluating candidates. It's… competitive."

Nun watches him closely. "You've done everything they asked. And more."

"It's not just about performance," Seth replies. "It's timing. Politics. Longevity."

"And optics," Marcus adds carefully.

Seth nods once. "Exactly."

Marcus lifts his glass. "You're the right man for it. They know it. It's coming."

Amri chimes in gently. "The universe has a way of aligning things when the foundation is solid."

Nun raises her glass. "God sees you."

They all echo the sentiment, nodding, affirming.

Zora watches her father's face soften just slightly at that. Pride flickers there. So does exhaustion.

Then Chae turns her attention to Zora.

"So," she says casually, "are you seeing anyone these days?"

Zora feels it before the words fully land. She sets her fork down slowly. "Not really," she replies. "Work has been full."

"When isn't it?" Marcus says lightly.

"Your career is impressive," Seth adds. "But balance matters." Zora silently considers that statement especially since her father hasn't been good at balancing his career and being the father she so desperately needs.

Zora smiles. "I'm working on that."

Nun tilts her head. "You know, I ran into Reese Parker the other day."

Zora's stomach tightens.

"He asked about you," Nun continues. "I took the liberty of inviting him to dinner next week. I thought it might be nice."

Reese Parker.

Of course.

Her face remains neutral. Inside, she freezes.

"I'm not really dating right now," Zora says carefully.

Nun waves a hand. "Just dinner. No pressure."

Marcus glances between them, sensing the shift. "Zora's been doing meaningful work," he says. "That takes energy."

Amri nods. "And timing."

Zora seizes the opening. "Actually," she says, leaning forward slightly, "we need to finalize plans for the heritage Zoom call at the end of the month."

Nun brightens immediately. "Yes. We need to confirm the elders' availability."

The conversation pivots, tension easing just enough for Zora to breathe.

Dinner winds down with laughter and shared stories. Plates are cleared. Hugs are exchanged.

When it's time to leave, Zora hugs everyone tightly, lingering just a moment longer with Marcus and Amri.

In the car, she exhales deeply, hands resting on the steering wheel. Contemplating.

The hunger stirs again. She is on full tilt focused on a fix.

She pushes the start button.

And drives…towards the hunger.

Chapter Eight

Zora glances at the clock glowing on her dashboard.

7:02 p.m.

Her jaw tightens. She bites her bottom lip, hard enough to sting. It is still early. Too early for her body to be acting like this. She knows she has back-to-back clients tomorrow. First one scheduled for 9 a.m. Mondays are always full. Counseling. Mentoring. Responsibility stacked neatly in her calendar.

But none of that quiets the knots twisting low in her abdomen.

Moisture gathers between her thighs, uninvited and relentless.

She is five minutes from home.

Five minutes from privacy.

Five minutes from relief.

Her foot presses harder on the accelerator.

As she pulls into the parking space behind her brownstone, she barely cuts the engine before rushing out of the car. The night air hits her skin, cool and useless against the heat crawling under it. She fumbles with her keys, heart racing, and slips inside.

The door shuts behind her.

She bolts up the stairs, every step urgent, her body vibrating like a live wire. Her purse lands on the bed with a dull thud as she peels off her coat and clothes in a frenzy, fabric pooling at her feet. There is no patience in her movements. No pause.

She heads straight for the bathroom.

The shower turns on, steam filling the space, but she does not linger. There is no savoring the water. No grounding. No ritual. This is not about calm.

She needs time.

She needs to transform.

She needs to satiate before she loses her mind.

When she steps out, towel wrapped tightly around her body, she goes directly to her closet.

Behind her everyday wardrobe, behind the pressed blouses and conservative dresses, a hidden door opens quietly.

Inside is the other her.

Lace. Leather. Sequins that catch the light. Fishnets. Halter tops. Mini dresses and skirts that never see daylight. Wigs in every texture, length, and color imaginable. Shoes too high for practicality. Too loud for her real life.

This is the wardrobe no one knows exists.

She runs her fingers along the fabrics, breathing unevenly, then settles on a black satin and sequin off-the-shoulder knit top. Leather pants. Four-inch silver heels.

She applies her makeup slowly now, deliberately. Darker eyes. Red lips. She dots the beauty mark just above her lip on the right. Silver hoop earrings. A thin chain with a ruby pendant resting just above the curve of her top. Black clutch bag large enough for her cell phone, keys, debit card, and license.

The blonde wig goes on last. Ultra-curly. Mid-length.

Zora stares at herself in the full-length mirror.

Skyy looks back.

It is 8:00 p.m. Dark chasing dark.

She leaves quietly. No neighbors watching. No familiar faces. That is the point.

***

The streets pull her northwest without conscious effort. Her GPS lights up as she types in the address.

The Mirror. 1413 K Street NW.

She has never been, but she has heard enough. Underground. Dark. Anonymous. A place where faces blur and intentions are unspoken.

Perfect.

She parks a block away and exhales in relief. *These heels are not built for distance.* She now regrets her shoe choice. The entrance to the club is discreet, down a short set of brick steps leading into something that feels deliberately hidden.

Inside, the space opens up. Low couches. A central bar. Chandeliers throwing fractured light across mirrors lining the walls. Music hums through the room, a fusion sound she cannot quite place.

Not classy.

But right.

She walks in like she belongs. Confidence as armor. Her eyes scan quickly, checking for recognition. None. And no one in her inner circle would recognize her in this disguise.

She takes a seat at the bar.

"What can I get for you, Miss?" the bartender asks.

She studies the menu briefly. "Hotel Nacional."

The drink arrives. Cold glass. Sweet burn. Enough to take the edge off, not enough to dull her senses.

She surveys the room.

Groups clustered together. A few too-loud laughs. Men posturing. Women watching. And then she sees him.

Alone. Two-top table. Beer in hand.

She glances once. Then turns away.

Moments later, a tap on her shoulder.

She does not turn right away. She takes a breath, lets the moment stretch just enough, then pivots slowly.

"Hello."

"Anyone sitting with you?" he asks.

"Not at the moment," Zora says. She is not about to indicate that she's in a bar after eight p.m. alone.

He gestures toward the small two-top behind him, his tone casual. He asks if she would join him at his table.

She smiles lightly, gathers her glass, and follows him to the table where he had been sitting. They settle in across from one another and slip into small talk immediately, voices raised slightly to compete with the music.

He leans in to speak. "You come here often?"

Slightly shouting above the music, she answers, "My first time. I'm waiting for my friends."

She lies easily. Too easily.

"I come on occasion when I need to wind down," he says. "Never been on a Sunday night. The vibe is much lighter than a Friday."

Zora nods, listening, but only halfway. Her attention is split. While he talks, she studies him carefully.

About five foot eleven. Maybe one seventy. Muscular, but not overstated. Olive skin. Medium brown colored hair; dyed she assumes because it doesn't quite match his complexion. Clean cut, but with an after-five shadowed beard that softens the edges. Green eyes. Supple lips. Rugged. Handsome. Just enough.

Just right for the night.

She is so absorbed in her quiet inventory of him that she misses his question entirely.

He asks again, louder this time.

"What's your name?"

"Skyy," she says, smiling as she lifts her glass and takes a sip. "My name is Skyy."

"Shelton," he replies. "Nice to meet you, Skyy."

She leans her head slightly. "You from around here? DC, that is. You from the DMV?"

"No. Just been here about four months. Moved here for work. I'm in tech, and my job relocated me from Pennsylvania."

Zora's thoughts flicker immediately.

Good. A transplant.

He doesn't know anyone she might know. No overlapping circles. No familiar faces. No cross-pollination of friend groups.

A perfect scenario.

She smiles again, this time slower, more deliberate, as the music shifts behind them and the night leans closer.

The music slows.

"Want to dance?"

She nods. "Sure."

His hand closes around hers. His arm tightens around her waist. They move together, bodies swaying. The hunger rises sharply now, electricity shooting through her at the simplest contact.

Too early, she tells herself. *Give it time.*

He looks down at her and smiles. There's a twinkle in his eye. Not sure if it is just the lights or if he is feeling what she is feeling.

He pulls her closer.

Her body answers before her mind does.

Before she knew it, her mouth was on his, tugging at his lips, begging for his tongue through soft moans. As they swayed and kissed, her nipples tightened, growing beneath her top. She can feel moisture soaking her panties. Right there on the dance floor. Lost in the moment. Shelton feeds

Skyy his wet tongue. Sweet. She tastes so sweet. Maybe it is the flavor of her drink, but he likes it. He likes it a lot. From the dark corner a voice rings out. "Get a room." The room erupts in cheers and laughter… "Get a room… Get a room…" they chant.

Realizing they are on full display, Zora pulls Shelton off the dance floor and out into the corridor. She frantically looks for a spot to satisfy her raging hunger. There, off to the side, is a door. *Is it locked? What's in there?* Zora aims for it and pulls.

Locked. Damn it!

Another door across from it. Shelton pulls. Locked.

Into the bathroom they go. A moody, dark green room with a two stalls, two sinks, a long gold gilded mirror above, polished concrete floors. Shelton can barely get the door closed and locked before Skyy is tugging at his pants. She is focused, trying to undo his belt. He lends her a hand. The button. The zipper. In this moment, Skyy regrets wearing pants. Too much work to get them off.

Dresses only she notes to herself.

Struggling to get her leather pants down, Shelton offers his assistance. With two hands, he gently glides her pants down, but she won't let him take them all the way off. She just allows one leg to get free. Her right leg. She then pulls down her wine-colored lacey panties with visible moisture in the crotch. The panties drop to the left where her pants are resting at her ankle on the floor, still on her leg. She reaches for her purse. Condom. She hands it to him. He puts it on.

Skyy looks at Shelton like he was a rib-eye steak. Meat to be devoured. She grabs him around his neck, and he forces her against the wall between the two sinks. The force nearly took her breath away, but she didn't care. She's tilting fast. He lifts her up and she spreads her legs across the two sinks. He reaches for her vagina and pushes a finger inside. She gasps in response. He slowly inserts another and pumps her with his hand, his manhood growing more stiff by the moment. Breathlessly she tells him, "Penis… Penis… I need your penis… Now! Right now!"

She knew they had very little time in the bathroom, so she needed him to get to business. Shelton followed her command and made his way between her thighs into her dripping vagina. He could actually see wetness glistening off her closely trimmed pubic hair. He slid himself effortlessly into her. *Damn. So wet.* She let out a moan that made the hair on his arms stand up. *WOW!* he thought to himself.

Slow strokes. Deliberate strokes. Deep strokes. His eyes are closed. Jaw tight. Skyy has intertwined her fingers into his hair and is holding onto him. He's not focused on the pain of his hair being pulled. He is focused on how hot her vagina is. How it fits perfectly around his bulging penis. She roughly whispers, "Harder, Shelton… Stoke me harder… Harder, damn it!" He follows her instructions and literally stokes her until her head hits the mirror on the wall behind her. She is pulling his hair and sucking his penis in deeper with her vaginal muscles. She is about to be "wasted." She can feel him stiffen inside her. He can feel her tightening. Almost simultaneously, they both explode. She muffles her scream in the crook of his neck as his face is now planted in her breasts to dampen his own moans.

Knock. Knock. Knock. "C'mon, what are you doing in there? The line is growing…"

Bang, bang, bang. "Someone needs the restroom…" They didn't realize how long they had been in there. Long enough, I suppose.

Skyy pulls up her panties and leather pants. She's trying to get her bearings. Spinning. Shelton pulls his pants from his knees, zips his pants, and buckles his belt. He smirks. The residue of the moment lingering. The scent of sex in the air. Her nectar caked on his fingers. He takes a deep whiff. No time to bask. Someone's coming through the door. The manager.

Skyy and Shelton spill into the corridor, adjusting clothes, breath uneven. The lobby is half full of patrons coming and going, but more specifically waiting for the restroom. Skyy thinks: *Why is there only one bathroom in this place?*

Management is about to reprimand them and throw them out, but Shelton apologized. The manager understood spontaneity and youthful passion, but he didn't want any parts of that type of action in his establishment.

"Next time you try that, you will be banned. Understood?"

"Understood, Sir. We apologize again," Shelton says.

Walking away from the crowd, Shelton looks at Skyy like she is everything he did not know he needed. Shelton is completely smitten. Enamored by Zora's sex drive. Her sex appeal. Electrifying. She's the kind of girl that drives him crazy in a good way. He wants to hold onto her.

She is internally resistant.

He is quietly insistent.

He grabs her arm.

Is he about to get physical with me? Is he becoming possessive off one tryst?

She pulls back hard. "Get off me!"

"Skyy, wait. We can go back to my place. Ya know, finish what we started…"

"No. Let go of me."

He releases her, startled. "I'm sorry. I didn't mean it like that. I wasn't trying to get rough. I'm just not ready for you to go."

She studies him, people passing by. "This was just fun," she says. "That's it. Just fun."

"Skyy, I want to see you again…"

"I don't think that's a good idea. I have to go, it's getting late."

"Let me give you my number. No pressure. Call when you want. When you can. Is that alright?"

She hesitates, sighs, opens her purse and then hands him her phone.

He types his name and number. Saved.

She knows she will not use it.

Or hopes she won't.

As she's walking away, Shelton says, "I had a great time, Skyy. Best time since I've been in the city. I hope to hear from you soon… when you have time."

Zora turns and shoots him a tender smile with pity in her eyes. "It was great to meet you, Shelton. I have to go. Take care."

With that, Zora headed out the door, up the brick steps and down the street to her car. Key fob in hand, she hits the start button. Not just to warm the car, but for a quicker get away. But not in these stupid heels.

***

In the car, the encounter lingers in her body. Her vagina is still pulsating. She can still feel the stroke of his penis. *Good girth* she thinks to herself. *Strong stroke* she recalls. She exhales shakily; grateful this time she had been prepared. She had condoms in her purse. She can't afford another situation like what happened at the market earlier that morning.

Seatbelt buckled. Car in drive. She pulls into traffic, radio on, volume up.

Two in one day.

She catches her reflection in the rearview mirror.

You are spiraling, Zora. Spiraling. Get help.

***

11:45 p.m. Back home, Zora peels of the residue of Skyy. She undresses and steps into the shower again. This one longer. Hotter.

Wash it off, she thinks. *Wash HER off.*

The hunger quiets but does not disappear.
She thinks of therapy. Two weeks since her last session.
Not ready.
Sleep comes eventually.
But hunger follows her into it.

Chapter Nine

Monday morning comes too soon.

Zora rises before her alarm, body heavy, mind already running. Clients to see. Notes to write. Youth mentoring later in the day. But first, she needs movement. She needs air. She needs to shake the residue of the weekend from her muscles and bones.

Zora slides out of bed, splashes water on her face, brushes her teeth, and puts on cool weather ready gear. Thick leggings. A fitted long-sleeve top. Sturdy running shoes. She pulls her long thick wavy hair into a high ponytail and puts on her earmuff wrap.

The mirror catches her briefly.

Tired eyes. Controlled face.

Recalibrate, Zora.

The weekend was too much. Even for her.

She thought she had control. Thought she had slowed the spiral. Instead, she let Skyy take over twice in one day. No restraint. No pause. Just hunger and surrender.

Shame flickers, sharp and unwelcome.

Refocus Zora.

You have too much to do. Too much to lose.

The thought lands heavy.

This is exhausting. And risky.

Trotting down the steps to the main floor of her home, she grabs her keys, license, a single earbud and cell phone. She usually listens to podcasts while running, but she's speaking at a conference at Spellman this week, so she needs to listen to her speech. Get it in her head so she can do it from memory. She hits play on her cell phone. Her voice begins to echo in her left ear bud.

Out on the street, she stretches. Calves. Quads. Hamstrings. Twists at the waist. Rolls her shoulders.

Then she's off.

Her route is familiar. Down Sixth Street NW. Over to Rhode Island Avenue NW toward Logan Circle. Across Sixteenth Street. Left onto Massachusetts Avenue NW toward Dupont Circle. Around the circle and back again, looping home.

Three miles. Every time.

Her breath steadies. Muscles warm. Thoughts quiet just enough to feel manageable.

Then she sees it.

The Cathedral of St. Matthew the Apostle.

She slows, almost without realizing it.

As she takes the left back onto Rhode Island, she passes the Cathedral of St. Matthew the Apostle. Her minds drifts upon seeing it. As often as she has taken that running route for the last three years or so, why had she not noticed it before?

How many times has she run this route? Years now. And yet, today, the building presses into her awareness, solid and unmoving, like it has been waiting for her to notice.

Her chest tightens.

She was raised Catholic but got away from the practice when she was old enough to voice her preference not to attend any longer. Every Sunday Mass. Mid-week Mass. Easter Mass. Christmas Mass. Confirmations. White dresses. Kneeling. Standing. Communion. Confession. All of it.

Rinse and repeat.

Year after year.

Routine without connection.

Inside, she never matched what was expected of her. Faith felt like performance. Like a costume. She believed in God, yes, but religion felt like a language she never quite learned to speak fluently.

So, she stepped away.

Her mother's disappointment lingered, quiet but present, but Zora was allowed her own path. Whatever that looked like.

Even if it did not resemble the one Nun had envisioned.

She shakes her head and pushes forward, picking up speed as she nears home.

Just as she turns onto her street, her phone rings in her ear.

She pulls it from her thigh pocket.

Libby.

Dr. Hanson's office.

She answers.

"Hello."

"Hi, Ms. Holley. This is Libby from Dr. Hanson's office. Did I catch you at a bad time?"

Breathless now, she jogs in place. "I'm just finishing my morning run. Is everything okay?"

"Yes, Ms. Holley. Dr. Hanson wanted to schedule your next appointment. You left rather abruptly last time, and we didn't get you back on the calendar. How does this Friday at nine a.m. look?"

Zora slows to a brisk walk, heart still racing.

"Unfortunately, I'll be out of town Wednesday through Saturday for a conference," she says, inhaling deeply. "Can I call you later when I can look at my calendar and confirm?"

She already knows she will not call.

"Of course," Libby replies easily. "I'll let Dr. Hanson know. Enjoy your conference, and good luck on your speech. I'll await your call."

The line clicks dead.

Zora stands on her stoop for a moment before unlocking the door.

Too much.

Too close.

Dr. Hanson sees too clearly. Pushes too hard. Zora convinces herself she can manage things for now.

Even she knows the lie is thin.

***

She showers quickly, efficiently and distracted, dropping her running clothes into the laundry basket before pulling on something professional but soft. Peach ribbed turtleneck. Chocolate wide-leg slacks. Brown block-heel boots. Gold teardrop earrings. A medium-length chain.

Natural makeup. Neutral lips.

She eats a small breakfast. Bagel half with avocado. Tea. Apple slices.

Downstairs, her office hums to life.

***

At 8:50 a.m. the office door chimes. Her first client. Single mother. Three children. Reeling from the unexpected death of her husband. Her immense grief is disrupting her children's lives. She's depressed. Anxious. Turning to alcohol.

At 10:30 a.m. Her next client. College student. Raped at a nighttime football game when in high school. Dealing with PTSD.

Twelve noon. Lunchtime. Zora goes upstairs and makes a small garden salad garnished with sunflower seeds, cranberries, and chicken. Water. She can't eat heavily. She has three more clients before the end of the day.

From 1:30 p.m. to 4:30 p.m. Zora's schedule is tight, but she handles each client with grace, empathy, and textbook techniques with individualized modifications.

Clients come and go. Stories heavy and raw. Grief. Trauma. Assault. Loss.

Zora is excellent at this.

She listens. Grounds. Guides. Holds space.

By late afternoon, her notes are complete, her body drained, her mind stretched thin.

She locks up and heads upstairs.

***

Mentally exhausted, Zora plops onto her couch with her usual evening cup of tea. She notices that she has a slew of missed calls and text messages. She taps in her security code and begins to read:

Text Message from Nico: Hey, Z, I'm just checking in on you. I hope you're still not mad at me. We are thick as thieves. Know that. Call me. Please.

Text Message from Lai: Z, where you at? I've been calling you since Saturday. You better not be ghosting me. Call me, girl. Want to run something past you.

Voicemail from Mommy: Hi, my Zora… You were on my mind. You seemed a little distant at dinner yesterday. Are you okay? I didn't want to bother you around family. Call me. Let's catch up. Love you!

Voicemail from Dr. Hanson: Good Day, Zora, Libby said that she called you, but I wanted to check back to see when you can come back in. We made a little headway the other day, even if it felt scary. We can do this. You can do this. Get on the schedule, please. Talk to you soon.

Scrolling through her phone, she's overwhelmed.

A slew of emails.

Four more voicemails.

Two more texts.

Concern wrapped in love. Concern wrapped in expectation.

Not tonight. I just don't want to be bothered.

Zora is mentally exhausted.

Skyy stirs.

Zora fights it. For a moment. For several moments.

Then she doesn't.

The closet opens. The transformation begins. Practical tonight. Calculated.

Purple sweater dress that lands just at the knee. Hugs her curves in all the right places. Not too presumptuous. Not too risky, but piques interest. Gold dangling earrings and a serpentine gold chain. Thigh-high black tights. Easy access. Black demi-heel boots. She learned her lesson yesterday with those damn 4-inch heels. Same wig as last night. Beauty mark in place over her right lip. Long black winter trench coat, scarf, and a beanie hat. No time for extravagancies. Her meter is running high. Revving through the sky. Literally through Skyy.

She looks in the full-length mirror one more time. *I don't know why I put so much effort into my outfits. These days I'm so tilted, I barely sit long enough for anyone to notice.*

She picks up her "fix" phone – the phone she uses for her encounters. She only carries that cell when she's Skyy. She'd never give her real cell phone to a "fix." She scrolls her contacts. She hesitates. Shelton. She dials. He doesn't recognize the number, but he answers anyway.

Damn you, Skyy!

"Hello?"

She hesitates and breathes in. "Is this Shelton?"

"Yes, who is asking?"

"Hi, Shelton. This is Skyy. We met at The Mirror last night… and…"

He strained to contain his excitement. "Heyyyy, Skyy! I'm so glad you called."

She tried not to be rude but got to the point. "You busy tonight? You want to meet somewhere?"

He is through the moon. In his mind, this is the open door to something more. To Zora it is just a fix. Just time to feed her roaring beast. "Sure. Same place? We can…"

"No," she says pointedly. "I don't think the manager would appreciate our presence." She ponders a moment. "Can you meet me at the entrance of Anacostia Park? We can park and go for a walk along the river."

"I'm not sure where that is, but I'll find it…"

"Good. See you there at 7?"

"Sure. 7 works for me. See you soon."

"Oh, Shelton, what are you driving?"

"A black BMW."

They both hang up. Zora locates her key fob, points out the window towards her car, and pushes the automatic start so that her car can heat up for 10 minutes. She then straightens up her bedroom a bit so that she doesn't come home to chaos. She is chaos enough on her own. At least one part of her life will be in order.

Chapter Ten

This part of the city looks different at night.

Zora notices it the moment she merges onto the main road. Streetlights blur into long ribbons of gold. Storefronts glow and dim in uneven rhythm. Music leaks from passing cars, bass thudding through closed windows. For a Monday night, the sidewalks are alive with movement. Laughter. Arguments. People going somewhere. People avoiding somewhere.

She grips the steering wheel, jaw tight.

The hunger is no longer subtle.

It sits low in her body, restless, demanding, pulsing with urgency. Her breath shortens. Her thoughts narrow. She tells herself to go back home. *Just go home, Zora.*

Her dash lights up with an incoming text. Nico.

She ignores it.

A bus stop billboard flashes by, half-naked bodies selling something she does not need to see. Her stomach flips. She turns the radio up, then down again. Nothing helps.

You can stop, she tells herself. *You always say that.*

The car moves as if it already knows where it is going.

***

She parks without thinking, slipping into a space she has used before. The area is dim but not empty. A couple argues quietly near the entrance. A group of friends laughs too loudly as they spill onto the sidewalk.

Zora sits in the car for a moment, forehead resting against the steering wheel.

Just one more time, she rationalizes. *Just to calm the hunger.*

She steps out, smoothing her coat, adjusting her posture. The door closes behind her with a soft, final click. She leans against the door and eyeballs every passing vehicle. A car slows, approaching in her direction but veers off. Not a black BMW. She's getting anxious. The tilt is getting intense. She starts stepping side to side, not just to keep warm, but to ward off the pressure brewing below.

Another car, then another.

Where is he?

She's getting frustrated.

She is warming quickly.

Her pubic area is saturated already. She fears she will grab the next person walking by and accost them right there on the parking lot.

Breathe, Zora. Breathe.

She leans her head back and exhales deeply releasing a plum of white smoke. "Where are you," she huffs. She's growing impatient. Just as she is about to get back into her car to call him, hc pulls up and parks a few spaces from her. *Finally*, she thinks to herself.

Not appearing too desperate, she approaches Shelton like she is on a mission. He's getting out of his car. A grin as wide as the Hudson River. She greets him and pulls him towards the water walk.

"Whoa! What's the hurry, Skyy?" he asks.

She doesn't respond. She just tugs at his coat. She is leading him toward the walkway that traces the river below. She finally speaks. "Sorry, just trying to warm up a bit." She lied. Again.

Laughing and grinning like he just won the lottery, Shelton remarks, "I can definitely keep you warm."

"That's what I'm counting on," Zora says with flirty resolve.

She leads him into the thick of the river walk. Tree are more bountiful. Not so sparce. Park benches strategically positioned facing the river. Across the river, life is a glow from condos, restaurants, and other establishments. But that is not her focus.

Zora pulls Shelton towards a large tree trunk and forces his back against it. This excites him because he can just about imagine what she wants and he is not going to fight her.

Before she can do anything, he leans in to kiss her and she receives him hungrily. Same fervor as in the bar bathroom. He can feel his manhood blooming in his pants. "Oh, God…Skyy…" he whispers against her mouth.

"No words," she barks back.

She slips her hands between his coat and pants. She grabs at his bulging penis and starts humping the air like a dog in heat. Humping and moaning. Her fire is intense as she is tearing at him. He unbuttons his pants. No belt this time. Too time-consuming. She can feel moisture on her inner thighs. The pressure. Her vagina is swelling. Wanting. "C'mon, Shelton… C'mon…"

"I'm ready, Skyy… How do you want…?"

Before he could finish his question, she turns from him, lifts her coat and dress.

No panties this time.

She spreads her legs and bends into him.

"Right to it, huh…?" he jokes.

She doesn't respond. She just keeps humping against him.

"Damn it, Shelton… Put it in… Put it in me, now… Pleeeeaaassse!"

"Okay, Okay… Don't you want to…?"

"Be quiet, Shelton… No talking…" she urges.

In one thrust, Shelton forces his engulfed penis into Zora's pulsating vagina. Hot. Slick. He can hear the sound of her wetness popping against him. Like a super moist kiss. More like a river. Holy hell! He is in heaven. She is pushing herself against him with reckless abandonment. Grunting. Groaning. Gyrating. He joins in the melody of the moment. A car drives by. She stops moving but doesn't disengage his penis. She stands slightly so people won't assume they are having sex in the park. Even though they are. The car passes.

She resumes her half bent over posture, bends her knees and shoves against Shelton's penis with power. Deep thrust. Deep thrust. He is fighting the pain of the bark against his butt cheeks. Pain versus pleasure. He chooses pleasure. He is giving her what she wants. Strong strokes. He already knows that's what she is looking for. Hard strokes. She is moaning. She has reached between her legs and grabbed his balls and is massaging them. This gets his attention. "Oh, Skyy… Ohhh…"

She squeezes them harder this time and thrusts against him. "Hurt me, Shelton… Hurt me…" He begins humping and thrusting in multiple angles and she is enjoying all of it. She is damn near singing when she hears a voice…

"What are you doing out here?"

Shelton stops thrusting, but Skyy is begging for more. "Keep going… Keep going, I'm almost there… Please…"

"Skyy? Skyy is that you?"

That voice. *Oh, no. No. No. No.*

Her blood runs cold.

Skyy hesitates then straightens up to see Nico standing there with his date. Hand in hand. They were on a stroll after dinner at a nearby restaurant.

She dislodges Shelton's penis and pulls down her dress and coat. Embarrassed.

Shelton is confused but turns away to put his penis back in his pants.

Nico walks over, still holding his date's hand. She is taking in the scene but says nothing. She's stunned. *People really have sex in parks at night,* she ponders.

"Hey, Skyy… Haven't seen you in a while. Where you been?" asks Nico. He already knows this is Zora's MO but he doesn't want to reveal her real identity to her "fixer."

"Nico? Umm, I've just been a little busy. Wanted to take in the river scene, but ummm…"

"Did you get my message? I texted you several times," Nico says sarcastically, but only Zora picked up on it.

Shelton steps forward and extends his hand. "Hi, I'm Shelton…"

"Nice to meet you," Nico says, but doesn't shake his hand. Knowing Zora, her feminine juices are all on his fingers.

Shelton puts his hands in his coat pocket, feeling a bit rejected.

"Well, we are headed back to the other side. I'll call you tomorrow. Make sure you answer, Sis!"

Through a shaky smile, Zora says, "Okay…Okay, I will. Have a good night."

Nico and his date walk away, but he looks back at Zora in disapproval and she can feel it. She really feels it. She is not ready for that conversation any time soon, but she knows it is coming.

Shelton asks, "Who was that? Your brother?"

"Something like that… You want to finish with me? I'm still horny…"

With a look of unbelief, Shelton says, "Are you serious!?! You want to pick back up so you can 'finish?' Don't you think one interruption for the night is enough?"

She huffs. "It was just Nico. C'mon, let's finish. Please."

Shelton steps back and looks at her. "Skyy, lets just get something to eat. Can we just go to a restaurant nearby?"

"I'm not hungry, Shelton," she says sharply before apologizing. "I'm sorry for snapping."

Her body is still vibrating. There's hunger still humming beneath her skin, in her vagina that needs to be soothed. She's looking around the park almost in a panic. "Please, Shelton… Just a few minutes and I promise we can get something to eat…"

"Okay, Skyy, but only in the car. I don't want to get caught having sex outside again."

"That's fair…" she says and follows him to his car.

Once inside, the passion ensues in the backseat of his BMW. Skyy mounts him, but he is not as hard as he was before. She is frustrated and it shows. "What's wrong? You don't want me?"

"Of course, I do, Skyy… I've never been in this type of situation before… Give me a moment."

"I don't have a moment. I'm ready now," she quips.

She gets off his lap and plants her face in his crotch. She takes his flaccid penis in her mouth and goes to work. She starts to lick him and suck him with a madness he's never known. He tosses his head back against the seat and closes his eyes, moaning. His penis begins to respond. Really respond. She keeps up her action until she can feel that he is stiff enough for entry. When she is satisfied with his strength, she mounts him facing him but doesn't kiss him. She inserts him into her aching vagina and begins to hump against him feverishly. Thrusting. Stroking. Moaning. Thrusting. He can sense that animalistic energy that he felt the night before and it is turning him on more. Together they are humping with such power that the car starts to rock. He stops, but she beckons him to keep going.

"I'm almost there… I'm almost there… Harder… Harder… Ahhhhh…"

Shelton's hips are thrusting up as high as he can get them in the confined space, but he is effective. Her energy is intoxicating. He is stiffening inside her and she can feel it. "Yes, Shelton… Yes… Ahhhh…" The car feels like it is about to break the parking brake loose, but they keep going. He is groaning. She is moaning. Ecstasy. They collapse in a heap on the backseat. The windows are all steamed up. She can feel that her wig is a little twisted, but she doesn't jump to fix it. Maybe he doesn't notice.

When all was said and done, she was no longer hungry and certainly not interested in food.

"You sure you don't want to get something to eat, Skyy?" Shelton asks again.

"I'm sure. It's getting late. I have to work early in the morning, but…"

"You said that last time… It's getting late. YOU called me to meet YOU at 7 p.m. and now it is after 9 p.m. and you want to tell me 'it's late?'"

In his frustration he asks, "What is this Skyy? Am I just a sex toy for you?"

Little did he know the answer was a resounding, *Yes!*

She apologizes and promises to make it up to him. She tells him that she will be out of town this week for her job but will catch up with him when she returns. She lied. Again.

Chapter Eleven

In her car, Zora drives. She pulls off her wig. Her natural hair is slightly undone from perspiration. Her lipstick gone. Damn. She forgot to use a condom again. *Zora you're being too reckless.*

Her body feels heavy, spent, but her chest is strangely calm. The hunger has quieted.

For now.

She watches the city pass by again, the same streets, the same lights, but she feels detached from it all. Like she is floating just above herself.

Pull it together, she tells herself. *You are better than this.*

The thought feels thin. Unconvincing.

Her dash lights up again.

A text from Rayven.

Rayven: You home?

At a stop light, Zora types, deletes, then types again.

Zora: Yeah. Just got in. Long day.

She tosses the phone onto the passenger seat.

The light turns green.

***

Home is quiet when she arrives. The brownstone greets her with stillness. She locks the door, leans against it for a moment, eyes closed.

Upstairs, her sanctuary waits.

She kicks off her shoes, shedding layers as she climbs. Each step feels deliberate. Slow. Heavy. From the third floor, lights glow warmly through the windows as she enters her bedroom.

She sits on the edge of the bed, hands resting on her thighs.

The calm is already fading.

She knows it will return.

She just does not know when.

Zora lies back, staring at the ceiling, the weight of what she has done settling over her in waves. Not shame exactly. Not regret.

Something emptier.

She closes her eyes.

Tomorrow, she tells herself, *she will do better*.

She always does.

Until she doesn't.

Chapter Twelve

Zora awakens to the ping of her phone on the nightstand.

6:40 a.m.

Who in the world is texting this early?

She rolls within her covers onto her side, still heavy from sleep, and reaches blindly for the phone. As soon as she sees the name, her chest tightens.

Nico.

"We need to talk. Today."

Zora stares at the screen. She knows she should respond, but the weight of the message presses down on her before her feet even touch the floor. It is too early for confrontation. Too early for truth.

She types back slowly.

"Got a full day, but we will."

The reply comes almost instantly.

"I mean it, Zora. Today. 4 p.m. My studio. Be there."

She does not argue. She does not negotiate.

A single thumbs up.

That is all she has to give.

Since she is awake, Zora throws back the covers and moves toward the window seat. She curls herself into the cushion and takes in the quiet unfolding of the morning.

Trees stretch upward, early signs of spring peeking through budding branches. Her neighbor sweeps the sidewalk with deliberate pride, as if the concrete belongs solely to her. Across the street, the small park stirs with life. Dogs tug at leashes. A man sits on a bench, coffee in hand, scrolling through his phone. A few cars pass by. A squirrel shimming up the nearest tree pausing before it takes a leap to the next branch. An elderly couple walks slowly, fingers interlaced, unhurried. From this vantage point, life looks simple. Unburdened. Manageable.

She catches her reflection in the glass and studies the woman staring back at her. Physically, she recognizes herself. Internally, she does not. Something in her feels altered, reshaped by years of desire that no longer obeys logic or restraint.

She exhales sharply and shakes herself.

Run. Now.

Her pace quickens as she reaches the final stretch of her route. As she slows to a jog, her eyes lift to the massive stone structure ahead.

The Cathedral of St. Matthew the Apostle.

It rises with quiet authority, its steps wide and deliberate, almost ceremonial. She slows further, then stops entirely. The building feels impossible to ignore this morning.

She looks around, then jogs up the steps, heart thudding louder than her feet. She pauses at the ornate doors.

Should she go inside?

Maybe just a peek.

She pulls one door open.

The interior steals her breath. Opulent. Painted ceilings. Regal columns. Humbling. Rows of polished pews dotted with people in silent prayer. The air feels heavier here, but also calmer.

She stands frozen, absorbing it all. She hasn't been in a church since she was 14 years old.

She turns to leave.

"Blessings to you," a voice says gently. "Would you like to come in and pray?"

Startled, Zora turns. A priest stands nearby, dressed casually in jeans and a clerical collar.

"Uh, no, thank you," she says quickly. "Just curious. Do you offer confession?"

"Yes. Monday through Friday, eleven to noon. Sundays four to five. Or by appointment." He smiles warmly and extends his hand. "I'm Father Vincent."

She shakes his hand. "Thank you. I'm here for a friend."

The lie slips out easily. In church of all places.

He hands her a pamphlet. "If you need anything, we are here."

She nods and steps back outside, the door closing softly behind her.

***

Back home, the quiet follows her upstairs. The thought lingers.

Confession.

More private than therapy, she reasons within.

No faces. No names. No exposure.

Maybe.

After her shower, she eats half a grapefruit, a slice of wheat toast, and drinks hot tea while the morning news hums in the background. Crime. Politics. A single feel-good story buried beneath everything else.

She shuts it off.

Why do I even turn the TV on?

She checks her Smart Watch. Class every Tuesday and Thursday at 11:35 a.m. She loves teaching, but with her hectic existence she couldn't add another class even if she wanted to.

She takes a final bite of her toast and cleans the dishes.

She grabs her purse, phone, and keys.

It is not as chilly today so she can wear her short Black Pea Coat.

Stepping out the backdoor to her car parked on the cement pad, she looks around for nosey neighbors. There's always one. There. Ms. Fitzpatrick, now waving. Zora gives a gracious and courteous wave with a smile. Just don't talk to me. I must be a terrible neighbor she thinks.

***

By midday, class has ended and her students file out, energized and engaged. As she packs her things, a familiar presence clears his throat.

She looks up to see Dr. Simmons standing near her desk.

"Hi, Dr. Holley."

"Hello, Dr. Simmons. Great to see you. How is your semester shaping up?" she asks.

"Rowdy bunch. Mostly athletes who need English Lit, but a good group," he smiles warmly.

Zora can feel a pull, but she pushes it away. No mixing business with pleasure she reminds herself. But she also knows that he's been indirectly chasing her for about a year.

"Um, I know you're busy and I don't typically make such bold invitations," he says, "But a group of staff are getting together tonight for happy hour at The Alchemist down on U Street, NW." He tosses her a soft smile, "We're just welcoming in the spring, if you know what I mean. No pressure. Just an invitation."

Zora considers and responds warmly, "Thank you, Dr. Simmons. I'm getting ready to speak at a conference in Georgia this week. Leaving tomorrow. Need to be fresh. You know."

"No worries. Just wanted to include you." He turns and starts to walk away, "Have a safe trip and knock 'em dead with your speech."

"Thank you, Dr. Simmons. I appreciate that. Have a great rest of your week."

With that Dr. Simmons was gone, leaving Zora with her thoughts. She exhaled. Clearly she was holding her breath.

Should she go?

Too risky.

She cannot allow her hunger to compromise her position at Howard.

***

Zora drives home, but not before stopping at Sweetgreen – healthy salad joint on W Street – to grab a Garlic Parm Cauli and Romesco bowl.

Something light, but filling. She can add some leftover chicken from the fridge.

2:40 p.m. Zora pulls up to the rear of her home. She kills the ignition but sits there in silence.

She is mentally drained. Hungry (for food this time).

Contemplative.

She opens the door and climbs the deck steps to enter her kitchen.

Clean.

Stylish but warm.

Inviting.

All hers.

She places her lunch on the counter and heads to the closet to hang her coat. She kicks off her shoes and leans against the kitchen island as she unpacks the bag. She plates half of the food and wraps the rest up for a later meal. She grabs a cup of water and plops in a cushy chair at the banquette table. She eats slowly.

She needs to call her mother. She sets up her phone to FaceTime her mother.

After three rings, her mother answers. "Ddara, sosik deureoseo bangapda." *My daughter, I'm glad to hear from you.*

"Annyeong, eomma! Akka jeonhwa mot haeseo mianhae. Ilhago sueop ttaemune neomu bappasseo." *Hi, Mommy! Sorry I couldn't call earlier. Work and classes kept me really busy.*

"Geurae, ihaehae, uri Zora. Hajiman gajogeun jung-yohae. Eonjena geugeol gieokhaeya haenda. Eolmana bappa-do gajogeul wihan siganeun naeya handan-da." *I understand, my Zora. But family is important. Always remember that. No matter how busy you are, you must make time for family.*

"Ne, eomma. Mianhae. Deo isang byeonmyeong-eun eopseo." *Yes, Mommy. I apologize. No more excuses.*

Her mother thanks her and permits the conversation to continue in English.

"You've done well, my daughter. We can use English now," she chuckles.

Laughing, "You are so funny, Mommy. Thank you for allowing us to use English," she says with a wide grin. "How have you been?" Zora is looking at her mother's environment. "You at the studio? Did I interrupt you?"

"Yes, I'm at the studio pulling together samples for a new job. A commercial space over in downtown Arlington." Her mother is clearly distracted as Chae is asking her questions in the background. "Yes, Chae… Okay…

Sorry…Just a little busy. I want to win this client's heart with this design. She's a bit persnickety," her mother says as she rolls her eyes.

"Oh, Mommy, I don't want to be in your way. Handle your business. I was just reaching out since we hadn't spoken since Sunday." Zora takes another bite of her lunch. "Finish what you're doing and call me later tonight. I have a 4 p.m. meeting with Nico. Something about community work. I think." She lied.

"Okay, my daughter. Let me get back to this. I'll call you this evening. Glad to see that you're eating. It makes my heart happy. Talk to you soon. I love you."

"I love you, too, Mommy!"

Zora hits the red phone button to disconnect the video. She finishes her lunch and leans back against the chair. She is actually full. She takes the final sip of her water and washes her dishes. Yes, she still washes dishes. No dishwasher for her. It is only her after all. No need for it.

Chapter Thirteen

She checks her watch again. It is 3:30 p.m. She has to get ready to go. Nico's studio is on the other side of Dupont Circle.

She rinses her mouth, puts on her shoes, grabs her purse, keys and coat and heads back out.

Anticipation.

Stomach is in knots.

Throat tightening.

In her car, she pauses and takes a few cleansing breaths. She looks in her rearview mirror, puts the car in reverse, then shifts to drive, and heads down the back alley. She is going over the conversation in her head.

He's so upset.

She doesn't want to be reprimanded.

He knows her.

He knows her 'why,' so she thinks he needs to cut her some slack.

Not likely.

She rounds the corner of the street where Nico's studio lives. Her palms are sweating. She can feel her hair start to cling to her neck from perspiration. *Breathe, Zora. It won't be that bad. He's your forever friend and brother. Breathe. You will survive this.*

***

3:56 p.m. She parks her car in the studio parking lot.

Nerves.

Fear.

Shame.

Excuses.

All hitting her at once.

She opens the car door and slowly walks to the studio entrance. Nico is waiting. Stern look on his face. She looks at him then lowers her eyes. He steps back to let her enter. No words. No greeting. No warmth.

Here we go.

Nico takes her coat and leads her back to his office. She is following him like a timid child. She knows she needs to brace herself.

Nico sits behind his desk. He points to the chair across from him for Zora to take a seat. He just stares at her.

"Talk…" he demands.

"Nico…I…"

"Stop it, Zora…" he snaps in frustration. "What are you thinking? You're spiraling and you don't even care."

"Let me explain…"

"No, Zora… We've talked about this too many times… too many, Zora."

He runs his hand through his hair and looks at the ceiling before looking back at her. "We've been friends for a long time, and I KNOW what's going on with you. You don't seem to care one bit. You're acting reckless. Absolutely, reckless…"

Zora tries to chime in. "I…"

"No excuses, Z. This is getting way out of control. Damn it… In a park? Really? What if I was a cop? What if I was Rayven or Lai? Did you think about that or is your ferocious appetite driving everything you do? Clearly it is…"

"Nico…please, let me…"

"I don't need explanations, Z. I need you to get help. I mean it," he shouts slamming his hand on the desk, nearly toppling over the lamp positioned on the corner. "We've been having this discussion for 19 years. Nineteen years, Z! Do you not think you have a problem? Do you not think of the consequences? What the hell, Zora?"

Zora just sits there. Eyes welling with tears. Hands folded in her lap. Shoulders bowed forward. She looks like she is in the principal's office and is about to be expelled from school.

"Nico, I'm sorry… I promise to get help… I pro…"

"Stop it, Z! You've been saying this for years. Sure, you go to therapy, but clearly you are not putting in the work." Nico breathes a deep sigh.

"It appears to me that you do NOT want help. You like being driven by this compulsion. You feed off of it. You hide within it. I'm not a therapist and even I can see through it."

Nico pauses before he continues…

"Zora Leigh Holley, you forget that I knew you when. I knew you when this started being an issue…"

"Nico, don't…"

"Yes, Zora… I'm going to remind you. You need to remember… before you crash and burn."

Zora closes her eyes as the tears begin to flow.

Chapter Fourteen

High school.

Nico was in the 10th grade.

Zora in the 9th grade.

Their lives literally collided in the hallway as she was rushing through between classes. She ran right into Nico. He should have been upset, but he joked about her asking, “Where’s the fire, girl?” She just apologized and kept moving through the hall. Little did he know that she was dealing with a private fire that no one knew about.

As they would run into one another at school events and gatherings, Nico and Zora became quick friends. Thick as thieves. He became someone steady that grounded her even though he didn’t know it. She thought he was funny but didn’t mince words. She learned to respect him for that.

One Saturday night at a party they were mingling with other classmates. Natural environment. Music playing. Laughter. People making out in corners, the porch, stairway, the entry to the kitchen. Nico was unaware of what was brewing within Zora. He was about to find out.

She grabs his arm and pulls him into the dimly lit dining room. Less traffic. Almost secluded. She planted a deep kiss on his mouth. He was caught off guard and tried to push her off, but she was insistent. He gave in. They kissed heavily. In his mind *she's like my baby sister. What is she doing? What are we doing?* He pushed the thoughts aside when he felt his own desire rise in his pants. Before he knew it, he and Zora were about to start a fire from their intense grinding session. Before they could go any farther, they heard a voice – one of the older kids – telling them, "Y'all can't 'go all the way' in here."

Zora took that as a cue and permission. She pulled Nico outside to the backyard. She found a dark corner behind the shed that was attached to the large deck. Right there, she pulls down her jeans and puts Nico's hand in her panties. Nico was surprised but intrigued. Innocent. He was a virgin. He was unaware that she was not. With her guidance, she let him explore inside her panties for just a moment. His trembling fingers fumbled with her labia. She kissed him hard and dropped to her knees to convince him that he wanted to do this. He had never felt anything like this before. He was getting wrapped up in what he was feeling, but she stopped. He looked confused.

Seeing the look in his eyes, Zora spins herself around, bends over and slips his innocent, engulfed penis inside her. He gasped. She thrust herself back against him creating that familiar friction that she was so used to. Nico is near tears because he was overwhelmed by pleasure. She kept forcing her hips back on him. Harder. Wild. This was his first sexual experience. He couldn't hold it. His penis stiffened. He exploded inside her with a scream.

"Shhhhhhh… be quiet…" she commands.

She keeps going, forcing him to fulfill her until she finally reaches her climax, which comes within the next 10 strokes. She collapses against him, hands on her knees. Hair hanging in her face. Both breathless.

When it was all over, Zora pulls up her panties and jeans and turns to look at Nico who appears to be in shock. Utter shock. So much so, he's standing there with his pants and underwear at his knees, penis fully exposed, and heaving for air. "Pull yourself together, Nico. Pull up your pants," she says laughing at him.

He was pleased and embarrassed at the same time. He looked at Zora and she looked *so normal*. Unaffected. Why isn't she affected like he was? Little did he know that this *was* normal for Zora.

From that first encounter, Nico was smitten. Protective of their friendship. They continued to have sex. Frequently. Always on the fly. Always unplanned. Always risky. Multiple times a day for months. Zora would just show up and tell him she was "hungry." He had no idea how insatiable her appetite was until it almost ruined their friendship.

"Zora, why don't you want to be my girlfriend? We are always together. Always having sex."

"Nico, we're too young to be in a serious relationship. I like that we are friends with benefits."

Nico scratches his head, bewildered. "You don't want more? More from me? For us?"

"Nico, you're too serious. We are having fun. Can't you just enjoy the ride?" she smiles at him.

He considers that. "Actually, no, Z. I want more. I'm falling in love with you… I want us to be a couple… I…"

She puts her fingers to his lips. "Shhhhhh, Nico! You want to ruin a good thing with a commitment? How many boys your age are getting this much ass for free? Enjoy yourself. I know I am."

This frustrated Nico.

"Zora, I can't keep doing this. We've never even had sex in a bed. You never want to talk about our intimacy. You never want to talk about commitment. You never want to snuggle or talk about deeper things. It is always just about sex. Although I enjoy being with you physically, I need more, Z. More of you…emotionally…Not just sex."

Zora is clearly frustrated. "Nico if you don't want this arrangement, I can find someone else who …"

He stops her. "Zora! So, is it that easy for you to find someone else? Don't I mean anything to you or am I just a 'warm tool' to you?"

She thinks carefully before she responds.

"Nico, I never told you we were exclusive. I never told you that we were a couple. You are just as much a part of this "warm tool" situation as I am. Don't act like you don't enjoy it with or without strings attached."

Nico's frustration grows. "Here's what I'm going to do, Z. I'm not going to make myself so readily available for your appetite. You are my best friend, but this is not a fair arrangement. At least not for me. I'm out..."

"Nico," Zora calls to him as he walks away. "You're going to miss this. Me. Wait and see. You'll be back..."

Nico continues to walk away. Zora stands there waiting for him to come back. He never does.

Six months later at basketball game, Nico runs into Zora coming out of one of her hungry stupors. He could tell. He knows *that look* on her all too well. He's seen it too many times. He checks in with her. "You doing okay, Zora?"

"Hi, Nico, I'm doing great!" she says glistening and breathless. "How are you doing?"

He can see she is flushed. He knows she just got "fixed." Probably under the bleachers right under unsuspecting fans seats. Her commands and moans drowned out by their stomps, cheers or boos.

"I'm doing great. Dating Marci Groom from music class."

Zora lets that settle. So, he is using his warming tool on her, huh? Nico interrupts her thoughts.

"I'll text you later so we can catch up... to talk." He makes sure she understands his intentions, so she gets no other ideas about them reconnecting.

Zora smiles and agrees. "That will be great, Nico." From that moment on, Nico has been covering for Zora's indiscretions and trying to get her some help. Nineteen years later, she's still on a crash course to destruction.

***

Back in Nico's studio office, he stares at Zora emotionlessly. She is weeping. He is not moved by her theatrics.

He interrupts her.

"Z, you know I love you, but I cannot keep covering for you. How long will you be able to keep this up, at this pace, which seems to be accelerating?"

Zora wipes at her face and looks up at him. "Nico, I want to be better, but sometimes I can't control it… can't control her – Skyy. I'm scared, but I don't know how to stop… I…"

Unconvinced, Nico leans forward.

"You *have* to want to be better. Words mean nothing, Z. Nothing. I'll always be here for you, but I'm going to step back from protecting you. I still won't tell the girls, but I will no longer cover for you. You have to live this thing out on your own."

"Thank you, I understand… I…"

"Don't thank me, Z. Get help! I mean it!" he says firmly. "I have a session in 15 minutes."

Nico stands and walks her to the door. Zora turns, heaviness in her heart. "I love you, Nico, and I'm trying even if you don't believe me. See you Friday at the next besties gathering."

With that, Zora gets in her car. She lays her head on the headrest with her eyes closed. Tears stinging her eyes. She is emotionally spent. Nico took her all the way back.

Reminded her of her salacious antics. She knows he's right. He's always been right.

I need a drink. Or something stronger.

She puts the car in drive and heads home.

Chapter Fifteen

At home, Zora leans her back against the kitchen door, the cool wood pressing into her spine as if it might hold her upright. Heavy. Exhausted. Drained in a way sleep doesn't touch. The meeting with Nico took more than she anticipated. It scraped at old places, places she'd boarded up and labeled *off-limits*.

She knows he's right.

She also knows he could never fully understand.

She was his first.

But to her, he had been just another fix.

Six months of sex without attachment. No names for what they were doing. No expectations. Nico was her friend. Her confidant, her ride-or-die but nothing more. She never allowed more.

Emotions were not allowed.

Trust was dangerous.

Satisfaction without commitment.

She liked it that way.

She needed it that way.

History taught her. And she learned.

The clock on the microwave blinks 6:15 p.m. She hasn't eaten since lunch. Her stomach tightens, but not with hunger for food. The pressure of the day has settled lower, deeper. Throbbing. Aching. Hot.

She inhales.

Exhales.

Repeats.

I need to blow off this pressure.

Her gaze drifts to the mini bar tucked neatly between the kitchen and living room, a small lounge moment she curated for guests. Four sherpa chairs. A round live-edge table on iron hairpin legs. Rum, vodka, gin lined up like a promise she rarely keeps. She isn't much of a drinker. When she does indulge, it's light. Controlled. Wine. A cocktail. Nothing that dulls the ever-present hum inside her.

She peels off her coat, kicks away her shoes, and scuffs barefoot through the house. Quiet. Comfortable. Fully furnished and hollow. Love has never been allowed to live here. Not physically. Not emotionally.

***

Upstairs, steam gathers as Zora steps into the shower and turns the water hot. She needs the heat; needs it to loosen the knot cinched tight across her neck and shoulders. Her body feels like it's been in a fight, though the blows were all verbal. Emotional. Invisible.

She exhales under the water. Both hands brace against the tile wall. Eyes closed. Head bowed. Water cascades over her shoulders, down her spine, soaking her hair until it falls forward, veiling her face.

Familiar.

Her hair always falls this way when she's getting *fixed.* Always turned away. Always hidden.

A mask?

Why does she never face them? What does that mean? The question flickers through her mind, but she doesn't linger. Digging leads to doors she isn't ready to open. Therapy would name it. Examine it. But not tonight.

She dismisses the thought and steps out of the steam.

***

Out of the shower, Zora is vibrating. Skin buzzing, nerves humming too loudly. Frazzled. Restless.

Just get a drink.

Breathe, Zora.

The pressure gnaws.

Ignore it.

Relax tonight.

You can do this.

She passes the bathroom mirror as the steam clears and catches her reflection.

Who am I kidding?

Her body answers before her mind does. She moves instinctively toward the closet, past the everyday clothes, into the inner space. Skyy's domain.

Red V-neck sweater with sequin cuffs. Black knit skirt. Gold shimmer thigh-high stockings. Black slingback heels. Only two inches. Gold heart pendant. Gold dangling earrings. A wig. Auburn, wavy bob. Sassy. Perfect. Smokey eyes. Bronze cheeks. Red lips. Beauty mark in place.

No panties.

She studies herself. Hesitation flickers.

Skyy is ecstatic.

Don't go, Zora.

Go, Zora.

She grabs a black clutch and heads downstairs. Spring has arrived, but the air still carries a bite. She slips on a short trench coat, keys in hand, and peeks out the back door.

She scans for neighbors. Especially Ms. Fitzpatrick, rumor mill incarnate.

The last thing I need is for her to see me leaving like this.

It isn't as dark as she prefers, but the internal heat is relentless. She removes the wig, tucks it into her coat pocket, and moves quickly down the deck steps, into the car.

Ignition. No warmup.

She needs to leave while she still can.

She checks the rearview mirror. No Ms. Fitzpatrick. Good.

The GPS lights up: **1334 U Street NW – The Alchemist Cocktail.**

At the next red light, she pulls the wig from her pocket, shakes it loose, and slides it on. The mirror reflects Skyy fully now. Sultry, wanton, hungry.

***

U Street feels too close. Too familiar. Zora checks every corner as she drives, nerves prickling beneath her skin. She hums with energy, pressure intensifying.

She parks in a paid lot. No street parking battles. Not tonight.

Inside, she chooses a bar seat near the end. Full view, controlled vantage point. The bartender approaches.

"What can I get for you, Miss?"

"I'll have a low alcohol Sex on the Beach, please."

"Comin' right up, Miss."

"Thank you," Zora says with a warm smile.

She scans the room. No familiar faces. Yet.

What are you doing, Zora? What if someone recognizes you?

Skyy pushes back.

Who would know you like this? Chill out, girl.

Nico's voice echoes anyway.

"…Words mean nothing, Z… I'm going to step back… Get help…"

"Miss? Miss? Your drink. Anything else?"

"Um, no, thank you. Thank you."

"Should I run a tab for you, Miss?"

"Not necessary. I won't be ordering anything else. I'll take the check, please."

Her heart races before she even sips.

Then… a tap on her shoulder.

"Excuse me, Miss. Is this seat taken?"

Her blood runs cold.

She turns slowly.

Dr. Simmons. Grinning. Charming.

"May I buy your drink? I'm Carl."

She shifts her voice, softens it, layers in a Korean inflection she knows well.

"Um, No thank you. One is my limit."

They exchange light pleasantries. Her discomfort deepens, not just from recognition, but from the heat pooling lower, demanding release.

She motions for the check. Dr. Simmons adds it to his tab. She thanks him and slides off the stool.

Too risky. Too close.

He offers to walk her out.

"Thank you, but I can manage."

"Miss, you should not be walking out on U Street at night alone. Let me be a gentleman, please."

She hesitates. Then asks, "Are you here alone?"

"I have a group of co-workers with me… May I walk you to your car, Miss…?"

She smiles.

"My name is Skyy."

"That's a beautiful name. A beautiful name for a beautiful woman."

She laughs lightly and moves toward the door.

Outside, the city hums. Streetlights, laughter, food scents curling through the air. He helps her with her coat.

"You okay?"

"Yes, Carl, just need to get to my car. It's been a long day."

They stop near the parking lot entrance. He steps closer.

"I'm sorry… but there's something about you that is intoxicating…"

She presses her fingers to his lips.

"Shhhhh… Where is your car?"

"On the next block."

"Let's go to your car…"

A silver Denali waits. Tinted windows, solid, perfect.

"Shhhhhh, Carl… No talking. Get in."

"Oh, my God. Are you a prostitute?"

"No. I am not a prostitute. Just a little fun. You up for this or not?"

He climbs into the back seat.

She pulls him to her and kisses him feverishly. He is surprised at her forwardness. Her strength. For such a petite woman, she commands a space. He leans into the kiss as she feeds him her tongue. Wet. Longing. She moans. He feels his manhood respond.

A group of people walk by laughing and frolicking. He opens his eyes and turns his head.

Skyy pulls his head back towards her mouth. "Focus, Carl… Focus."

He's turned on and almost scared at the same time. He's never been manhandled before. It is new, but he likes it. He really likes it.

Skyy continues her ravenous quest.

"Open your pants…" she pants against his mouth. "Open your pants…"

He fumbles for his belt, gets it unbuckled. Unzips his slacks. She starts to rhythmically hump the air waiting for him. "Hurry… Hurry, please…"

He's growing harder by the second at her desperate commands.

"Pull it out… Pull it out…" she says biting his bottom lip and trying to mount him at the same time.

He's pulling at his slacks, feeling his own heat and the slickness of her lips as she starts stroking against his hands. She hands him a condom that she pulled from her clutch while he was preparing. He rolls the condom onto his stiffened penis.

Damn. This woman is wet and wild. Literally.

"Here… Here it is… This what you wa–?"

In one motion, Skyy was shoving his erect penis inside her pulsating vagina. She begins humping him frantically. Moaning. Groaning. Grinding it out. Extinguishing her fire.

"You like that? Huh, you like that?" Carl asks.

"No… talking…" she snaps as she is taking him for all he is giving to her. Strong strokes. Deep thrusts. She is so wet he thinks she peed on him. She is responding to his power.

Huge black penis.

Thick.

Hot.

Thumping.

Humping.

Stroking.

Feeding her desire.

He is pushing up into her with the same force that she is delivering to him. The Danali is rugged, holding up to the motion. To the rocking without being noticeable to the average person.

Skyy tosses her head back against the front seat behind her. Holding onto the collar of his shirt for leverage.

"Bang me… Bang me harder," she barks. "Bang me, damn it…"

Carl obliges. They go at that pace until the both of them explode.

Skyy unfolds herself from his lap, breath ragged. He stares.

Something is off.

"Do I know you?"

Before the realization can settle, she bolts out the door, down the street, heart pounding.

Shit. Shit. Shit. Shit.

CHAPTER SIXTEEN

Zora has never driven so fast in her life.

The city dissolves into streaks of light and shadow. Everything blurs together. The four miles home vanish beneath her tires in less than ten minutes.

Traffic lights.

Did she stop?

Stop signs.

Did she even see them?

Her hands grip the steering wheel so tightly her fingers ache. Her breath comes in sharp, uneven pulls. Her chest feels too small for her lungs.

She does not remember turning down her street.

She only remembers pulling in behind the house, the car landing crooked in its space. Half in. Half out.

She does not care.

She bolts up the deck steps, fumbling with the door, slamming it shut behind her the moment she is inside. The sound echoes too loudly in the quiet house.

Her legs give out.

She slides down the door until she hits the floor.

Panic crashes over her in a violent wave.

Her heart slams against her ribs, frantic and unrelenting. Her ears ring so loudly it feels like pressure building inside her skull. The room spins. Her hands tremble uncontrollably. Her legs feel heavy, useless.

Her face goes numb.

Her breath stutters, shallow and fast.

I can't breathe.

I can't breathe.

Emotion detonates inside her.

She sobs. Deep, uncontrollable sobs that tear out of her chest. Real tears. Hot and relentless. They soak her face and drip down into the collar of her trench coat.

She rips the wig from her head and flings it away, not caring where it lands. Her fingers claw into her natural hair, yanking hard, desperate for pain sharp enough to override everything else.

Ahhhh. Uhhhhhh.

"No. No. No. No."

Her voice cracks.

"What did I do? What the hell did I do?"

Her chest heaves as shame floods her.

"Stupid, Zora. Stupid. Stupid. Stupid."

Her hands cover her face as she screams into her palms, over and over again. Louder each time. As if volume might erase the moment. As if sound could drown out humiliation and fear.

"I hate you, Skyy. I hate you!"

Her body betrays her again.

Nausea surges violently.

She gags.

I have to throw up now.

She scrambles toward the powder room on her hands and knees. The distance feels impossible. The floor tilts beneath her.

Don't throw up.

Please don't throw up.

She barely makes it.

Her fingers fumble with the toilet seat before everything comes up. Her body folds over itself as she vomits into the bowl. Her hair spills forward, dipping into the water.

The irony does not escape her.

Her addiction has her facedown in the toilet.

She convulses until there is nothing left, dry heaving until her throat burns and bile coats her mouth. Her forearms brace her weight as her body shakes.

Her hair is wet.

Her stomach aches.

Her head throbs.

And between her legs, her body still remembers.

The sensation hits her like another blow, dragging her back to the moment that dropped her to her knees.

She collapses onto the bathroom floor, curling into herself, knees pulled tight to her chest. Fetal. Small. Broken.

This could ruin everything.

Her career.

Her reputation.

Her life.

Disgust settles deep in her bones.

Through tears and shallow breaths, her voice emerges. Barely audible.

"You need help, Zora," she whispers.

"Get help."

Chapter Seventeen

The ache in her hips and shoulders tells Zora she has been on the bathroom floor longer than she realized. Her body speaks before her mind catches up.

What time is it?

She presses her palms against the cool tile and pushes herself upright, every movement deliberate, cautious. The taste of bile still clings to the back of her throat. Her stomach twists in protest as she steadies herself and begins the slow walk to her bedroom.

Streetlights spill through the tall windows, casting long amber streaks across the walls, the bed, the floor. The room feels exposed in the glow, stripped bare of comfort. She does not turn on the light.

She undresses in silence.

Her coat slips from her shoulders. Clothes fall where they land, abandoned in a loose heap on the floor. She does not care. She moves straight to the bathroom.

The overhead light snaps on.

Her reflection stops her cold.

Mascara streaks her cheeks in uneven lines. Her eyes are swollen, dark, rimmed like bruises. Lipstick smeared, broken. Her hair is tangled, pulled, wild. She barely recognizes the woman staring back at her.

Tears rise instantly, sharp and hot, but she blinks them back.

No.

Not tonight.

She did this to herself.

The shower is necessary, but it is not cleansing. The water runs hot, beating against her skin, rinsing away sweat and makeup and the physical remnants of the night, but it cannot touch the truth underneath. That stays. Lodged deep.

Pajamas on, she sits heavily on the edge of the bed and reaches for her phone. Her real phone. The one she leaves behind when Skyy takes over.

Three missed calls.

Lai.

The hotel confirming her reservation.

A co-worker.

More messages wait. The Besties group chat. Lai, of course, leading the thread.

Lai: "Hey, Besties! I'm excited to see you all this Friday night. Instead of going to a different restaurant, I wanted to invite you to Jazz-n-Gems for a special night of entertainment. I'm hosting an up-and-coming group from the city. They are f-i-y-a for real. So proud of them. 7 pm. Don't be late. Confirm you got this."

Rayven: "I'm in. Loving I don't have to drive outside of the city for a change to enjoy my besties. LOL! Got a lot to share. Luv y'all!"

Nico: "I'll be there. About 30 minutes late. Have a last-minute session with my youth band for their Spring Fling concert. #Excited"

Zora stares at the screen, her thumb hovering just above the glass. Her pulse kicks up again.

They have no idea.

They cannot know.

Not yet.

She types carefully, deliberately, crafting distance with words.

Zora: "Hey, Besties... Sorry, just seeing this. Been preparing for my speech on Thursday in Georgia. I'll be back in time for our rendezvous. BIG love to all!"

The message sends.

And the guilt lands immediately.

She feels like an imposter inside her own life, performing competence while quietly unraveling. Grieving something she cannot name out loud.

She forces herself to focus.

Emails next.

She checks that her Out of Office reply is active. Confirms that her Wednesday and Friday counseling clients have been notified and rescheduled. She verifies that her students have received the message in the portal. Thursday's class cancelled. Assignment posted.

Responsible.

Efficient.

Put together.

She sets her alarm.

5:00 a.m.

Flight at 11:00.

Zora eases back onto the pillow, eyes fixed on the ceiling above her. The room is silent now, except for the hum of the city outside and the soft thudding of her own heart.

She needs to sleep.

She needs rest.

She needs to rest.

Her eyes finally close.

Sleep does not come easily.

Chapter Eighteen

Zora drives on autopilot. The stretch of 295 unfurls beneath her tires, asphalt humming like white noise, but she barely registers it. The steering wheel feels distant under her palms. Her eyes are open, focused forward, yet her mind is everywhere else.

Thoughts stack on top of one another, overlapping and colliding.

Her behavior.

Her speech.

Skyy.

Nico's voice.

Her parents' expectations.

Her body.

Her need.

Her shame.

She feels suspended between tears and screaming, between the urge to disappear and the urge to be touched again. The internal tug-of-war exhausts her.

She knows which side will win.

Desire always does.

She pulls into daily parking at BWI without remembering the drive. The car stops. The engine cuts. She sits there, staring ahead, heart thudding, breath shallow, as if she has arrived somewhere she never meant to go.

The shuttle bus pulls up with a hiss of brakes. She boards mechanically, luggage rolling behind her, eyes scanning nothing. At the terminal, people rush past with purpose. Conversations overlap. Coffee steams in paper cups. Children cry while parents negotiate patience. Laughter bubbles up near the gates. Life, in motion.

Zora watches it all like an observer behind glass.

In her mind, she is counseling every one of them.

Slow down.

Breathe.

You are allowed to rest.

You are not alone.

Why can't I take my own advice?

The flight is uneventful. Atlanta greets her with warmth and movement. Hartsfield-Jackson buzzes with energy, but it feels contained, manageable. The Hilton Atlanta Airport Hotel is close enough to feel safe. Convenient. Controlled.

She checks into her suite and sends a text to the Besties group:

"Hi, Besties. Just landed in Atlanta. Meet-n-Greet tonight, 5 p.m., lobby of the Spelman Wellness Center. Conference and Plenary Panel in Sisters Chapel tomorrow at 10 a.m. Wish me luck on my speech!"

She sets the phone down and exhales.

***

Wednesday evening.

Zora rides the elevator down, dressed professionally, intentionally understated. Soft fabrics. Clean lines. Approachable. Her stomach twists with nerves. This conference matters. The inaugural Mental Health Conference hosted by the Counseling Center. Post-pandemic, youth mental health is no longer theoretical. It is urgent. Lived. Raw.

She is proud to be here. Grateful that her Delta Sigma Theta Soror thought of her.

At 6:10 p.m., she enters the Wellness Center.

Students greet her warmly, directing her toward hors d'oeuvres and beverages. The room hums with conversation. Soft jazz floats beneath the noise. Healing feels possible here, tangible in the air.

She pours herself a glass of white wine, selects a small plate of cheese, crackers, and turkey, and drifts toward a high-top table. No chair. She prefers to stay mobile. Observant.

She takes it all in.

Professors. Counselors. Students. Educators. Laughter spills from one corner while serious conversations anchor another. This is what community looks like, she thinks.

I needed this.

People approach her, introduce themselves, share their anticipation for her speech. She smiles, thanks them, grounds herself in the moment.

Then two men step into her orbit.

"Hello, my name is Jenson, and this is my friend and colleague, Damian," one of them says brightly. "He's my voice of reason."

Jenson is light-skinned, about five-ten, medium build, sharply dressed. His smile is easy. His eyes sparkle with something warmer than charm. Zora clocks it immediately.

Damian stands slightly back. Medium-brown skin. Six feet even. Solid, muscular frame. Bald head. Low-cut beard. Quiet presence. His eyes are deep, searching, respectful. Too perceptive.

She resists the urge to hold his gaze.

"Nice to meet you both," she says. "My friends call me Zee."

They exchange pleasantries. Compliments about the conference theme: "Mental Health Momentum: Moving at the Speed of Life."

"Hope we can talk more tomorrow," Jenson says.

"I'd like that," Zora replies, a little too softly. "Let's catch up then."

They move on. Zora releases a breath she did not realize she was holding.

No, Zora. Not here.

She catches Jenson's eye over her wine glass, quickly looks away. A student approaches her, eager, grateful, grounding.

Thank you, Sis.

She makes her rounds, then requests an Uber back to the hotel, adding a stop for a salad. It is nearly 7 p.m. She needs real food.

***

Back in her room, wrapped in a lounging robe, Zora eats her salad slowly. She FaceTimes her parents.

Her mother answers first. Warm. Familiar. Loving.

Her father appears briefly. Formal. Efficient.

"Lock your door. Be safe. Love you."

And then he is gone.

The familiar ache settles in her chest.

She tells herself she will address it Sunday. She has to.

After the call, she checks the time.

8:10 p.m.

Not too late.

The heat stirs.

She tells herself it is less risky here. New city. New faces. No Skyy attire, but the hunger does not require costume. It lives in her body.

She dresses again. Soft top. Same skirt. Easy access. Freshens her makeup. Perfume. Heels. Purse.

As the elevator descends, doubt flickers. The elevator doors slide open. Jenson steps inside, smiling too easily.

"Where you headed, Zee?"

She keeps her eyes forward. "Restaurant. Just a nightcap. Nerves."

He chuckles softly. “Same. Speaking never gets easier.”

The doors close. The elevator begins its slow descent.

“Mind if I join you?” he asks.

She hesitates a beat too long. “I do not plan to stay.”

“That makes two of us,” he says lightly.

Silence settles. The hum of the elevator grows louder. The doors open again. People step in. Too many. Too close. Zora is pushed back. Her shoulders press into Jenson’s chest.

“Sorry,” she murmurs automatically, trying to shift.

“There’s nowhere to go,” he says quietly, almost apologetic.

Another stop. More bodies. The space tightens.

Her breath shortens.

He smells like clean linen and something warm. Bourbon. Soap.

“You okay?” he asks near her ear.

“Yes,” she says too quickly.

She feels the heat of him. Feels her body betray her. She stiffens, then stills.

The elevator jolts slightly.

His breath catches.

She tells herself to move. To step forward. To do anything. She does not.

Third floor. A few people exit.

There is more space now. Enough to move. She doesn’t.

He shifts. Barely. Testing.

Her pulse spikes.

“Zee,” he says softly. “If this is too much…”

She shakes her head once. A small, dangerous no.

The elevator slows.

Fourth floor.

The doors slide open.

This is his floor.

He turns slightly, blocking the exit.

"Come with me," he says, low. Not demanding. Inviting. "Just for a minute."

Her mind screams stop.

Her body steps forward.

The room door closes behind them.

She can feel the wetness on her inner thighs. She wants to stop, but she has passed her threshold.

He reaches for her blouse, but she catches his hands and commands, "Unzip your pants…"

Without hesitation, he works on his pants until they are at his knees. Her eyes widen. *Damn. He is massive.* His penis is thick and has a slight bend to the left. He pulls a condom from his wallet. *He's prepared.* She appreciates that.

His back against the room door, he slides the condom onto his thick, erect penis. Before he can say anything, Zora lifts her skirt, bends herself over and shoves herself onto him, taking him in one thrust.

"Oh, my God… you are so damn wet… I…" He whispers.

"Shhhhhh… No talking… just… work … me…" she says as she widens her stance and thrust herself on him with vigor. Holding her screams to herself. Hands touching the floor. Hair hanging in her face. He is banging her hard. She is loving it. Taking all of him in.

"Deeper… deeper… ahhhhh… go deeper, please… deeper…" she pleads with him.

"I'm about to… I'm about…" he says fighting the urge to cum.

"Shhhhhh. Be quiet… not yet… not yet…" she commands.

She gives him about five more powerful thrusts and the both of them cum at the same time.

They stay there. Connected. Heavy breathing. Bodies tingling. Her hanging upside down. Her hair is damp on the neck. His chest heaving for air. He's holding onto her hips giving small grinds against her.

She dislodges his penis from her vagina, stands up, and pulls her skirt down. She composes herself without looking at him.

The fifth floor is quiet when she exits the elevator.

Shame crashes over her.

She showers. Pulls the drapes closed. Crawls into bed.

10:07 p.m.

Her body relaxes despite herself. The throbbing reminder in her vagina lingers.

Again.

Chapter Nineteen

Zora rises to the alarm on her phone. She sits up slowly, wincing at the ache between her legs. A dull reminder she did not ask for. She swings her feet to the floor and heads into the bathroom.

She stares at herself in the mirror.

She sees Zora.

But she feels too much like Skyy.

"I thought I left you in DC," she whispers to her reflection.

Shame settles in her chest. Heavy. Persistent.

She dresses carefully. A mid-calf tan floral dress. Chocolate blazer. Brown heels. Minimal jewelry. Modest makeup. Maybe if she tones everything down, the raging part of her will quiet too. Maybe she will feel less like the woman she does not want to be.

She orders her Uber and makes her way to Spelman. Watching the city slide past the window, her anxiety builds. It is not just the speech. Not just the plenary.

I hope I do not run into Jenson.
I need to focus.

***

Zora arrives at Sisters Chapel at 9:00 a.m., intentionally early. An hour to settle herself. To breathe.

She is greeted by Shumi, one of the students assigned as her assistant for the day. Shumi moves with grace and ease, anticipating Zora's needs before they are voiced.

"I am so not used to all of this," Zora says with a soft laugh.

"This is how we treat our sisters, Dr. Zee," Shumi replies warmly. "You are family. We want you comfortable."

"Well, thank you, Shumi. I truly appreciate your care."

They walk together toward the green room, a smaller chapel tucked near the Chaplain's office. Along the corridor, Zora is greeted with smiles and nods. Then she sees them.

Jenson.

Damian.

Her stomach tightens.

They exchange brief greetings as Shumi continues forward. Zora glances back. Jenson holds her gaze a beat too long before looking away.

Do not say a word.
I mean it.

***

At 9:50 a.m., Zora is introduced as Dr. Zee, the name her students use with affection. She requested anonymity. Less formality. Less exposure. She takes the podium:

"Mental health momentum is not about speed," Zora says, her voice steady. *"It is about direction. Too many of us confuse survival with healing. We move quickly through life without ever stopping to ask what we are carrying with us...*

"...Trauma does not disappear because we succeed. It does not dissolve because we smile, achieve, or lead. Trauma waits patiently in the places we refuse to name. Healing begins when we acknowledge those spaces, not with shame, but with honesty...

"...Recovery is not linear. It requires courage to revisit what hurt us, and compassion to forgive ourselves for how we learned to cope. Therapy, community, and accountability are not signs of weakness. They are tools of freedom...

"...When we slow down long enough to face what shaped us, we reclaim agency over our lives. That is momentum. Moving not faster, but wiser. Toward a life that is whole, grounded, and free."

Her speech lands.
The room responds.
A standing ovation.
Unexpected.
Humbling.
Even Jenson is on his feet.

She later joins the plenary panel. Thoughtful discussion. Honest questions. Students lean in. The room feels hopeful.

For the first time in a long while, Zora feels normal. Present. Unburdened by the version of herself waiting back in DC.

Maybe I could have this there too.

Maybe I could.

***

After the session, Jenson and Damian approach her.

Dinner invitation.

Professional. Casual. Loaded.

Zora holds her breath beneath a practiced smile.

"Dr. Zee, you should join us," Jenson says. "Just a few speakers sharing reflections. By George Restaurant, six o'clock. I'll give you my number."

Time stalls.

"Dr. Zee?" he presses.

Damian remains a step back. Observant. Quiet. Seeing everything.

"Damian, give her your number too," Jenson adds. "We should collaborate."

"I am sure Dr. Zee does not need my number," Damian replies gently.

Jenson laughs as Zora hands her phone to him. He adds both their contacts with a grin.

Her stomach churns.

Breathe.

"Thank you," Zora finally says. "I will let you know."

***

By George Restaurant hums with warmth. White tablecloths. Ambient light. Jazz floating low beneath conversation.

Zora arrives alongside another female colleague. Relief floods her.

Introductions. Professors. Doctors. Educators. An advisor.

When introductions circle the table, Damian speaks briefly.

"Damian," he says evenly. "I live in Bowie, Maryland. I work part-time as an advisor at Trinity College. I travel with Jenson when needed."

Something about the way he says *when needed* registers with Zora.

Not boastful. Not casual.

Deliberate.

Bowie. Close enough to touch DC.

She files it away without knowing why.

The evening moves smoothly. Professional banter. Reflections on trauma. Education. Responsibility.

Each insight cuts deeper than Zora expects.

How can I counsel healing when I am unraveling?

Dinner winds down after ten. Numbers are exchanged. Polite hugs are given.

Zora pulls out her phone to order an Uber.

"You can ride back with us," Jenson says.

It is not a question.

She forces a smile. "Thank you. I just need the Ladies Room."

She moves quickly. Heart racing.

Only Jenson and Damian remain when she returns.

***

Back at the hotel, the three of them – Jenson, Damian, and Zora – wave to the night concierge staff and make their way to the elevator. Damian stops at the convenience store to grab a bag of trail mix and a flavored water for a snack.

"Hey, I'll catch up with you. I'll be right up," he says.

Oh, no! I'll be on the elevator alone with Jenson.

She doesn't want or need another encounter with him.

The elevator doors slide shut. Jenson stands too close. Then closer. His hand presses against her lower back. His breath brushes her ear.

"Relax," he murmurs. "You liked it last night."

She shifts away. He follows.

"Jenson, stop."

He smiles. Slow. Ugly.

"You do not get to turn it on and off like that," he says. "You do not get me worked up and then play holy professor."

Her pulse spikes.

"I said stop."

The elevator dings. Fourth floor.

The doors open.

He grabs her wrist and yanks her out.

Hard.

"Let go of me!" she shouts, clawing at his arm.

He shoves her against the wall, his forearm across her chest.

"You think you are special?" he snarls. "You think you can tease a man and walk away?"

He curses and slaps her across the mouth. Her head snaps sideways. Pain blooms. Metal floods her mouth.

Her heel slips off. Skids across the hallway. Her hair comes loose, wild around her face. She scratches his neck, his cheek, anything she can reach.

"Let me go!" she screams. "Let me go, you bastard!"

He clamps his hand over her mouth, dragging her toward his door.

She bites his hand.

Hard.

"You wanted this," he growls. "Do not pretend now, bitch."

The door is half open.

Her foot catches the frame.

She kicks. Thrashes. Tries to scream through his palm.

Damian appears from the stairwell. He never takes the elevator. He sees what is happening.

"Jenson."

The voice is calm. Firm.

Damian.

"Let her go."

Jenson freezes but does not release her.

"She wanted it," he snaps. "She is playing games."

"Let. Her. Go."

Zora's eyes lock on Damian's. Terror. Pleading. No words needed.

Damian steps closer. Hands slightly lifted, palms facing outward.

"You are not thinking," Damian says. "Let her go."

Jenson shakes his head, breathing hard. Caught in a flurry of his thoughts and urges. Looking from Damian to Zora and back again.

"She owes me," he pleads.

Damian's voice sharpens.

"Jenson. Focus. Let her go. Now."

Silence stretches.

Jenson's grip loosens.

Damian moves fast, pulling Zora free and placing himself between them.

"Get in your room," Damian orders. "Lock the door. Do not come out."

Jenson hesitates.

Damian does not blink.

"Now."

Jenson backs away like a child caught doing something unforgivable. He shuts the room door.

Damian turns to Zora.

She is shaking. Hair tangled. One shoe missing. Lip bleeding.

He checks her quickly. Gently. Like someone who has done this before.

"You are safe," he says. "I have you."

***

Damian reluctantly rides the elevator with Zora to the fifth floor and walks beside her down the quiet corridor. The carpet muffles their footsteps. The lights feel too bright. She keeps her arms folded close to her body, shoulders drawn inward. He does not crowd her. Does not rush her. Every few steps, he glances over, silently checking in.

Tears streak her face now. Her cheek is swelling. One side of her mouth is tender and beginning to darken.

At her room door, 515, Damian pauses. "May I see your phone?" he asks gently. "I'll open the door for you."

Her hand trembles as she places it in his. He opens the door and steps back, giving her space. "Call me if you need anything," he says quietly.

She hesitates, turns, then reaches for his forearm, her fingers barely grazing his sleeve. "Wait," she says, her voice unsteady. "Don't. Don't leave me alone. Not yet. Please."

Damian exhales slowly. "Dr. Zee, I don't go into women's rooms. I don't want to give the wrong impression. I…"

"Please," she says again, tears spilling over now. "Just for a little while. I don't want any trouble. I just… I just don't want to be alone."

He looks down the hallway, then back at her. After a moment, he nods. He steps inside but remains near the door, hands tucked into his pockets, posture guarded but open.

"Come in," she says softly, motioning toward the couch. "Please. Just sit with me for a while."

He hesitates. "Until you fall asleep," he says carefully. "That's it. Is that fair?"

"That's fair," she replies, her voice breaking.

She walks into the bathroom and turns on the light. The mirror reflects back a version of herself she does not recognize. Her hair is disheveled. Her lip swollen. A bruise is forming along her cheek.

"I can't believe he did this," she whispers, leaning closer to the mirror. "He hit me."

From the couch, Damian asks, "Do you have any ice in the freezer?"

"I'm not sure," she calls out softly. "I never looked."

He moves into the kitchenette, careful not to linger, though his eyes take in the room despite himself. The open suitcase. Jewelry lay neatly on the dresser. Shoes lined up. A book resting on the bed. Night clothes folded across the pillow. The air carries the faint scent of honey and hibiscus.

He shakes his head once. *Stop it, Damian.*

"I found ice," he says. "Do you have a washcloth?"

She hands one to him from the bathroom doorway. He wraps several ice cubes inside, wets it at the sink, and returns to the couch.

She comes out slowly, looking like the aftermath of a storm. He offers her the cloth. She hesitates, then says quietly, "Could you… please do it for me?"

He pauses. "Only if that's okay with you."

"Yes," she says. "Please."

He gestures for her to sit. "Lean your head back," he instructs gently. "It might hurt a little. I'll use light pressure. Tell me if it's too much."

She closes her eyes. "I'm ready."

With careful hands, he holds the cold cloth against her cheek. She inhales sharply, then exhales. Her breathing begins to slow. When she opens her eyes, she catches him watching her with concern and tenderness. He notices and starts to look away.

"Don't," she says softly. "Please don't look away. Thank you. For being here."

"I'm glad I was," he replies quietly. "I wish you hadn't gone through that."

After a moment, she sits up. He pulls the cloth back, but she gently places his hand against her cheek again, anchoring herself.

"May I ask you something?" she asks.

"Anything."

"Is this why you travel with Jenson?" Her voice is careful. "Does he… does he have a problem?"

Damian takes a breath. "Yes. He needs monitoring around women. He knows it. He just doesn't always control it."

"Is it an addiction?" she asks quietly, understanding her own question relates to herself.

"You could say that," he replies. "His impulses take over. He doesn't handle rejection well. That's why he has a chaperone. His sponsor requires it. His regular one couldn't travel this week, so I flew down from Bowie, Maryland and filled in."

That lands differently for her. Close. Not far. Human.

"Everyone is fighting something," Damian continues. "It comes down to how badly you want to conquer it."

The words settle into her.

He studies her face again. "Are you okay? Do you want to report this?"

She shakes her head slowly, tears brimming her eyes. "I just want to go home."

"I understand," he says. "Rest. I'll leave once you're asleep."

"Please," she says. "Just wait until I fall asleep."

He nods. "I will."

She hugs him suddenly, tightly, her body shaking. "Thank you," she whispers. "Thank you so much."

He sits still, allowing the embrace, then gently releases her.

She changes for bed and curls beneath the covers. Damian remains seated, quiet, present. He watches her breathing slow. Her shoulders soften. Her face relaxes. When her breaths even out and sleep finally takes her, he rises silently.

He leaves the room without a sound.

And even as the door closes, he carries her presence with him.

***

Later, Damian handles Jenson. Man to man. Closed doors.

Jenson never speaks of Zora again.

Chapter Twenty

Late Friday morning, Hartsfield-Jackson Airport is alive with motion. Travelers move with purpose, eyes trained on departure boards, rolling suitcases trailing behind them like obedient shadows. Coffee cups steam in hurried hands. The scent of baked goods, fried food, and cinnamon pretzels drifts through the corridors, mixing with jet fuel and recycled air.

Zora moves through it all quietly, almost invisibly. Her body is present, but her mind is somewhere between what just happened and what comes next.

Three days.

Three long, unraveling days.

The speaking assignment had been a success. Applause. Validation. Purpose.

And then there was Jenson.

Damian.

The bruise on her face, still tender beneath makeup, pulsing faintly like a warning light.

Gate D.

Flight 2487.

11:05 a.m.

Once the plane lifts off, Zora presses her forehead lightly against the window. Atlanta shrinks beneath her, buildings flattening into grids, streets dissolving into lines. The higher they climb, the smaller it all becomes, until the last three days are nothing more than shapes and color.

The flight is uneventful.

Landing at BWI, reality rushes back in the moment her feet touch the ground. Home. Familiar. Heavy.

In her car, she studies her reflection in the rearview mirror. The woman staring back at her looks composed. Professional. Fine.

But inside, she feels scattered. Fragmented.

Who am I?

Who am I becoming?

She puts the car in drive and merges onto 295, heading south toward DC, the road stretching out ahead of her like an unanswered question.

***

Pulling into her space behind the brownstone, Zora exhales deeply. The kind of breath that empties her lungs and her chest at the same time. She pops the trunk, lifts her suitcase, and climbs the back steps slowly, deliberately.

Inside, the house feels unfamiliar, as if it has been waiting for her longer than she realized.

Her last memory here flashes uninvited.

The panic attack.

The bathroom floor.

Her body folded in on itself.

She moves through the kitchen, hanging her trench coat in the hall closet. Keys on the hook. A small, grounding ritual. Then upstairs, into her sanctuary.

Mentally exhausted, she pauses before unpacking. Picks up her phone. Holds it there, palm warm against the screen. Head tipped back. Eyes closed. Heart racing.

Damian.

Her thumb hovers before she finally types.

"Hi, Damian. This is Zee, from the Atlanta conference. Just wanted to thank you again for watching over me the other day. I'm back home in DC."

She sends it, then immediately wonders why she feels exposed for doing so.

No response.

She sighs, shakes it off, and begins unpacking. Shoes lined up. Clothes folded. A quiet attempt at control.

Her phone chimes.

"Hi, Zee. Glad you had a safe flight! Take care of yourself. We all need a friend. If you ever need to talk, I'm here."

She stares at the words.

We all need a friend.

The sentence lands gently, but it lands deep.

She carefully texts back. "I would appreciate a good friend. Thank you, again. Talk soon."

She sets the phone down, changed into soft lounging clothes, and decides she will not leave the house again until Besties night.

In the kitchen, she makes tea and washes green grapes, her favorite. She settles into the living room, a space she rarely allows herself to occupy without distraction.

She calls her mother.

"Hi, Mommy. I'm back home."

They talk for fifteen minutes. About Atlanta. The speech. Her mother's new design client. The family dinner on Sunday.

"Just bring yourself," her mother says, smiling through the phone.

When the call ends, Zora sits quietly, tea cooling in her hands.

She loves her parents deeply. She always has.

She just wishes she could feel her father's love in the way she needs it. Emotional. Unguarded. Soft.

She closes her eyes and imagines it. Just once.

The thought leaves her chest aching.

She picks up her phone again and calls Dr. Hanson's office, requesting a video appointment. No deep dive yet. Just a place to begin. To unpack the father wound she has carried quietly for decades.

She will wait for Libby's call to schedule the appointment.

From the sofa, she looks out the front window at the small park across the street. People walking. Sitting.

Laughing. Living. She wonders what secrets they carry beneath their ordinary movements.

Her tea goes untouched.

She closes her eyes.

***

Two hours later, Zora jolts awake, heart pounding, breath shallow. Disoriented. Afraid. She forgets, for a moment, where she is.

Breathe, Zora.

In through your nose.

Out through your mouth.

She repeats it until the panic loosens its grip. She refuses to let it take over today.

***

After a shower, she dresses for Besties night. A cream, lightweight sweater slipping off one shoulder. Cream slacks. Bronze jewelry. Heels. Careful makeup to conceal the bruise. Bronze lipstick. One last look in the mirror.

Besties ready.

At 7 p.m., Jazz-n-Gems hums with energy. Lai greets each of them as they arrive, radiant with pride over the group she is featuring tonight.

Rayven chats animatedly. Zora listens, responds, laughs in the right places. They trade stories from the day, catching up until Nico arrives.

Drinks are ordered. Nico notices the discoloration on Zora's face. She dismisses it easily. Too easily.

Looks are exchanged.

Nico asks her to join him at the bar.

At the bar, his voice lowers. "You look tired, Z. You okay?"

"Yes. Of course. Spelman was amazing. The students walked away with real tools. Real healing. I loved it."

He studies her. "What's with the bruise?"

"It's nothing. I'm fine."

He does not believe her.

Lai interrupts with perfect timing, ushering them back to the table as her new group, Velvet Rue, takes the stage. The lighting shifts. Purple. Fuchsia. Gold. The room leans forward.

The band electrifies the space. Applause explodes.

When Lai returns to the stage and sings. The room stills.

Verse

I learned how to smile with a crack in my chest
Learned how to carry what wouldn't rest
I folded my pain in the pockets of pride
Called it surviving, called it my stride
But silence gets heavy when it sleeps in your bones
And the heart knows the truth even when it won't be told

Refrain

So tell the truth softly
Let it fall slow

You don't have to bleed it
Just let it show
Healing ain't loud
It don't need proof
Just a willing heart
And a whispered truth

Verse
I ain't asking you to bare it all tonight
Just loosen your grip, let yourself breathe right
You don't owe the world your deepest scar
But you owe your soul who you really are
And grace ain't scared of the mess you made
It meets you right where the truth gets brave

So tell the truth softly
Let it heal you whole
Piece by piece
Let the hard parts go
You are not your shame
You are not your youth
You are still worthy
Of a healed-up truth

Lai's voice carries truth. Healing. Vulnerability.

A hush wraps the audience. People lean into one another. Tears fall freely. The lyrics settle deep into bones and breath.

When Lai steps offstage, tears in her eyes, the Besties gather her in silent awe. No words needed. Warm embraces are exchanged and whispered "I love you" in each other's ear.

Nico leans into Zora's ear. "Can I get a ride home?"

In Zora's mind, despite the tenderness of the moment, a familiar thought flickers.

Here we go again.

She agrees.

In the car, he turns toward her. "Talk to me, Zora."

She exhales and tells him everything. Skyy. Jenson. The slap. The near rape. The man who stepped in.

"I'm getting help," she says quietly. "Therapy. Confession."

Nico listens. Then says, calmly, "I'll believe it when I see it."

***

Back home, those words echo.

She hangs up her coat. Drinks a glass of water. Climbs the stairs. The house is quiet. The night is quiet.

In her bedroom, she undresses and prepares for bed. Lai's song plays on repeat in her spirit, pressing against places she has avoided.

Truth.

Healing.

Softly spoken.

She stretches as she climbs under the covers. She ponders if she should read or rest. She picks up her phone at the bottom of the bed.

Missed text.

Damian.

Her heart jumps. She exhales. "Just friends," she reminds herself.

She texts him back. They exchange a few light messages. Nothing heavy. Nothing loaded. A quasi promise to talk again soon. Good night.

She chooses rest.

The bedside lamp clicks off. Streetlight filters through the drapes, painting shadows on the walls.

Alone in the dark, Zora reflects on Georgia. On who she is becoming. On how tired she feels.

Zora closes her eyes.

Skyy is still restless.

Chapter Twenty-One

Sleep does not come as Zora hoped it would after her evening with the Besties. She rolls onto her back and releases an exasperated sigh into the quiet room. The clock glows beside her bed. 10:15 p.m.

Her body is tired, but her mind refuses rest. Beneath the exhaustion, Skyy stirs. Familiar. Insistent.

She knows she should resist the heat that is building, but tonight she does not fight it. Instead, she sits up in the darkness and opens her nightstand drawer. Her fingers close around the second phone. The fixer phone.

Someone should be up on a Friday night.

She scrolls through the names, weighing her options. Tonight she does not want the unpredictability of a bar. A regular feels safer. Easier. Contained.

Brandon.

She sends a text.

"Hey, you up to some fun tonight?"

Three dots appear, then disappear. A response follows.

"Sorry, I'm in the middle of something. Maybe next time. Hit me up later."

A frustrated breath slips from her lips. Skyy grows restless. The ache between her legs sharpens, more demanding now.

She moves on.

Anthony.

"You up for some fun tonight?"

His reply comes quickly.

"Not tonight, Skyy. I'm on a date. Sorry."

Zora exhales sharply and drops back against the mattress. Skyy does not like rejection. The tightness in her groin pulses, insistent. She needs relief. Soon.

One more.

Milo.

Her fingers hover for a second before typing.

"Hi, Milo, you busy? Want some company?"

Nothing.

She lets out a near scream and drops her arm across her eyes. Then her phone dings.

She sits up fast.

"Hey, Skyy, great to hear from you. I'm off in about 30 minutes. Meet me at the rear of the restaurant. I'm at your service. LOL."

Milo knows the rules. He always has. No expectations. No emotions. No attachments. Just release. In his mind, it is simple. Mutually beneficial. No harm, no foul.

"See you at 11 p.m. Same spot," she texts back.

She is on her feet instantly, moving with purpose. The bathroom light flicks on. She washes quickly. Face. Underarms. Pubic area. Behind. Efficient. Ritualistic. She brushes her teeth and moves into the inner closet.

The air outside is warmer now, though not quite summer. She chooses a long-sleeved burgundy jersey knit dress that stops just above her knees. No panties. She checks her notes as a reminder of what wig she wears with Milo. She pulls the brunette wig from its stand. Wavy. Center part. Mid-back length. Consistency matters.

She dresses. Applies light makeup. Conceals the bruise on her cheek with care. Smoky burgundy and black shadow. Beauty mark placed above her lip. Gold necklace. Earrings. Flat shoes. This will be quick.

She slips a condom and the fixer phone into her clutch.

She moves down the steps with intention. Skyy is fully present now. Focused. Hungry. She needs this. Tonight. Most nights, if she is honest.

At the kitchen door, she pauses. Peeks outside. No Ms. Fitzpatrick. No movement. No witnesses.

All clear.

She gets into her car and heads toward the bistro where Milo works.

***

Friday night lights blur past her windshield. Desire narrows her vision. There is no space for scenery or thought, only the urgency building between her thighs. The drive feels endless. Every red light an insult.

"Come on," she mutters to herself.

She pulls into the rear of the restaurant. Milo is already there, leaning against the brick wall near the dumpsters. White chef's jacket. Black and white checkered pants. He sees her and moves without greeting, slipping into the dim corner of the lot where they are hidden from view.

She approaches him.

"Hi, Milo. You look tired. You up for this?"

He grins.

"Up for it? My penis responded before my fingers did."

She smiles and tilts her head.

"Let's go. I'm..."

He does not let her finish. Milo grabs her and kisses her deeply. Not tender. Not romantic. A kiss of want. Of need.

Zora responds readily. She is already moist and can feel her juices start to travel to her inner thighs. She moans into his kiss. Their tongues intertwine. He groans against her mouth. She can feel his penis stiffen, pushing hot against her. Her breath is heavy. She lets out a deep groan from her throat.

Because Milo knows what she wants and how she wants it, he spins her around. She reaches into her jacket pocket and hands him a condom. While he rolls it onto his penis, she lifts her dress and starts swaying her hips trying to stave off the throbbing between her legs. "Milo... Milo, hurry..." He grabs her hips and widens his stance. "Ready?" he asks.

Through staggered breathing, she bends over and replies… "Fill me, Milo… Fill me…"

He sticks two fingers into her slick vagina then sucks his fingers. "Miloooo…" she begs. He can feel how wet she is. No effort needed on his part to work himself inside her. Her vagina is a waterfall, and he slides his hot penis in with one push. She gasps. She thrusts her hips back. Hard. He can feel her power. He can tell that she really needs this. He gives it to her. Together they are thrusting and thrashing. The rhythm of their movements creating familiar sounds as his penis strokes inside her wetness. She is going wild. He is pumping her like a madman, and she is taking all of him. Her legs are wide and she is holding her ankles. Her hair is covering her face.

Occasionally, she will bend her knees and then quickly straighten them with a powerful thrust onto his penis. He yelps every time she does it. He is loving every moment of it. They go at it for a little longer when she can feel his penis stiffen more. A signal that he is ready to release. She wines, "No… not yet, Milo… A little longer… Fill me… Please… Not yet…" He bites his bottom lip for restraint. Holds onto her hips for leverage as he concentrates. She continues to receive him. In and out. Stoking. Deep thrusts she's been longing for. He works with her until she lets him know it's time. "Milo… Miloooo… I'm… I'm…" At once they both release in explosive ecstasy. She can feel his penis throbbing as he releases. He can feel her exaggerated movements as she releases. They keep the motion going until neither of them has anything left to give.

She hangs there, almost upside down. His penis still locked in her vagina. He is leaning against the brick wall, both hands on the top of his head. Panting. His hips are moving slightly. Enjoying every moment.

Zora interrupts his moment of meditation as she dislodges his penis from her vagina, pulling the condom off at the same time. She reaches between her legs and pulls the condom out of her and hands it to him. He chuckles. "Really, Skyy?"

She turns to look at him, pulling her dress down at the same time. Her face is glistening. He can tell that she is satisfied. He pulls his pants back up and gives her a look. "You good?" he asks.

She smiles softly.

"Better than good. Thank you."

"My pleasure," he says, grinning. "And I *really mean* my pleasure."

She scans the lot. He knows what that means.

"See you next time, Skyy," he calls as she walks away.

She gives a small wave and gets into her car.

***

Back in the driver's seat, Zora catches her reflection in the rearview mirror. Smudged lipstick. Wig slightly askew. Skin still glowing. Body humming.

She stares at herself.

Haven't you learned your lesson yet?

Apparently not.

The drive home is quiet. Heavy. The release has already begun to fade, replaced by the familiar gnawing conflict. Even as the ache dulls, anticipation stirs again.

She is already thinking about the next fix.

Chapter Twenty-Two

Saturday morning, Zora stares up at the ceiling, unmoving.

Her body remembers the night with Milo before her mind fully catches up. A dull ache. A low hum. Heat that hasn't fully dissipated. She lets the sensation linger for a moment, neither indulging it nor rejecting it. Just noticing. As if observation alone might give her control.

She exhales slowly and rolls out of bed, bare feet padding across the floor toward the window. She parts the curtain just enough to peer out at the neighborhood coming to life. Joggers pass in steady rhythm. A man walks a dog that refuses to cooperate. Across the street, a couple stands on their stoop, coffee cups in hand, arguing softly, the kind of argument that never quite rises to a fight.

Life continuing. Ordinary. Uninterrupted.

She needs something different today.

The idea of going for a run crosses her mind and immediately feels heavy. Too quiet. Too much time inside her own head. Then she remembers Rayven's open African dance class, held every third Saturday. No commitment. No expectation. Just movement. Rhythm. Sweat. Rayven always said it was part outreach, part invitation, part healing. Zora had always believed her.

She checks the time.

10:40 a.m.

She sighs softly. *I needed the sleep, I suppose.*

The class starts at 11:30, and Steps Studio is only twelve minutes away. Her body responds before her mind can overthink it. She moves quickly now, shaking off the fog. A short shower. Steam filling the bathroom. The familiar scent of soap grounding her as water runs down her shoulders and spine.

She pulls on a pink and beige running suit, tugs her hair into a high ponytail, and slips into her pink New Balance sneakers.

Grabbing her gym bag, she chuckles quietly. "When was the last time I went to the gym?"

She tosses in biker shorts, a T-shirt, a tank. Toiletries. A towel. Flip-flops.

Phone. Wallet. Bag.

She bounces down the steps and reaches for the kitchen door.

"Hi, Zora. You heading out?"

Ms. Fitzpatrick's voice carries from down the block, as if summoned by movement alone.

Zora gives a brief wave without slowing, unlocking her car. *Of course I'm heading out. Why else would I be dressed like this?* She shakes her head, tosses the bag into the back seat, and settles behind the wheel.

No need to warm up the car. Spring has finally decided to stay.

As she drives toward Steps Studio, there's a lightness in her chest she hasn't felt in a while. Rare. Unexpected. She actually feels good. A smile creeps across her face, followed by a quiet laugh.

Milo fixed her good.

She laughs under her breath. *I might need to move him to the top of my fixer list.*

The streets hum with Saturday energy. Sunlight bounces off storefront windows. A soft breeze lifts banners and jackets alike. People look awake. Alive. As if the city itself has exhaled after winter.

***

Zora pulls into the rear lot of Steps Studio.

Inside, the space buzzes with anticipation. Dancers stretch in small clusters, laughter rising and falling. Some lean against the ballet bar, calves flexing, conversation flowing easily. Others sit on the floor, rolling ankles, warming joints.

Zora heads straight for the locker room and changes into dance-ready clothes.

Rayven strides into the room and claps her hands sharply.

"Welcome to Steps! So glad you decided to start your day off with movement. We'll begin in five minutes."

She turns and freezes.

Zora stands there grinning, breathless already. Rayven lets out a squeal and wraps her in a tight bear hug.

"What are you doing here, Z? You haven't been to class in almost two years."

Zora lifts her hands, palms up, shoulders shrugged. "I know. I wanted to surprise you. I needed something different today. Something fun."

They giggle like teenagers.

"Well, I'm glad you're here," Rayven says, stepping back. "Get ready, girl."

Zora isn't sure what that means, but she nods anyway.

The music drops heavy and deep. African rhythms thump through the floor, vibrating straight into her chest. Arms lift. Feet stomp. Bodies move in unison, grounded and powerful. Rayven calls out the steps while demonstrating, sweat already glistening along her temples.

Zora keeps up as best she can. Awkward at first. Rusty. It's been too long. But her body remembers more than she expects. Her hips loosen. Her breath deepens. Sweat pours freely, unapologetic.

By the end of the hour, everything in her feels alive. On fire. Good and aching all at once.

She sinks to the wood floor, back against the brick wall, towel pressed to her face. Her hair is soaked. Her lungs pull in air greedily as she sips water.

Rayven drops down beside her.

"You did good," she says, laughing. "For someone who's been out of step for almost two years."

Zora shoves her lightly. "You better be glad I still know how to move. And that I love you."

"This was nice," Rayven says, quieter now. "I miss you, Sis."

She studies Zora for a moment. "You good?"

Zora wipes sweat from her neck. "Yeah. Just a lot going on. Clients. Students. Life."

Rayven leans back on her hands, eyes serious. "You know you can tell me anything, right?"

Zora nods. Hesitates. "I know. We'll talk. I promise."

They seal it with a pinky swear.

"So, where you headed now?" Rayven asks.

"I need to go check on my condo. My last tenant's 6-month lease ended last week. I need to restock, clean, and get it ready to be an Airbnb until I get another tenant in there," she shares.

The property was Zora's first house. A one bedroom, one bathroom condo off 12th Street that she purchased with her parents help when she graduated from college. When she purchased her current brownstone two years ago, she has been using the condo as a short-term Executive Rental that helps to pay the mortgage and gives her passive income.

Zora smiles. "My father wouldn't have it any other way."

"That's what's up, Z. That was a smart move. I wish our people thought like that. Building financial legacy." Rayven pauses. "That's why I'm working so hard with Steps. Even more so to get funding for the nonprofit Keeping Step. I want to leave a legacy of the arts. You know? I'm just waiting to hear back about the grant funding I applied for two months ago."

Zora puts a tender hand on Rayven's shoulder. "You'll get it, Ray! You're doing great work for this community. Keep your head up," she says with a smile.

"Thank you, Z. Go handle your business. Let's catch up later this week," Rayven offers.

Rayven tells Zora that she loves her. She's her bestie and she is just concerned about her.

Rayven rises off the floor and tells Zora she has to get ready for her next class but needs to grab a quick bite first. Zora rises off the floor as well, hugs Rayven and grabs her bag then heads to the shower.

She looks over to Rayven and says with a gentle smile, "Thanks for the class. My body is already cursing you." They both chuckle and go off in different directions.

***

Showered and back in her pink and beige running suit, hair now hanging in its usual style, Zora is ready for the next task at hand. Checking on the condo. She realized that she hadn't eaten at all today. She stops into a familiar mom-and-pop bakery a block away from the condo. They remember her from her when she used to frequent their establishment when she lived in the neighborhood. They exchange pleasantries. Catch up a bit and she grabs a warmed banana nut muffin and a large Chai tea with hazelnut creamer.

Yes, she still drinks tea when it is warm.

She sits at one of the small round tables and thumbs through her emails as she forks her muffin into her mouth. Nothing pressing. Thank God. Student emails she will handle on Monday. An email from Libby at Dr. Hanson's office. She will deal with that when she gets back home.

She checks her smartwatch. Almost 2 p.m. She takes the last few bites of her muffin. Grabs her tea and heads out the door. Her phone dings and she checks the notification. As she walks out onto the sidewalk, she is walking with her head down, eyes on her screen.

SLAM!!! SPLASH!!!

She runs smack into someone! Her tea crashes into her chest and starts soaking through her jogging suit jacket onto her T-shirt underneath.

"Agggggh…" she exclaimed. In her frustration, she yells, "Watch…"

Before she finishes her accusation, she realizes that she just ran into Damian.

He grabs her shoulders and apologizes profusely. "I'm so sorry, Ma'am… I…" Then he realized who it was. "Zee?"

"Damian?" she asks.

"I'm sorry, Zee. I was rushing and I…" he starts.

"No, no, I wasn't paying attention. I should not have been reading my phone and walking," she returns.

They both chuckle. He looks at her clothes. "I ruined your outfit," he says apologetically.

She stops him. "No, it was my fault."

She looked for a nearby trashcan, and he headed into the bakery and came back with a handful of napkins. He hands them to her, and she dabs at her top trying to soak up the tea.

While she is attempting to clean herself up, he asks, "Where you headed? You live on this side of town?"

She looks up briefly from wiping her top. "No, I actually used to live up the block. I own a condo off 12th Street, but I rent it out as an Executive Rental." She dabs at her top again then looks back at Damian. "I'm headed over there now to check it out and take inventory since my last 6-month lessee just moved out. I need to get it ready for either another tenant or list it as an Airbnb. Either way, I need to get going," she says with a smile.

He pauses. "You mind if I walk with you? I sometimes have students or interns who need short-term rentals. I may be able to get your next tenant lined up."

She leans back and folds her arms across her chest with a smile. "Why, thank you, Damian. That would be amazing. That will keep my mortgage paid and also keep the passive income flowing."

He returns the smile and a mocked bow. "You're welcome, Ma'am. I am here to please."

The two of them have a good laugh then Zora asks, "What are you doing on this side of town? Don't you live in Bowie?"

"Yes, I do, but I had a meeting with some colleagues to discuss plans for a late summer event leading up to Fall semester," he says. "It helps keep things operating smoothly.

Less stressful trying to do it in a vacuum without proper planning."

"That's great," she says. "You sure visiting the condo won't disrupt your plans for the day?"

"I'm sure. Nothing else on my schedule," he says. "A light day for me. Rest and relaxation is the order for the evening for me."

"I know that's right," she says with a chuckle.

He looks at her warmly. She returns the look then says, "Follow me."

***

They pause at the elevator. Damian is searching the lobby. Zora looks at Damian.

"You okay?" she asks.

He shuffles his feet. "I don't take elevators," he says softly. "Mind if I take the stairs?"

She lifts an eyebrow at him. "Oooookaaaay," she drags. "Afraid of elevators, are you?"

"Not afraid. Trauma," he says looking at the floor.

No more prying from Zora. She points to the steps in back corner. "I'll meet you on the second floor. Unit 21A," she says warmly.

"Thanks," he says almost embarrassingly.

On the second floor, Zora opens the door and Damian follows her inside. The door closes behind them, and she is already making her way into the living space. She takes out her phone to take notes of what needs to be done and what needs to be stocked.

Damian looks around. Impressed. "Beautiful place," he says. "How long you been renting it out?"

She's listening, but focused. "About two years. When I purchased my brownstone, I wanted to keep this as a financial investment." She continues walking through the living room, checking for damage that may have occurred by the last tenant.

"Hey, Zee," Damian says interrupting her process. "Why don't you walk through, and I can type the notes into your phone for you."

She turns and looks at him, putting her hand on her hip. "Aren't you the handy helper," she says smiling. "Sure. That would be helpful. I appreciate it. We can go room to room," she instructs. "Let's start in the back and work our way to the front."

So, that's what they do. The two of them working in tandem identifying and annotating. No damage other than general wear and tear. She calls back to Damian. "Add replace towels, linens… Mini-split filters… dry clean sofa accent pillows…"

They move into the kitchen and Zora starts opening cabinet doors. She takes inventory of the dishes. Then the lower cabinets. Pots and pans are good. Drawers. Silverware and other smaller kitchen devices are good. Damian is taking notes then says, "Excuse me. May I use the restroom?"

She turns to him. "Yes, of course. I still need to have everything deep cleaned. I'll call for a maid service next week."

While he is in the restroom, Zora grabs a small step ladder from the broom closet to check the overhead cabinet above the refrigerator. She stretches on her tiptoes and loses her balance. Before she knows it, she is falling. Damian catches her in the nick of time.

Resting too comfortably in his arms, she shyly says to him, "You should be sick of rescuing me, don't you think."

He looks in her eyes and smiles gently and says, "Stay out of trouble." They both laughed as he lightly placed her feet first to the floor. They stood there for a moment. Closer than either of them thought they would be. Quiet. Neither know what to do next. He goes to step around the island to the left, but she unintentionally stepped in the same direction. Their bodies gently collide. They both feel it. Electricity.

"Can't seem to get away from you," she says looking into his eyes.

He clears his throat and says, "Looks that way."

Time stood still. No words. Just breath. Little air between them.

Damian is confused as to what to do next.

Zora is taking in the moment without pressing.

Skyy is not invited. Not here. Not with him.

He speaks. "Ummm, Zee, I'm sorry. I haven't stood this close to a woman in years." He puts his hand on his forehead.

"Please excuse me." He steps back until he is leaning against the counter behind him.

She looks at him and teases, "Damian, I don't bite." At least he doesn't know that she does.

She steps closer to him until she is leaning against him. He inhales deeply and closes his eyes. His hands clutching the counter behind him.

Zora rests her head on his chest. Nothing more. The two just stand there. Quiet. Absorbing the moment.

He puts his hands on her shoulders. She looks up at him. He moves a lock of hair from her face. He starts to speak. She reaches up and kisses him gently on the lips. No tongue. He doesn't respond. He can't respond. He doesn't know how to respond. Conflicted.

"Zee, please… I …." He feels like he can't breathe.

"Damian, I'm not going to do anything if you don't want me to do," she says looking in his eyes.

Neither moved. The heat surge is noticeable. Tangible.

Damian rolls his eyes slightly then leans down and kisses her back. Gently. A little tongue this time. Curated tenderness that she hasn't felt in almost 16 years. She leans in. He wraps his arms around her waist. She can feel his heartbeat racing against hers.

He whispers against her mouth, "Zee, we are friends… we shouldn't…"

Kissing him back softly, she whispers against his mouth, "Are you sure about that, Damian?"

He grabs her shoulders and gently puts space between them. He moves to the other side of the kitchen. By the elevation in the front of his grey sweatpants, she can clearly see that he is definitely affected by her. By her presence. Her touch. Her kiss.

"Zee, I can't do this… we can't… I haven't had…"

She walks over to him and puts her finger to his lips. He closes his eyes but doesn't move. He is breathing heavily.

"Damian, there's no pressure," she says to him softly. "I know you feel what I feel, but I will not disrupt your life." He looks at her. "I promise," she says.

Too late.

She has no idea that she already has disrupted his life.

She steps away from him slowly and leans against the island. Her arms folded. Guarded. Head down. They both stand there for a moment before Damian speaks again.

"I need to go, Zee." Confusion is washed over his face. He is conflicted by what he feels.

"Thank you for showing me the condo. Send me the listing and I'll post it on the bulletin board in the Student Union."

She is lost in her thoughts. He speaks again. "Zee?"

"Yes, of course, Damian. I would appreciate that," she says with a gentle smile.

He walks away, leaving her in the kitchen but turns and says, "I'll talk to you soon. Let me know you made it home safely."

The door closes and Zora is frozen. Standing in the kitchen, mind racing. Heart processing.

Damian.

Chapter Twenty-Three

An hour passes. The sun has shifted in the sky. Zora is still standing inside the condo. Inventory complete. Notes made. Nothing left to do.

And yet, there is a weight pressing against her chest that makes it difficult to move. She feels suspended in the space, rooted to the floor by something she can't quite name. She knows she needs to leave. Staying any longer won't change anything. But her body doesn't cooperate right away.

She finally reaches for her keys and purse and walks toward the door. Her hand closes around the doorknob. She stops. She turns and looks back toward the living room.

The air feels different now. Charged. Heavy with something that lingers.

She can still feel his presence.

Something happened here.

Something she didn't expect.

Something she didn't know she needed.

Something she had been longing for without admitting it.

Touch.

Not hungry kisses that bruised her lips.

Gentleness.

Not her bent over, being pummeled from behind by a random man.

Tenderness.

Not driving away afterward with emptiness and an aching vagina.

Acknowledgment.

Not brokenness wrapped in unbridled desire.

Damian.

She exhales slowly, turns the doorknob, and leaves.

***

Damian is beside himself.

The forty-minute drive back to Bowie feels endless, stretched thin like time itself has slowed to mock him. Traffic moves normally around him, but inside his car, everything feels thick and sluggish. Like molasses in a North Dakota winter.

His mind won't quiet.

His heart is still pounding.

He grips the steering wheel tighter than necessary, jaw clenched.

What did you just do?

What were you thinking?

He shakes his head, muttering under his breath.

"You weren't thinking."

The thought of calling his mentor crosses his mind. The impulse is strong. But he dismisses it just as quickly. This is something he needs to sit with on his own. Something he needs to understand before pulling anyone else into it.

He needs to consider his actions. The consequences. The line he nearly crossed.

The last thing he wants is to ruin a friendship that hasn't even fully formed yet.

He catches his reflection in the rearview mirror at a stoplight. His own eyes stare back at him. Serious. Unsettled.

"You have to be more responsible," he says quietly. "Use more restraint."

Then, firmer: "It is imperative."

The light turns green. He drives on.

***

Zora arrives home without remembering much of the drive.

She doesn't even check to see if her self-appointed neighborhood watchdog is lurking nearby. She just pulls into her space, steps out of the car, and makes her way inside.

The moment the door closes behind her, she leans back against it.

That door has held her upright more times than she cares to admit.

Although the condo is only two miles away, her body feels like she's been stuck in traffic for hours. Everything aches, not in the way it does after physical exertion, but deeper. Heavier. As if she'd been in a fight she didn't realize she was having.

She pushes herself away from the door and moves slowly through the kitchen and sitting area, then climbs the stairs to her sanctuary.

Her legs feel weighted. Not sore. Not tired. Just… anchored.

She changes out of her tea-stained running suit, immediately soaking it in cold water with pre-wash to keep the stain from setting. Practical. Controlled. Something she can manage.

Then she runs herself a hot bath.

She needs it.

Her body needs to loosen. To settle.

Those few moments with Damian have left her spent. Drained. Stirred in a way she can't articulate.

Emotional.

The word gives her pause.

Emotional?

What does that even mean?

Emotions are not allowed.

Never.

She steps carefully into the tub, letting the hot, oil-scented water envelop her skin. Lavender fills the air. Calming. Grounding. She closes her eyes and sinks lower, allowing the warmth to seep into her muscles.

Her fingers rise unconsciously to her lips. She can still feel his there.

The softness. The restraint.

His breath against her mouth.

"When was the last time I was kissed like that?" she whispers.

Her mind tries to wander back to search for a memory, but she pulls herself up short.

No time for that. Not now.

After nearly forty-five minutes, she climbs out of the tub and dresses in comfort: blue floral leggings, a blue three-quarter-length top, white footies, slippers.

It's too early to retreat upstairs, so she opts for quiet time in the living room. She grabs both phones – yes, both – and heads down to the kitchen to make tea.

While waiting for the kettle, she rummages through the junk drawer until she finds the Chinese Garden menu. She orders without hesitation: sesame chicken, non-spicy, fried rice, a spring roll.

Thirty-five minutes.

She settles onto the chaise lounge and pulls a throw blanket over her legs. Comfort. Security.

With tea in hand, she checks her personal phone.

Texts from Rayven.

A check-in from Nico.

Emails.

Voicemails.

She listens.

"Hi, Ms. Holley, this is Libby from Dr. Hanson's office confirming your video appointment for Tuesday at 1:30 p.m… I sent a video link to your email."

She exhales.

Then the second message plays.

"Hi, this is The Cathedral of St. Matthew the Apostle… Your confession appointment is scheduled for Monday at 11 a.m… Your assigned confessional booth is labeled "Angel." Bless you."

Zora freezes. Her chest tightens. Panic flutters just beneath the surface. She whispers, "Is this a mistake? Should you really go through with this?"

She lifts her tea and takes a slow sip, cradling the mug in both hands as steam rises. She breathes deeply. Five counts in, five counts out. Again. And again.

You can do this.

You need to do this.

She opens her calendar and enters both appointments, setting multiple alerts.

The doorbell chimes.

Dinner.

She plates her food and returns to the chaise, eating slowly, distracted. Everything is pulling at her. Mentally, emotionally. "Ugh," she thinks to herself.

Her phone pings.

Damian.

Her stomach flips.

"Hey, Zee, I'm checking to see if you made it home safely. You never texted. Not trying to stalk you or anything. Just confirming."

She stares at the text for a minute. She hesitates.

Then another message.

"Are you okay? I hope I didn't push you away. Talk to you later."

She reads the texts again carefully before responding.

Thumbs hovering over the keyboard, she considers her response and texts back.

The exchange is easy. Tentative. Honest.

"I apologize. I was at the condo longer than intended. Made it home safely. Thanks for checking in."

"That's great. How are you feeling? Ya know, after…" he says.

"I'm still processing to be honest. Not sure what to do with my thoughts at the moment. You?"

"Same. I wasn't prepared for that. I should have been more of a gentleman."

"You were the perfect gentleman… until you kissed me. LOL"

"I kissed you? Wow! Jokes."

"Just say'n… you kissed me back," she chuckled.

"I didn't mean to cross the line. That is not me…"

"Did you cross the line, Damian? IF it wasn't you, then who was it? LOL"

"Zee, you got mad jokes today. I'm being serious."

"I know you are. I'm not. Lighten up."

"I'm trying."

Zora was about to respond to him when her phone rings. A video call coming in.

Damian.

When his video call comes through, she answers before she can overthink it.

His face fills the screen. Warm eyes. Gentle smile.

She finds herself smiling back.

Their conversation flows, light teasing layered over sincerity.

"Sooooo, what makes you think I wanted to see your face again today?" she laughs.

"All that texting is time consuming. Thought it better to talk face-to-face," he says with a smile.

"What if I didn't want you know where I am? Are you stalking me, Mister?" she chuckles.

"Not at all. Just wanted to make sure you knew I was serious. I try to be a better man than I've known and seen in my life. I don't want to be one of those guys. You know?"

"What is one of *those* guys? What does that mean to you? Explain," she says with a smirk.

"I mean I'm not a typical guy who preys on women. I've stayed away from relationships for years because I wanted to make sure that I understood who I was as a man; not a societal generalization. I guess I want to break the mold, so to speak."

"Interesting. Never heard a man say that before. Most of them would have taken that kiss and pushed it all the way to sex."

Damian didn't know how to respond to that comment, but he adjusted for his response.

"Well, that is not me. I want to respect women. Male examples in my life showed me who I didn't want to be... I..."

His voice trails off. He gets quiet. Just staring at the screen.

"What's the matter, Damian? Why did you stop?"

He held his head down and took a deep breath then continued.

"Zee, I don't typically open up to people, women in particular. I'm guarded on purpose. I don't want to bore you with my life's details. At least not yet."

"So, there's more to you than meets the eye is what you're saying," she chides with a smile.

"That is the case with everyone," he offers. "Everyone has a backstory. How many people do you know jumps out the gate with all of their sorted details?"

Zora considers that question. That truth.

"As a therapist, I understand that entire process of peeling back the layers to find one's truth while trying to trust others to receive it. It is dicey, but we all need it at some point."

She heard herself say that and shuttered within. She needs to take her own advice.

Stop talking, Zora!

Damian ponders her words. Taking them in. Leaning in as she speaks.

"That's powerful, Zee. Deep and true. One day when we are both ready, we can pull back some layers. No pressure. No expectation."

"You say that now, but once those walls come down everything is free game," she says laughing out loud. "I'm gonna make you spill your beans," she says with a single eyebrow lifted and a diabolical smile.

"I'm sure you'll try," he says smiling back. "Step-by-step. We can start there." He looks up at his screen, no longer looking at Zora. "Zee, I need to take this call coming in. Can we catch up tomorrow?"

"Sure. Everything okay?"

"Yes, my mentor is calling. We've been missing each other. Gotta take this. Tomorrow?"

"Okay. Take your call. We will talk soon."

When the call ends, silence settles around her again. She sits there, replaying the exchange. She holds onto it. She's intrigued. Something in her chest softens.

What is it about him?

She shakes her head and mutters aloud, "Girl, you are hiding something too."

Her food and tea have gone cold. She reheats them and finishes eating, unsure how to spend the rest of the evening. Damian has been a welcome distraction.

Her fixer phone pings. Milo. Her new favorite fixer. She exhales slowly, a familiar pull awakening. Skyy has been quiet all day, but she stirs now.

The invitation is simple. Easy. Tempting.

Zora glances at the clock.

8:25 p.m.

She texts back.

Plans made.

She heads upstairs, already moving toward the familiar ritual. The "Milo" wig. Skirt. Perfume. Makeup. No panties.

Skyy stretches, yawns, and steps forward.

Out the door. Into the car. Zora smiles to herself.

She's about to be "Milo-ed."

Chapter Twenty-Four

Skyy is already on the move.

The meeting place is strategic. A park after dark. Familiar enough to blend in. Isolated enough to disappear. Milo texts Skyy to let her know he is behind the old sports storage building, tucked between a line of trees. No lights. No foot traffic. Obscured.

Perfect.

Skyy rounds the corner and spots him immediately. Milo is leaning against the brick wall, hands in his pockets, the widest grin stretched across his face like he has been waiting all night.

"So, you're scheduling these drive-by booty calls now?" she asks with a smirk.

"You didn't refuse the invitation," he replies, chuckling softly.

"Touche," she says. "Touche."

He pulls her to himself and covers her mouth with his. Full. Warm. Wet. Hungry. She matches the energy of his kisses. She moans against his mouth and he does the same. Her own moisture is apparent to her, and her hips are responding to the pressure of his penis against her abdomen. She pushes against him harder. He pushes back. He breathes over her mouth. "You hungry, Skyy? What do you want?"

She doesn't speak. She hands him a condom that she tucked into her bra. She is jumpy like a kid in a candy store. He rolls the condom onto his engorged penis and gives her a sheepish smile. She looks at him and spins around, pulls up her skirt, and bends over. He can see her ass in full view. Her pubic hair is drenched. Moist. He gives her cheek a quick tap as she begs him to "feed her."

"C'mon, Milo… I need it… Feed me, Milo… Feed me, please…" she pleads.

Happy to oblige, Milo slides his penis into Skyy's soaked vagina in one thrust. She gasps and then grunts. He lets out an exhaled "ahhhhhh" and commences with a steady rhythm filling her with his girth. She grinds against him with each stroke. Hands on her knees, hips lifted. She thrusts back against him. Deeper. Harder. Moaning with each push and pull of his penis. He is breathing heavily. She is biting her bottom lip. No words. He knows the rules. Just the sound of moisture and meat in the dark. She can feel him stiffening. She protests.

"No, Milo… No… Not yet… Feed me… Go deeper…" she instructs.

"Skyy, I'm trying not to… Skyy…" he struggles.

"A few more strokes… deeper, please… deeper…"

He holds out from his release. He closes his eyes and bites his own lip but keeps the strokes long and strong.

Skyy responds. "That's it… that's it…" He continues his stroke at her bidding. "That's it, Milo… get ready… I'm… I'm… Ohhhhhhh…."

Milo grabs her hips with what feels like death grips, and he thrusts deeper and in one full push, he releases. Grunting in his throat. She is working on his penis as they are both releasing. Her own wetness is combined with his cum and she is working against him with fervor, jerking with the fulfillment of her own orgasm.

Both are breathless. Milo leans back against the brick wall, chest heaving for air, still hanging onto her hips. Skyy remains bent forward, hair falling into her face, hips still moving as she draws every last sensation from the moment. He exhales slowly and runs his hands over his face.

Skyy dislodges from his penis and takes her time standing. The aftershocks of her orgasm still ripple through her. She pulls down her skirt, then turns to face him. Her wig is damp against her neck. She is still breathing heavily. She just looks at him. He just looks at her. And then they both start laughing.

She places her fingers on his lips. "Shhhhhh… people are going to hear you."

"Me?" he asks. "You're laughing just as hard," he says, still chuckling.

She nods, covering her mouth with her hand. "So good… You are soooooo good, Milo."

He pulls up his pants. "You're not too bad yourself, Skyy… Not too bad at all," he says with a wide grin.

She steps closer and plants a kiss on his cheek. "I gotta go. Thank you for the invitation, Mr. Fix It," she says, suddenly shy.

"You're welcome, Skyy," he replies. "My tool is your tool. Your place or mine next time?" he asks with a giggle.

She presses a finger into his chest. "I'll let you know. That is if you don't call me first," she says, laughing softly.

He catches her hand. "Next time…"

"Next time," she returns.

She scans the area quickly for peering eyes and slips back into the darkness toward her car.

***

On the ride home, Zora removes the wet wig, tossing it onto the passenger seat. The city hums around her. Late-night movement. Windows glowing. People heading somewhere or coming from somewhere. She wonders how many of them are getting fixed just like she did.

Then she questions herself.

Did I really need to be fixed?

No.

But Skyy never passes up the opportunity.

At a red light, her mind drifts.

Damian.

Damn him.

Intriguing, but not consuming. Familiar, but not known. She likes the way he lingers in her thoughts and resents it at the same time. She doesn't need confusion layered on top of control. Her realities feel contradictory, public versus private, composed versus unraveling.

Don't fall for it, Zora.

He's just another man.

Stay guarded.

You don't need kindness undoing what's worked for you all these years.

She reminds herself firmly. *Addiction does not disappear just because tenderness shows up.* Guard stays up.

***

Once home, a warm shower eases the noise in Zora's body, but it does nothing for the emotional pull. She doesn't like that at all.

One thing she knows about herself. Being fixed works. It has always worked. It is her coping mechanism. Her navigation system. It keeps her away from the shadows. It soothes wounds she refuses to name. Most days, she doesn't want to put Skyy away.

Skyy is safer.

Skyy is effective.

Skyy delivers.

Skyy protects.

Zora climbs into bed and pulls the sheet up to her chest, staring at the ceiling. Physically satisfied. Remembering the logic she has rehearsed for years. It all makes sense.

At least that is what she tells herself, hoping one day it will feel true.

Don't count on it.

***

Sunday morning arrives quietly. Heavy clouds. Damp air. Zora slept deeply enough to miss the rain entirely. She peers out the window. The street is still. Sparse movement. Perfect running weather.

A splash of water on her face. Teeth brushed. Hair pulled into a high ponytail. Green jogging leggings. Light jacket. Running shoes.

Out the door.

She jogs down the steps, stretches briefly, slips one earbud in, scrolls until a podcast catches her attention, and presses play.

The rhythm of her feet against the pavement steadies her breathing. The scenery hasn't changed, but her perception has.

On the final stretch of her three-mile run, The Cathedral of St. Matthew rises into view. She slows to a jog in place at the base of the steps. The thought flickers.

Confession.

Her stomach tightens. She shakes her head and dismisses it. Not today. Maybe not at all.

The voice in her ear cuts through her resistance.

"…noting changes without effort… nothing gets better until you want it to get better…"

She nearly curses aloud, but she knows the voice is right.

She turns and heads home.

***

Back inside, she showers and slips into lounging clothes. Breakfast is simple. Maple brown sugar oatmeal with half an apple. Tea, as always. Dishes cleaned. She settles onto the chaise with a book.

She glances at the page and exhales. "It's sad that it's taken me two months to read a 300-page book."

Ten minutes later, her phone rings.

Nico.

"Hey, Z. You got my text. You didn't respond."

"Sorry, Nico," she replies calmly. "Yesterday was full. I meant to respond. You okay?"

"Yeah. You been out lately?" His tone sharpens her awareness.

"What makes you ask?" she counters. "I was home most of the day handling some things."

"Just asking," he says. "Thought I saw your car at the park last night."

Her pulse spikes. "I was out with friends for a little while…"

"Z, stop lying," he interrupts. "I saw you coming from behind the old sports storage building. Don't tell me it wasn't you. I know you."

Silence stretches.

"What do you want me to say, Nico? I am…"

"You're getting reckless," he cuts in. "Public places. Too often. Not smart, Z."

"I have appointments this week," she insists. "I'm getting help."

"I hope so," he says quietly. "I really do."

The call ends.

Zora sits still, the weight of being seen settling heavily in her chest. Truth is exhausting.

She naps.

1:18 p.m.

She wakes disoriented, then remembers. Family dinner at four.

Another shower. Butter yellow cardigan. White wide-legged slacks. Soft knit top. Yellow flats. Pearl drop earrings. Cross necklace.

She studies herself in the mirror. "Family ready."

***

At 3:05 p.m., Zora pulls into her parents' driveway. Familiar. Routine. The Stiths are not there yet. Just her parents.

She knocks once, then lets herself in.

"Hello, Mommy. Daddy. I'm early."

"In the kitchen," her mother calls.

Zora kisses her mother's cheek, breathing in comfort and memory. "Where's Daddy?"

"In the office."

She taps lightly. "Daddy, may I come in?"

"Sure."

She sits across from him, heart tight. "How are you? Any word on the promotion?"

"Still waiting," he replies, not looking at her.

"I wanted some time with you before everyone arrived."

The doorbell rings.

Shit.

"Better greet our guests," he says.

She nods, swallowing the familiar ache.

Dinner unfolds. Laughter. Family rhythms. Until the doorbell rings again.

"Get that, daughter," her mother says.

Zora opens the door.

Reese Parker.

She invites him in, already bracing herself.

Dinner becomes a subtle performance. Praise. Positioning. Pressure.

Reese seated beside her. Her mother nudging the narrative forward.

Zora remains polite. Unmoved.

"Reese has been nominated as a Top Lawyer," her mother beams. "He can bring a plus one."

Zora smiles gently.

Never happening.

Dinner ends. Hugs exchanged.
"Reese, walk Zora to her car," her mother insists.
In the driveway, Reese opens her door.
"I'd love for you to join me at the ceremony," he says.
"I'll let you know," Zora replies.
Hope lingers on his face.
Irritation settles in her chest.

Chapter Twenty-Five

Monday. Sunshine filters through the window. Birds chirp with reckless optimism. The temperature reads eighty degrees by midmorning.

"It feels like we skipped over spring," Zora says aloud. "Just jumped straight into the middle of May."

Her three-mile run is done. Sweat dried. Shower complete. She dresses and heads into the kitchen for breakfast. Whole grain toast. Avocado spread. A glass of orange juice. Standing at the island, she reviews her schedule for the day.

Only four clients.

And one appointment that sits heavy in her chest.

11:00 a.m.

The Cathedral of St. Matthew the Apostle.

The thought alone flips her stomach.

She exhales slowly. *Breathe, Zora.*

She checks her watch. 8:45 a.m. Her first client arrives at nine. She finishes her toast quickly and takes the back steps down to her private office. The blinds are opened wide, inviting in the morning light. A scented candle is lit. Sandalwood. The green noise machine hums softly. She is meticulous about creating a space that feels safe. Controlled. Grounded.

By 10:15 a.m., her first client had left. Zora locks the office door and heads upstairs to her bathroom. She brushes her hair into a slick, tight bun low at the nape of her neck. Clean. Restrained. She removes her jewelry. Wipes away her makeup. Pulls on a skirt that falls below her knees.

She studies herself in the full-length mirror.

"What are you doing, Zora?"

She believes she needs to look pure. Demure. Less worldly.

Skyy quietly mocks her.

Zora adds dark square-framed glasses and heads downstairs.

In the car, driving the short distance to The Cathedral, her body betrays her resolve. Sweat beads along her hairline. Her hands slip slightly on the steering wheel. Her mouth is dry. Her stomach twists.

Less than ten minutes later, she parks as far back in the rear lot as possible.

"That won't make for a quick getaway," she mutters.

Too late now.

***

Inside the church, Zora keeps her head down. Shoulders folded inward.

"This is crazy. This is crazy," she whispers.

Her eyes flick upward despite herself. Stained glass windows scatter light across wooden pews. People kneel. Others sit quietly. Candles flicker along the walls.

You still have time to leave.

A tap on her shoulder makes her jump. She clutches her chest.

A woman smiles kindly and offers assistance. Zora explains that she is new and looking for the Angel confessional for an eleven o'clock appointment. The woman walks her halfway, then stops, pointing gently while placing a reassuring hand on Zora's shoulder.

Zora thanks her and continues alone.

Her throat tightens. Each step feels like quicksand.

Skyy whispers, *You don't need to do this.*

"Shhhhh," Zora mutters under her breath. "Be quiet."

Inside the confessional, the lighting is dim. She cannot see the priest. He cannot see her.

Thank God.

Her nerves unravel as she sits. It has been fourteen years since her last confession.

A sound on the other side.

Her chest tightens.

The small door slides open.

Silence.

Then the priest speaks, beginning with the sign of the cross.

> *"In the name of the Father, and of the Son, and of the Holy Spirit. Amen. May God, who has enlightened every heart, help you to know your sins and trust in His mercy."*

Zora clears her throat and speaks with a Korean accent to disguise her voice.

"Bless me, Father, for I have sinned. It has been fourteen years since my last confession." She swallows. "I am a twenty-eight-year-old single woman, and I do not know where to start. I am living a double life. My addiction is winning."

A pause.

"What is your addiction?" the priest asks gently.

Zora's voice breaks. "I don't think I can do this. I should go."

"Daughter," he says, calm and steady, "do you believe God can forgive you? Do you want to be forgiven?"

"I'm not sure," she admits. "I've been trapped for so long. It's second nature. Sometimes it's more first nature. It's where I hide. It's comfortable."

"I see," he says softly. "How does your addiction show up?"

Tears spill over. Zora covers her mouth.

"I have a sex addiction," she confesses.

"How does this addiction control your life, my child?"

"I'm sorry, Father," she whispers.

"How often have you fallen into this sin?"

Her head bows. Shame rises.

"Five times a week," she says. "Sometimes twice a day. With random men. Sometimes a regular."

"Is this the act of prostitution?"

"No," she says quickly. "No money is exchanged. It's just an intense, unhealthy need. And the satisfaction doesn't last."

"How do you plan to stop practicing this sin?"

"Therapy," she says. "Returning to my faith. I see no other way."

He instructs her to read the Act of Contrition. Her voice trembles as she reads the words aloud, each sentence landing heavier than the last.

When she finishes, the priest assigns her penance.

Three Hail Marys in the morning, afternoon, and evening. Ten more throughout the day.

"You are welcome to return as often as necessary," he tells her. "God bless you. Go in peace."

Zora exits the confessional with her hand shielding her face.

In her car, she exhales and then breaks into a wail. Her breathing turns shallow. Rapid. Panic sets in.

She grips the steering wheel, forehead resting against it.

"I'm sorry," she whispers. "I'm sorry. I'm sorry."

She said it out loud.

To someone else.

To God.

***

12:15 p.m.

Zora sits motionless on her chaise lounge. Numb. Disconnected. The emotional release reverberates through her body like an aftershock.

A phone notification pulls her back.

1:00 p.m. client.

She rises slowly and heads to the bathroom. The mirror reflects a woman hollowed out by truth.

You look like hell.

She splashes water on her face again and again. Modest makeup. Hair released from the bun. Small hoops. Nude gloss.

She keeps the same clothes on.

The reminder matters.

By 4:30 p.m., her last client leaves. Notes logged. Computer shut down. Lights off. Door locked.

She is exhausted.

***

The bath is hot. Lavender oil beads on the surface. Candles glow softly. Music plays without words. A glass of wine. Half a bottle gone before she notices.

She soaks. Thinks. Cries.

No Hail Marys yet.

After an hour, she gets out, dresses in a long jersey knit house dress, and heads to the kitchen. She missed lunch. Hunger beckons. Leftover Chinese. Water bottle. Back to the chaise.

Her body is here. Her mind is not.
She reaches for her phone.
Nico.
"Hey," she says when he answers. "Are you busy?"
"Just heading home. You okay?"
"Can you stop by?" she asks. "I need to talk."
A pause. "I'll be there in twenty."
The call ends.
Zora stares at the ceiling.
Waiting.

Chapter Twenty-Six

Nico arrives rapping on the front door as he uses his key to enter. The sound is familiar. Comforting. He steps inside and closes the door behind him, locking it out of habit. Zora rises slightly from the chaise as they greet one another, exchanging a brief hug before he takes a seat in the side chair closest to her.

"What's up, Z? Should I be concerned?" he asks.

"No," she responds softly. "I just need my friend. I didn't want to talk on the phone."

He studies her for a moment. The way she's holding herself. The tension in her shoulders. The redness around her eyes. Nico leans forward, elbows resting on his knees, hands clasped together. Fully present. Fully attentive.

"Talk to me, Sis," he says gently.

It catches her off guard. She hasn't heard *that* tone from him in a while. With everything she's put him through lately, she expected guarded frustration, not tenderness. His gentleness feels like a gift she didn't know she needed tonight.

She straightens on the chaise, smoothing her dress nervously. "I went to confession today," she says, almost in a whisper.

Nico sits up immediately, surprise softening his expression.

"Really?" he says. "How did it go?"

She inhales deeply, then exhales. "It was scary. I hadn't been to confession in fourteen years. It was private, but that didn't make it any less nerve-wracking."

"That's normal," he reassures her. "Nerves are normal even for people who go regularly. You're not alone in that."

"Yeah… well," she pauses. Swallows hard. Then looks directly at him. "The priest asked what my sin was." Her voice trembles. "I said it. I said it out loud, Nico. I…"

"What did you say, Z?" he asks quietly.

"I said…" She clears her throat. "I said I have a sex addiction."

She closes her eyes, bracing herself.

Nico doesn't flinch.

Instead, he shifts closer and kneels beside her. His hand rests gently on her knee, grounding her. She opens her eyes.

"Z," he says softly, "I know that was hard. But you did it. You really did it." His voice thickens slightly as he adds, "I'm proud of you. So proud."

He moves a lock of her hair that has fallen into her face. She leans her head into his hand, tears spilling freely now. No restraint. No shame.

Nico says nothing else. He doesn't rush her. He lets the moment breathe. Silence becomes a shelter. Acceptance fills the space between them.

The stillness breaks when her phone rings.

Nico glances at it. "You want me to answer that for you?"

"No," she says quickly. "Let me take it. Just a minute."

She sees it's a video call. Damian.

Her chest tightens. She wipes her face, straightens slightly, and answers.

"Hey," Damian says, his eyes already searching her face.

Those eyes.

"Hey… can I—"

"Zee, are you okay?" he interrupts gently. "You've been crying."

He notices everything.

"I'm fine," she replies, though her voice betrays her. "Can I call you back? If it's not too late?"

"Anytime," he says. "Call me back, please."

"I will," she promises, barely above a whisper.

She ends the call.

Nico is watching her carefully.

"Was that one of your—"

"No," Zora cuts in. "It wasn't. None of them call my personal phone. And certainly not on video."

She doesn't elaborate. She doesn't have to. Nico understands the rules. Skyy always wears a disguise.

He checks his watch. "I need to head out, Z." He pauses. "Thank you for trusting me with this."

"Thank *you*," she says. "I love you, Nico."

"Love you too," he replies, moving toward the door. "Lock it behind me."

She nods.

After he leaves, Zora sinks back into the chaise. The day presses down on her all at once. Confession. Truth. Relief. Fear. She closes her eyes and begins her breathing exercises.

In… one, two, three, four, five.

Out… five, four, three, two, one.

Again.

***

Upstairs, Zora slips out of her lounge dress and into a soft nightgown. The house feels quieter now. Still.

She thinks about the Hail Marys she's supposed to say. She hasn't yet.

She opens her bedside drawer.

The fixer phone.

Two missed texts. Brandon. Milo.

She reads them both. Doesn't respond. Her lips part slightly at the thought of the other night.

Mmmmmm, Milo.

She puts the phone back in the drawer and closes it. She exhales slowly.

> *"Hail Mary, full of grace, the Lord is with thee…*
> *Blessed art thou among women, and blessed is*
> *the fruit of thy womb, Jesus. Holy Mary, Mother*

of God, pray for us sinners, now and at the hour of our death. Amen."

She keeps going. One after another. Ten in total. Her voice steady, though her mind drifts.

When she finishes, she notices another message on her personal cell.

Damian.

"I hope you're okay, Zee. I'm getting concerned."

She types back carefully.

"Long day. I'll reach out tomorrow," she promises. "I'm available after three. Good night."

She placed the phone face down on the bedside table.

The room darkens as she turns off the lamp. The darkness feels comforting tonight. Necessary.

She pulls the covers up and closes her eyes.

Tomorrow will come soon enough.

Chapter Twenty-Seven

Tuesday morning has started off well. A refreshing run. A hearty breakfast. And then, off to her final class for the semester at Howard.

The students have proven themselves formidable. Their presentations reflect competence, confidence, and genuine readiness for the helping services fields. Zora listens intently as each group presents, pride swelling quietly in her chest. These are not just students anymore. They are emerging professionals.

She closes her laptop at the end of class, satisfied.

It is 12:15 p.m.

Zora packs up quickly, hoping she does not run into Dr. Simmons. If she does, it will be too soon for her own sake. She moves with purpose, sliding papers into her bag, shutting off the podium monitor, mentally rehearsing her exit.

A tap at the classroom door.

Dr. Simmons.

Too late.

"Hey, Dr. Holley. Haven't seen you in a while," he says easily.

"Oh, hi, Dr. Simmons. I was out of town at a conference for several days," she replies with a gentle smile, hoping the explanation will be enough.

"Oh yeah, I heard about the Spelman conference," he says. "I'm sure you knocked it out of the park."

"It was an amazing experience," she says. "The young women were enriched and empowered. I've been invited back next year."

"That's great," he says. "Any plans for the summer?"

"I always have something going on," she responds as she finishes packing her bag. "Especially if it helps the students."

"That's right. You're spearhead the THRIVE program, don't you?"

"Yes. In fact, I need to get going," she says gently. "I have two meetings scheduled over the next couple of hours. If you'll excuse me."

"Sure. Maybe we can catch up over the summer," he says, hopeful.

"Maybe," she replies. "I'll see you at the THRIVE event next week?"

"I'll be there. Have a good day, Dr. Holley."

"You as well," she says, already walking away.

Dr. Simmons remains standing in the classroom, alone.

Thank God he did not inquire further. Thank God he did not look too closely. God knows Zora is trying desperately to forget that experience. The memory is still too raw. Too close.

She has little time to get home.

***

Back at home, Zora eats a quick lunch.

Sliced cucumber drizzled with vinaigrette.

Green grapes.

She washes the dishes immediately, needing the sense of order. At 1:30 p.m. she has a video call scheduled with Dr. Hanson. Her stomach tightens as she reflects on their last appointment, the one that ended in a panic attack.

She gives herself a quiet pep talk.

This is necessary.

This is part of healing.

This is how you get to the root.

She does not want the energy of her trauma lingering in her personal space, so she heads to her private office on the first floor. She lights a sandalwood candle, the same way she does for her clients, and turns on the green noise machine. The familiar routine steadies her. She powers up her laptop, opens her email, and locates the link Libby sent last week.

1:25 p.m. She clicks the link and waits.

Breathe, Zora. It's going to be alright. Breathe.

1:28 p.m. Dr. Hanson appears on the screen.

"Hi, Zora. It's great to see you again," she says warmly.

"Hi, Dr. Hanson. It's great to see you as well," Zora replies.

"I understand we had a bit of a setback at our last session," Dr. Hanson says carefully, "but I also understand that you want to drive the direction of today's session. Is that correct?"

"Yes, ma'am," Zora says, nervous but resolute. "Thank you for giving me autonomy. I know myself, and I think I need to start at a particular point so that I can build from there."

"Of course," Dr. Hanson says. "This session belongs to you. Whenever you're ready."

Zora closes her eyes and softly clears her throat.

"I know my current issues stem from my daddy issues," she begins. "I know that my father loves me, but I've long known that he desired a son and settled for the daughter he received. I wasn't his choice in terms of gender. He loved me. He provided for me. But there was always a distance."

She continues, voice steady but weighted.

"His military career kept him away often. And when he was home, I thought that time would be spent with me. Building a connection. A relationship. You and I both understand the importance of a father's presence in a child's life. When that presence is missing, even partially, it creates doubt, inadequacy, and an inferiority complex."

Her breath catches.

"My father's distance was especially felt through his involvement with little league football. Boys eight to ten years old. He mentored them with joy. I watched him with them. He looked like a different man. He acted like a different man. I saw how engaged he was with those boys when they came to our house for sleepovers or when he had one boy come over for one-on-one attention."

She swallows.

"He tolerated my presence. I always felt like I was in the way. Like I was a mistake. I wasn't allowed to cry. I wasn't allowed to tell him I needed him. Or that I loved him. His disappointment in receiving a girl, paired with his military bearing, left little room for humanity. For feeling. For expression."

Her voice trembles now.

"I internalized my father's emotional abandonment. And I see now how that made me a vulnerable little girl and a disconnected, messed up adult."

She pauses. A lump forms in her throat.

Dr. Hanson speaks gently. "Thank you for sharing that, Zora. I know that was difficult. Would you like to continue?"

Zora dabs at the tear falling down her cheek.

"Even now," she continues, "when I visit my parents every Sunday, I am still trying to win my father's attention. Yes, he speaks to me. He engages when others initiate conversation. But he never pulls me close. His love feels transactional. Not emotional."

Her voice breaks.

"As an only child, that leaves a void. A deep one. I fill it with other vices that I'm not ready to discuss today."

Dr. Hanson remains attentive.

"My mother pressures me to get married. To have children. But I don't trust that type of relationship. For reasons I understand now stem from this first layer. My father's distance. Not feeling chosen. Not feeling enough. Not feeling worthy of love."

Tears fall freely now.

"It is very difficult to know that I wasn't chosen because of my gender."

Zora weeps openly.

Dr. Hanson speaks with care. "Zora, that devaluing is not your fault. I need you to hear that. You are not responsible for your father's inability to show up emotionally. His limitations are not a reflection of your worth."

She pauses.

"You are meaningful. Your existence is meaningful."

Silence settles between them. And it is necessary. Truth needs space.

After a moment, Dr. Hanson asks, "What are you feeling right now, Zora?"

Zora wipes her face.

"I understand the truth intellectually," she says softly. "I just need to learn how to live it. To accept it. To stop needing my father's emotional validation to feel valuable. To appreciate what he gives, even if it's not what I want."

She inhales deeply.

"I need to accept that he may not be capable of meeting my expectations and be okay with that."

"That's right," Dr. Hanson affirms. "Be responsible for you. Only you."

She pauses. "Is there anything else you'd like to share today?"

"No," Zora says quietly. "This was challenging, but it was good. It was a start."

"You did very well today," Dr. Hanson says. "We will wait for you to take the lead moving forward."

The call ends.

Zora leans back in her chair, eyes closed, allowing the truth to reverberate. It hurts. But it needed to be spoken.

After fifteen minutes, she shuts down the laptop, blows out the candle, turns off the noise machine, locks the office, and heads upstairs.

She feels lighter.

Two admissions in two days.

Two releases in two days.

That is growth.

Growth through it, Zora.

Chapter Twenty-Eight

Back in her home, Zora allows herself to slow down. The day has been an emotional lift, the kind that leaves muscles sore you didn't know you were using. She is not accustomed to expressing emotion. Her childhood trained her otherwise. Feelings were acknowledged internally, never displayed. But something is shifting. Subtle. Persistent. She is stepping into a new perspective, even if she doesn't yet know what to call it.

She makes herself a cup of tea, the familiar ritual grounding her. Steam curls upward as she carries the mug to her chaise lounge and lets the cushions cradle her body. Nestle is the right word. She sinks into it gratefully. Recovery time. Space to let this week, only two days in, reshape her internally before it ever shows on the outside.

Quiet.

Calm.

Introspection.

3:40 p.m. Her phone rings, cutting through the stillness. The sound jars her, sharp and intrusive. Her first instinct is to ignore it. She has earned this silence. But something tells her it could be important.

She looks at the screen.

A video call.

Damian.

She exhales, then answers.

"Hello," he says, his face filling the screen, a gentle smile already in place.

"Hello back at you," she replies. "What if I wasn't dressed? What if I looked a mess? What if I was entertaining a male suitor?" she jokes, her tone light, playful.

"Oh, I'm so sorry. I… I wasn't thinking…" he starts, clearly flustered.

"Chill out, man. I'm just messing with you," she chuckles. "I just notice that you always video call me is all," she adds with a smile.

"I apologize," he says, straightening slightly. "Texting feels a little impersonal to me. It's fine for quick conversations, but nothing more, in my opinion."

They banter easily, the rhythm familiar now. Comfortable. When Zora tilts her head and says teasingly, "You just want to see my face. Admit it."

He counters without missing a beat. "Evidently, you want to see my face too, otherwise you would not have answered," he says, laughing.

She laughs openly. "Right. You got me on that one."

They laugh together, the kind that lingers, the kind that fills the spaces between words. A friendship is forming, unmistakably. Something else is forming too. Quiet. Unspoken. Beneath the surface. Neither of them names it. They don't need to. There's an ease between them. No expectations. No pressure.

Just friends.

Yeah, right.

"Seriously though, Zee," he says, gently steering them back. "A colleague of mine has a daughter who may be interested in renting your condo. She's starting a PhD residency program at Howard in August."

Zora's face brightens immediately. "Really? That's amazing. I'd be happy to show her the place, especially since it's so close to Howard University."

He hesitates. "Here's the catch."

Zora lifts an eyebrow. "Okay…" she says, waiting.

"She wants to see it today. She's only in town this week to find housing."

"Oh, that's not a problem," Zora responds easily. "What time?"

He exhales, relief clear. "Is 5 p.m. too soon?"

She glances at the clock. 4:08 p.m. "Sure. Five is good. I'll meet you there."

"Thank you, Zee. This really means a lot," he says. "They've been searching online, but everything affordable was way out in the suburbs. She doesn't have a car yet."

***

Zora arrives at the condo on 12th Street at 4:30 p.m. She opens windows, straightens pillows, makes sure the space smells welcoming. It's already clean, but she wants it to *feel* cared for.

At 4:50 p.m., Damian knocks on the door of 21A. She opens it and welcomes him in with a gentle smile.

"Hi, Zee. Thank you again for the short notice," he says, grinning. "Kira is coming on her own."

At exactly 5 p.m., Kira arrives. Zora walks her through the condo, explaining the layout and the contract details. Damian stays back, observing quietly. He notices how Zora moves through the space. Confident. Professional. At ease. When she catches his eye, he looks away. She smiles to herself.

Kira narrates the tour to her father over video call. "Daddy, it's available the first of July."

Zora listens quietly. She gives Kira her number and explains next steps. She can't help but feel a twinge of envy as she watches Kira interact with her father. Attentive. Present. Gentle. Not that her own father wouldn't provide financially. But the emotional availability. That's different.

The tour wraps after about forty-five minutes. Kira thanks them both and leaves hopeful.

Zora and Damian are alone now.

Damian leans against the back of the sofa, arms folded, a closed-mouth grin lingering. Zora finishes turning off the lights in the other rooms and returns, hands on her hips.

"What are you grinning about?" she asks.

"You're a natural," he replies.

"A natural at what?"

He tells her she has a realtor presence. They laugh. She pulls out her phone and makes a note to schedule a deep clean.

"You know," he adds, "if Kira didn't take the place, I might have considered it. It's a lot closer than Bowie."

"Really?" Zora asks.

"Yeah," he says thoughtfully.

Interesting, she thinks.

She checks the time. 6 p.m.

"You gotta go?" he asks.

"Not really. Just checking. Near dinner time."

He suggests they order in. She raises an eyebrow.

"You sure you feel safe being in here alone with me?" she jokes, pushing his shoulder lightly.

"Safe? You're harmless, Zee," he smirks.

They order pizza and drinks. Her a small thin crust white pizza with chicken, tomatoes, spinach and a Lipton's Green Tea. Him a large thin crust meat lovers and a Lipton's Lemonade.

"Hearty appetite," she jokes.

"Gives me lunch for a few days," he says.

"True. True," she says in agreement.

Pizza arrives and they plate themselves a couple of slices each and sit on the couch to eat with their drinks.

They talk about work, hobbies, favorite foods. Nothing heavy. Nothing forced. Just learning one another.

Eventually, he asks how she became a therapist.

She thinks before answering. "I wanted to help people. I know what it's like to carry wounds that go untreated. Helping others heal helps me too."

He takes that in. "That's incredible, Zee. I believe you make a real difference."

"Thank you, Damian. That means a lot," she says taking a sip of her Green Tea. "Sometimes it takes a while to know if your purpose has presence. I'm just coming into my acceptance of mine."

He leans back against the couch cushion. "That's deep, Zee," he says. "I've been considering a career change. I've always wanted to help young boys, especially those who have no father figure in their lives." He pauses in reflection. "I know what that feels like and I wouldn't wish that on anyone. I figure catching them at the beginning of the pipeline before they become a statistic that society throws away."

Zora puts her hand to her chest empathetically. "That's so powerful, Damian. I wish more people felt like you do. Wanting to stop the pain before the bleeding becomes irreparable."

He swallows what is in his mouth. "I mean it, Zee. People are living with their younger selves as adults, but they haven't been able to change the trajectory because no one cared enough to notice the fractures."

"Wow!" she says expressively. "You sure you don't want to be a therapist?" she jokes.

"Nah. I want the young boys to feel seen before they need to sit in front of someone who psychoanalyzes them without understanding. That's all."

Zora shakes her head in agreement. "Damian, you never cease to amaze me. You will do well. Keep me posted on that career shift. I'd love to see where it takes you."

He smiles warmly. "Thank you, Zee. I appreciate you listening. I really do."

They take in the moment. They embrace the connection.

***

By 8 p.m., Damian checks his watch. He needs to go. Zora carries plates to the kitchen. He grabs his pizza box. She walks him to the door.

He thanks her again.

"No problem," she replies warmly.

He notices a smudge of white sauce on her chin. Without thinking, he reaches up and wipes it away with his thumb. Their eyes lock. The air shifts.

"Damian…"

"Yes?"

They stand closer now.

"I… ummmm…"

"Yes?"

He steps closer without thinking. Her breath catches. She can feel his breath on her face. Sweet. Warm. Scented with lemonade. He inhales, fighting his urge, but loses. He dips his head down and kisses her softly. She responds to him softly. Different from their first kiss. This one was almost conversational. Saying what words never said. Almost communion. A culmination of a silent drawing. Attraction. Understanding. Not animalistic like Zora is used to. Gentle acknowledgment that something is there without words.

The kiss continues for what seemed like an hour, but it was only about five minutes. Damian steps back. Head tilted down. Eyes still closed.

"Zee…" he says breathless.

"Yes?" she breathes back.

Before he knew it, he pulls her into his arms this time and wraps them gently around her waist. She reaches up and puts her arms around his neck. A more intentional kiss. Something *is* there. Something behind the rhythm of their kiss. Soft breathing. Safely locked together. Lips still in contact, he moves her towards the couch, walking her slowly backwards. She lets him.

He carefully placed his pizza box on the table. Walking desire. Tamed, but understood. He gently pulls at her knit sweater. She helps him. She pulls at his polo shirt. Both now shirtless.

She's soft. Silky skin that looks like honey.

He's muscular, but not bulky. Smooth chocolate.

He dips to kiss her collar bone. Her shoulder. She tilts her head back and feels the fire of his lips against her skin. She removes her bra and he kisses lower until he is almost at her breast, but he pulls up. She looks at him as if to say "Don't stop…"

Seeing the look in her eyes, he lays her back on the couch and lays on top of her.

He is fighting his flesh and his conviction.

She is happy that Skyy hasn't entered the room.

He hasn't been intimate in so long.

She doesn't know intimacy.

He knows it is wrong, but it just feels so right.

She feels right with him but is unsure.

Their bodies sway together. She lifts her hips to meet his. He pushes his hips to meet hers.

Longing released. For Zora, she hasn't known touch that isn't initiated by a booty call.

Damian hasn't known touch that wasn't a ploy for everything except emotional fulfillment.

They continue in this vein, but his phone pings.

Saved by the bell. Literally.

He stops and realizes what he was doing. He was so engrossed in this tenderness of the moment that he completely forgot that he had a mentor check-in. He apologizes as he pulls himself off Zora, pulling on his shirt.

"Why are you apologizing?" she asks, confused. "You leaving?"

"Can we talk tomorrow?" he says tenderly as he rises from the couch. Embarrassed by the noticeable bulge in his pants.

He grabs his pizza box and turns to her before reaching for the doorknob.

"We really need to talk, Zee."

Damian dashes down the steps like they are on fire. He finds his car hallway up the block and slams the door shut. He hits the steering wheel with the butt of his hand over and over.

Frustration. Confusion. Desire. Interest. Embarrassment.

Everything is hitting him at once.

He grabs the steering wheel with both hands, lets out a real scream, and hits his forehead on the wheel a few times, hoping to knock some sense into his head. It is not working.

He pulls off and points his car towards Bowie. Before he gets to the corner, his car Bluetooth rings. He looks at the name.

Shoot. Shoot. Shoot.

He hesitates, but he answers. The voice looming through the car says, "Damian, where are you? We were supposed to have a video meeting at 8:30 p.m. You alright?"

"Yes, Sir. I'm alright. An appointment ran late." He lied. Can we reschedule for tomorrow? I'm driving and I really need to talk to you."

The man's voice confirms they can talk tomorrow at 11 a.m.

The call ends.

Damian is disappointed in himself. He knows better. His thoughts taunt him the remainder of his ride home.

Chapter Twenty-Nine

Back in the condo, Zora cleans up the kitchen. She stands leaning against the counter in deep thought. Her body is humming. Her mind is racing.

Why does this keep happening?

Friends my ass.

There's something between them. Something almost tangible. Unmistakable.

She can't believe he left her feeling like this. A second time.

All hot and bothered. Skyy begins to whisper to her.

You can fix that feeling, you know. Call him.

She holds her hands to both of her ears trying to quiet Skyy's voice in her head, but her body is betraying her efforts. She cannot go to bed like this. She needs a release.

***

Within seven minutes she is back home and frantically digging through her inner closet. A quick cleaning of her lady parts, armpits, she brushes her teeth. She chooses a navy-blue sundress. An auburn-colored wavy wig. Smokey eye makeup. Beauty mark. A dash of perfume for good measure. She goes to her bedside table and opens the top drawer. Fixer phone in hand. She checks her messages. She texts Brandon this time. She needs a distraction within a distraction. Milo is getting too used to her and she is getting too used to him. She needs a different meal tonight. Brandon responds.

"Hi, Skyy. Long time," he says. "What you up to tonight?"

"Hey, Brandon, you busy? Sorry I missed your text yesterday," she says. "I am really hungry tonight. Can we meet. Please?"

"Yeah. Say less."

"Where are you now?" she asks.

"Getting off work. I'm just leaving Georgia Avenue, passing by Howard University."

"Stay there. I'll meet you," she says. "You have your truck tonight?"

"Yeah, I do," he says. "That where you want it? In my FedEx truck?"

"Yes. Private. Obscure. Roomy," she says. "Is that okay with you?"

"Hell, yeah. Meet me one block from the old warehouse park. You remember the spot?"

"Yes. See you in 20," she says. "Be ready."

"Oh, trust me, I will," he says with a chuckle.

The call ends.

She grabs a pouch purse, puts her fixer phone and regular cell in it. She tucks a condom in her bra for easy access.

Within 2 minutes she is out the back door and, in her car, headed for the location. She doesn't even care if Mrs. Fitzpatrick is looking. She's shuttering, heat growing more intense by the minute. Skyy is in rare form tonight. Skyy knows Zora wants to do better, but she doesn't plan on making it easy.

Damn Damian for getting me all worked up.

Skyy wins tonight.

***

Zora sees Brandon's truck parked as promised. She pulls into a nearby space on the street and almost sprints to the truck.

He's already in the back, roller door open, waiting with a chessy cat grin on his face. She hops in. Brandon can see her fire.

"Damn, Skyy," he exclaims. "You look like you're on a mission tonight."

She shoots him a look. "Brandon, you know what this is about," she says anxiously. "I'm burning bad. Just help me. Please."

He holds both hands up palms facing outward. "Okay, okay. I got you."

"Good," she says. "Close the door."

Inside the truck she is squirming, waiting for him to ease her fire. She charges him, almost knocking him down. She takes his mouth viciously, kissing him with purpose. He matches what she's giving him. Kisses so intense the noise echoed within the truck.

"I can't take it, Brandon… help me…" she begs.

She starts grinding on him. No rhythm just erratic movement. She feels out of control. He's trying to open his pants, but she is up on him tight humping on him. Moaning. Panting. Skyy is intensifying.

He gives her a gentle nudge. "Let me get it out, Skyy… Damn, you that horny?" he says chuckling.

She's not laughing. Skyy is laughing at her. This is not a laughing matter to her. She is spiraling hard.

As he works on his pants, she passes him the condom from her bra as she is humping the air like a dog in heat.

"Brannnnnndon… Hurry… Hurry…" she pleads.

"I'm ready… I…"

Midsentence, she spins around and pulls up her dress. She bends over and spreads her legs wide. He can see the wetness dripping from her vagina. This pushes him to respond.

"WOW!"

One thrust and he is inside. Thick and stiff.

"Damn, Skyy… You're so…"

"Please… Stop… Talking…" she breathes as she thrusts against him.

He should know the rules. No words. Just the melodious sounds of unbridled sex.

Her wetness. His stroke. His hips slapping against her ass. Both bodies working together. He isn't as grand as Milo. Brandon's penis is shorter and thick, but she will work with it for tonight.

He is giving her all that he has. The thickness is working for her. He is unable to go deeper, but she makes the best of it. She is holding her ankles and thrusting against him as he leans against the shelves of the truck wall.

He spreads her butt cheeks, licks his finger, and slides it into her anus. She gasps upon entry. She forgot he is an anus man. She can take it or leave it, but tonight she'll take anything.

He teases her. Pulling out and pausing. Making her beg while deeply stroking her anus. He thrusts his penis back inside her vagina. Quick thrusts then slow thrusts. His finger mimics the movement in her anus. She is shuttering. Enjoying the fix.

She can feel him starting to stiffen inside her vagina. She doesn't fight him to hold off. She's going to have to work for hers. He's not long enough to hit her G-spot so she has to rely on dual stimulation to make her cum. She does what she needs to do. She reaches between her legs and strokes her clitoris. In rhythm. With intensity. She can feel it enlarge with each stroke. He's thrusting her in her vagina and her anus at the same time. She is stroking him and her clitoris at the same time. The movements are getting more purposeful for both of them. Audible pleasure is heard from both. The truck is now visibly rocking.

"Let's go, Brandon… Let's… go… Ahhhh…" she starts screaming.

"Here we go," he says. "Here… we… gooooooo."

With the next stroke, both release with cataclysmic expression. Him growling. Her screaming.

Hip movement continues to work through the vaginal and clitoral shocks she feels. His penile thumps continue as she thrusts against him. "Ahhhh…Ahhhh…" he voices as she works him down.

Finally. They stopped moving. The truck stopped moving. All that is heard is deep breathing and soft moans. The residue of pleasure.

He removes his finger from her anus, and she dislodges his penis from her vagina and stands up, while pulling her dress down. She is still breathing hard. Almost frantic. He taps her shoulder and she turns to him.

"You alright, Skyy?" he asks.

She feels like she is about to have a panic attack, but manages, "Yes… Yes, I am," she says chest heaving, eyes closed.

"You seem out of control tonight. That was different from times before," he acknowledges.

She looks at him. "A lot going on. Had to release. 9-1-1 level release needed."

He lifts his eyebrows as he's closing his belt. "Oh, okay… Just never seen you like this before."

"I'm fine, Brandon," she says with a slight smile. Her face glowing. Wig disheveled. Eyes enlarged like cat's eyes at night. "I gotta go," she says apologetically.

He shakes his head. "I get it. I know what this arrangement is about. Get home safely, Skyy."

"Thank you, Brandon. Really. For everything."

***

Driving back home, Zora sees a wrecked version of herself in the rearview mirror. She doesn't even recognize herself as Zora or as Skyy. She's almost beastly. It scares her.

The city lights blur past her windshield. Tuesday night is quiet. The hum of the road beneath her tires is the only constant.

In the silence, one thing rings true in Zora's mind: *Confession doesn't cure her addiction. It only exposes it. Making it more real. Louder. Hungrier. And sometimes that exposure increases the urge before it quiets it.*

She laughs once. Sharp. Humorless.

What Hail Marys?

She's not sorry!

Chapter Thirty

Wednesday morning sunshine greets Zora through the parted drapes. She feels likc she was run over by a mac truck. Her body protests as soon as she shifts beneath the sheets. A deep soreness lingers in places she does not want to think about yet. Vagina. Clitoris. Anus. Her head. Her spirit. Every inch of her feels tender, bruised by pleasure and punishment alike.

With everything she experienced last night, she still feels unsatisfied.

That realization irritates her.

Skyy mocks her quietly from somewhere beneath her ribs.

No time to entertain her.

Zora swings her legs over the side of the bed and forces herself upright. Discipline first. Always. She moves through her familiar morning routine with muscle memory doing most of the work. Shoes on. Hair pulled back. Jacket zipped. Door closed behind her. Stretch. Podcast in her ear.

Her three-mile run grounds her. The warmth of the rising sun kisses her skin. The fragrance of blooming flowers drifts through the air. The city hums awake around her. Cars begin to crowd the streets. Buses hiss at corners. Life moves forward whether she is ready or not.

By the time she returns home, sweat-damp and breathless, she feels steadier.

She thinks to herself. *I need to schedule these clients after 10 a.m. so I can sleep in a little later.* Skyy steps into her thoughts: *you need to get fixed earlier in the day instead of so late at night.* She chuckles to herself. She knows that is not realistic. Every client is her paycheck. So, the more clients she sees, the more stable her lifestyle.

She showers, dresses for the workday, and heads to the kitchen for a light breakfast. Turkey sausage patties, multigrain toast with a little spread of margarine and Chai tea steaming by her plate.

She checks her watch. 8:37 a.m. She finishes up and cleans her dishes before descending to her office and welcoming her first client for the day.

The hours blur together.

By the time her final session ends at 5 p.m., Zora feels hollowed out. Emotionally wrung. Her clients needed everything she had today, and she gave it willingly.

"Whew. Today was heavy," she says aloud.

Her mind aches. Her chest feels tight. Too bad she cannot counsel herself out of her own turmoil. And even if she could, she knows the truth.

She would not take her own advice.

Facts.

She grabs her phone. Missed texts light up the screen. The Besties. Lai is reminding everyone about Besties night on Friday and informs the group that it is Zora's turn to choose the location.

Zora types slowly.

"Heyyyy, Besties. Excited about our get together."

She pauses.

"I want to make a suggestion. I'd like everyone to meet me at my house and bring a dish to share. I'm thinking about something more intimate. Just us. No noise. No distractions. I'll provide the drinks as well. Everyone good with that?"

The replies come quickly.

Lai responds first.

"Gurrrrrl, potluck? That's different. Me like it. Me like it. LOL!"

Rayven follows.

"Potluck? You KNOW I don't cook on the weekends. I'll pick up something and bring it," she texts with a laughing emoji.

Then Nico.

"I'm all for the potluck and the intimate setting. I'll bring something as well. You REALLY don't want my cooking. LOL!"

Zora smiles softly and responds.

"Glad you all are on board. We need this. I need this. See you all soon. Love u!"

Each responds with their version of affection. Hearts. Laughs. Familiar comfort.

When the texts stop, hunger creeps in. She checks the refrigerator, but nothing speaks to her. Nothing feels right. It is already 6:20 p.m., later than she prefers to eat.

She opens GrubHub and orders a Mediterranean salad and a small slice of orange olive oil cake. Delivery in twenty minutes.

Enough time to change.

At 7 p.m. the doorbell rings.

"Thank God. I'm starving," she says with a small smile as she tips the driver.

She watches him walk back to his car a little too long.

"Mmmm. Nice," she thinks quietly.

She portions the salad into a bowl, grabs a water bottle, and sinks into her favorite place.

The chaise.

That chair holds her like nothing else does. It does not question her. Does not ask her to explain. It simply supports her weight and her worries without judgment.

As she eats, her thoughts drift in the stillness.

Confession.

Should she schedule another appointment?

What good would it do?

Skyy is still very much alive. Louder. More demanding.

Should she confess something she is clearly not ready to release?

Probably not.

***

7:18 p.m. Forty minutes away, Damian sits on his leather couch with his head in his hands. He has not moved in nearly an hour since arriving home from work.

His head throbs. His chest feels constricted. His thoughts spiral endlessly.

His career. His living situation. His life.

Zora.

He leans back and stares at the ceiling, replaying the video meeting with his mentor earlier that day. The conversation was not long, but it stripped him bare.

"Hi, Damian," Pastor Hayden says with a smile. "How are you doing?"

"Hi, Sir," he responds. His face betrays him. Tension etched in his brow. "I just need to talk. So much going on I don't know where to start."

"Start with one thing at a time," Pastor Hayden encourages. "No need to unpack everything all at once."

Damian exhales deeply, so deeply it could be felt. The kind of breath that empties the chest. Pastor Hayden can feel the weight of the exasperated sigh.

"Talk to me, Damian," he says gently. "I'm here."

Damian closes his eyes and takes a few cleansing breaths.

"I met someone. We are not dating or anything, but there is something there. Something that I can't shake." He looks into the camera for Pastor Hayden's response. There is none.

Just a mentor sitting in the moment with his mentee. Damian continues.

"I met her in Atlanta when I was chaperoning for Jenson. She was one of the speakers. I stayed out of the way. There only on assignment, but then I had to rescue her." He said clearing his throat slightly.

"Rescue her?" Pastor Hayden asks.

"Yes, Sir," he says painfully. "Jenson was trying to force her into his room when I was coming upstairs from the convenience store. I caught him just in time, but not before he frazzled her and slapped her."

Damian swallows in reflection then continued.

"I walked her to her room, but not to go in…" he adds quickly as he checks Pastor Hayden's face and continues. "…but she insisted I stay until she fell asleep…"

"Damian, you know that is outside of the rules of a chaperone," Pastor Hayden interjects.

"I know. I know. I promise you I didn't do anything. I sat on the sofa and watched until I knew she was asleep and I slipped out without waking her." He rubbed his face with both hands and continued.

"We are just friends, Sir. I have or had no intention of crossing the line with her. I promise. I know what my therapy requires and I'm sticking to that… At least, I thought I was…" his voice trails off.

"What do you mean by 'at least, I thought I was,' Damian?" Pastor Hayden leans closer to his screen.

Damian lowers his head.

Silence.

"Damian, what did you do, son?" Pastor Hayden asks concerned. "Did you…?"

"No, Sir. I didn't," Damian says quickly. Then softer. "But I kissed her. Well, she kissed me and I kissed her back… I didn't mean…"

Pastor Hayden exhales sharply.

"Damian, you know the rules, man," Pastor Hayden confronts. "You are not to be in any kind of relationship as a requirement of your therapy among other things. You know that. How did this happen?"

"I know, Sir. I'm sorry. It just… It just… happened. The first time, we ran into each other, and I was helping her with listing her condo." He clears his throat again. "The second time… yesterday… I was at her condo showing it to a new student who is interested in renting. The student left. She and I had pizza. Talked. I kissed her and she kissed me back. This time… I…"

"What did you do, Damian?" Pastor Hayden asks irritation creeping into his voice.

Damian closed his eyes. He pauses and continues softly, "I laid her on the couch, both of our shirts came off, we kissed heavily and started grinding… we… I stopped… I stopped when my phone rang… It was you calling because I missed our appointment." He looks up at the screen to see Pastor Hayden cupping his forehead in frustration.

"I'm sorry, Sir. I'm so sorry… I just… I…"

"Damian," Pastor Hayden says sternly. "What were you thinking? What if your phone hadn't rang? How far would you have gone?" Pastor Hayden is clearly disappointed.

"You cannot see her again. You hear me? You cannot risk your recovery and everything else attached to it." Pastor Hayden looks at Damian. Damian is clearly affected. His eyes filled with tears that flowed down his cheeks.

"Damian, do you hear me?" Pastor Hayden asks again.

He clears his throat and whispers, "Yes, Sir…"

"Call your sponsor. Call him tonight. This risky behavior is not going to end well for you if you don't get control."

"Yes, Sir…" Damian responds.

"In fact, call him now while I'm here. Use your program phone. Call him right now!"

Pastor Hayden meant business. He leaned back in his chair; arms folded across his chest as Damian dialed his sponsor. He listened to the conversation and his sponsor's instructions on what he needs to do.

"Damian, you must come back to group. You need support. You cannot do this alone. Don't trust yourself. You are not as strong as you think," his sponsor offers.

Damian wipes tears from his face and agrees to his sponsor's requirement. Not a request. An expectation to return to group.

Damian ends the call with his sponsor and looks into the screen at Pastor Hayden who has not changed his position. Damian can see the disappointment on his face, but Pastor Hayden doesn't say anything further in judgment.

"Damian, we need to meet more often for accountability. Once a week is not going to work. Please put me on the calendar for Monday, Wednesday, and Friday 2 p.m. until I and your sponsor feel you can handle things better."

All Damian could say was a timid, “Yes, Sir.”

With that, the call ends.

Damian realizes that he needs to talk to Zora soon. He has really been enjoying their time together. A little too much he reminds himself. He cannot undo years of work for a moment of weakness. He cannot allow himself to fall. To crumble against all that he has done internally.

He picks up his phone to dial Zora. Incoming call.

Jenson.

Jenson tells Damian that he has to go out of town this weekend and that his sponsor just spoke Damian’s sponsor, and they both agreed that Jenson needs Damian to travel with him as a chaperone.

How convenient.

Since classes have ended for the semester, Damian doesn’t have anything on his work calendar at least until summer classes begin. He confirms travel arrangements with Jenson and sends a text to his own sponsor agreeing to chaperone Jenson on this trip.

“Good! This will be good for both of you,” his sponsor texts back. “This will help get you back on track and focused. Let me know when you arrive and when you return home.”

“I will” Damian responds.

Damian feels the familiar tightening in his chest. The old oversight. The loss of autonomy. A trigger he still struggles to shake.

He dials Zora.

Chapter Thirty-One

Zora lays awake staring up at the ceiling while the world has been on the move since the break of dawn. She has no thought of the weather outside her window. Birds that may be chirping. Wind may be blowing lightly. People moseying about their day, some with fervor and purpose, while others just take it step-by-step, moment by moment without a care.

None of that reaches her.

Her thoughts consume her. The ceiling feels closer than usual, heavy with questions that refuse to quiet. No class today. The only thing on her calendar is a 3:00 p.m. Zoom meeting for the THRIVE Employment Empowerment program next week. A reminder that life continues even when her inner world feels tangled.

She needs to keep busy.

Her mind shifts. She runs through the brief conversation she had with Damian last night. No typical video. He actually called. His voice sounded different. Serious. Careful. Almost weighted.

He wants to meet with her today.

11:30 a.m.

He insisted on a public place.

The therapist in her tries to analyze his movements, his motives, the sudden shift in tone. But she is too clouded by her own inquisitive nature. Her professional instincts are dulled by personal curiosity. By anticipation she does not want to admit.

She sits up and leans against the tufted headboard. She folds her knees up to her chest, arms around her shins as if anchoring herself.

What does he want to talk about?

Did she do something?

Is he upset with her?

No answers come. Only the ticking of time.

It is 8:43 a.m. The waiting feels cruel. Stretching. Pressing against her ribs. But she has no choice except to wait it out.

In the meantime, she takes a late run to clear her mind. Not sure how much success she will have, but she needs a mental distraction. Needs something to push against the anxiety tightening her insides.

***

11:18 a.m. Zora arrives at the agreed meeting place. The mom-and-pop bakery on 12th Street. She doesn't know why he wants to meet there.

Too close to the condo.

The place where nothing and everything happens.

She steps into the bakery. The familiar scent of baked goods greets her. She exchanges pleasantries with her long-time friends. She orders her usual warmed banana nut muffin and Chai tea.

As she is paying, she hears the door chime behind her.

Damian.

Her stomach tightens instantly. She does not turn right away. She steadies herself, camouflages her reaction with a light smile, then pivots.

"Hi, Damian," she says." I've already ordered. I wasn't sure what you wanted."

He smiles back at her. "Not a problem," he says before turning to the counter to order an orange raspberry scone and a small coffee with French vanilla creamer.

Zora finds a table in front of a window where sunlight spills warmly across the surface. Damian joins her with his order and a gentle smile.

Not wanting to meet his eyes, Zora plays with her muffin and stares out the window like it holds answers she cannot find inside herself. He interrupts her failed avoidance tactic.

"Zee," he says gently stirring his coffee. "Thank you for agreeing to meet me today. I know it is short notice, but I..."

She looks directly at him and says nervously, "You seem to have a knack for short notices."

A faint smile curls his mouth. "That's been happening a lot lately. I apologize. I'm not typically a last-minute person. A lot going on."

"I see," she says taking in a forkful of her muffin.

He bites his scone and takes a sip of his coffee, eyeing her the entire time.

"Zee, look at me, please," he says softly.

She puts her fork down, folds her hands on her lap, leans back in her chair and looks at him.

"What's up, Damian," she quips. "You said you wanted to talk. Talk."

The chill in her tone lands immediately. He regroups, wipes his mouth and continues.

"Zee, I do not want to give you the wrong impression. I do not want to confuse you. I…"

"Too late, Damian," her voice is sharper than she intended. She looked around to see if anyone in the room heard her response.

"What am I supposed to think? How should I feel, Damian?" she asks through a tightened smile.

"Let me explain, Zee," he pleads with softened eyes.

"Explain," she says crossing her arms across her chest.

He scans the bakery. Too many eyes. Too many ears. He makes a suggestion.

"Zee, do you mind if we finish our food and then go for a walk or go to your condo? I need you to really hear me. To understand me."

Clearly frustrated, Zora leans forward. "Let me get this straight. You invite me here to talk. Now you want to talk somewhere else. A walk. The condo." She sighs heavily. "Stop jerking me around Damian. I don't have time for this," she says as she grabs her purse and rises to leave.

He gently reaches for her arm, but she snatches away from him.

To ground himself, he sips his coffee and takes a final bite of his scone before rising slowly, trying not to draw attention to himself or the situation.

"Zee, please," he says softly. "I don't want to make a scene, but we really need to talk. I thought this would be easy in a public place, but I was mistaken." He reaches for her hand and asks her again, "Zee can we please go for a walk? Please."

Despite her irritation, she looks in his eyes and can tell that he is sincere.

"Come on, Damian," she says as she drops the rest of her food items into the trash and heads for the door. He follows doing the same after a final bite of his scone.

Outside, the sun feels too bright. Too warm. It does nothing to cool her irritation. She starts walking towards the condo, leaving Damian behind.

He catches up to her. "Zee, wait…," he says touching her shoulder. Clearly irritated with him, she stops walking and turns to him.

"What do you want from me, Damian? All of this… this… whatever it is… it's too much," she says as tears start to brim her eyes.

"Zee, I'm not trying to make this too much." He puts both hands gently on her shoulders and dips his head to focus on her eye-to-eye. "Can we please go inside the condo? Please."

She consents and they go to the condo. She opens the door and walks in leaving Damian in the hallway. "Come in, Damian, before my neighbors starts lurking."

He comes in and shuts the door quietly behind him. He leans against the door waiting for her to welcome him in. She extends her arm with a "welcoming" sweep and he comes in further. Zora plops on the couch, arms folded across her chest, legs crossed, and a pout on her mouth.

Damian clears his throat and sits across from her with space between them. He takes a deep breath and turns to her, folding his leg under himself. He reaches for her hand after reassuring her that he is not going to try anything.

"Talk, Damian," she says looking away with tears on her cheek.

He scoots closer to her, but not to overwhelm or crowd her.

"Zee, this is new for me. All of this…" he says softly and continues. "I haven't been in a relationship with a woman in almost 10 years."

She shoots him an alarmed look. "Are…are you… gay?" she asks, eyes wider than usual.

He quickly responds, "No, no I am not gay." He looks at her deeply in her eyes. "Look at me, Zee… I need you to see me and hear me. Please."

She shifts towards him and focuses on his face. *Damn those eyes.*

"I need to explain a few things. First, I am very… and I mean VERY attracted to you. I know you think that I am not because I pull away from you… I…"

"How would you feel if I always ran away whenever things get too close… too intimate?" she asks in frustration. "You keep abandoning me, drawing me in and then leaving me hanging, Damian. What am I…"

"I know, Zee… I promise you I'm not abandoning you. There is an explanation. I'm not asking you to understand, but I am asking that you hear me out, please."

He swallows. She leans in to hear, but not necessarily to listen.

"I am part of a program that stresses celibacy for men who have been… for lack of better terms… in trouble. When I was younger, I couldn't restrain my urges and one time I found myself going beyond a girl's 'no' and it landed me in juvenile detention for a few years. As part of my rehabilitation, recovery, and to keep me from serving actual prison time, I had to participate in this program. The Anchor Project. Rules. Restraint. Accountability. Celibacy. No options."

Zora is now looking at him open-mouthed. Looking for an escape. He can feel her panic. And grabs both of her hands, cupping them softly within his.

"Zee, that is not me anymore. I'm not here to hurt you or to take advantage of you. The program teaches men how to redirect sexual urges and one of those mandates, if you will, is not to be in any relationship until our sponsor and mentor agree that we are ready."

"But…you…" she starts.

"I have been in this program for most of my adult life… But you have thrown a wrench in my program," he smiles lightly.

"What does that even mean, Damian?" she pouts.

"What I mean is I let my guard down. I came into your space without a chaperone. That is not allowed. I am not supposed to put myself in the presence of a woman without having an accountability partner with me…"

She interrupts. "Is that why you were there with Jenson?

"Yes," he says. "Jenson doesn't run his program with integrity. I must say that it is challenging when a beautiful woman enters your orbit and hijacks everything about you without permission," he chuckles softly.

He reaches up and touches Zora's cheek. She leans her head against his hand and closes her eyes.

He continues gracefully. "Zee, I never expected to break any standards of my program. I was doing so well, but you looped me in. You aren't like others who tried to push me out of my process. They tried to test me. My boundaries. My weakness as a man. They would force themselves even after I told them I was celibate. They thought it was a game and would get mad at me. I was always afraid they would cry rape and I would find myself in prison for breaking probation."

He pauses and checks her face. She is all in. Listening. Taking in everything he is saying.

"Zee, you did something to me. In me. I didn't expect that. It's not about sex for me. At least, not anymore. That was the old me. It's deeper. You stir something in me. You pull on me differently. That is not to say that you aren't sexy. Trust me, you are sexy. VERY sexy. Irresistible, even." He pauses briefly to ask, "You okay? May I continue?"

She nods 'yes' in silence, eyes locked in on him. Holding his hands like a life preserver.

"When I saw you in trouble in Atlanta and you asked me to stay with until you fell asleep, I was captured just watching you. When I slipped out of your room, I went to the gym that night to shake off what I was feeling. I knew better than going into your room, but I did. I knew better than to come to this condo with you alone every time, even now, but I did… I have."

"Did I force you? Why didn't you tell me? I'm sorry…"

"Zee, you didn't know. You wouldn't know. It is not something that we advertise as part of our covenant of restraint. We don't announce our stand. We *just stand* in our celibacy. That's it."

He closes his eyes. Fighting back tears. Zora notices and touches his cheek and he responds to her touch. He kisses the palm of her hand and opens his eyes.

"Damian, I never want to be the reason that you break covenant with your program. I admit that you stir something in me that is foreign yet comforting. Something I've not had but didn't know I wanted or needed until you blew into my world. When you are near me, I don't feel like myself and it unnerves me, to be honest. I don't do emotions, but you have a way of making me pay attention to them and that drives me nuts."

She can feel her eyes growing with tears but continues.

"I am very, very attracted to you, Damian, but not like others. I'm not saying that I'm celibate because I'm not. Those moments of sexual engagement are not at all about intimacy. They are only about satisfaction, but I'm finding that it is getting more difficult to reach satisfaction." She pauses. "Am I making sense?"

He wipes his cheek and nods 'yes' in agreement.

"Zee, this is a lot for me. It seems it is a lot for you, too." He clears his throat. "I know what I'm supposed to do and not supposed to do, but being around you makes it very difficult for me."

He locks in on her. "My sponsor and my mentor have forbidden me to see you again. They told me that I need to go back to the group meetings twice a week. I now have to meet with my mentor three times a week as opposed to just once because I had to confess what's been happening between us even without being sure what *is* happening between us." He drops his head and inhales.

He continues softly. "I know they are trying to protect me, but to be honest, I don't want to be protected, Zee. I *want* to be around you… *with* you. Again, it is not about sex for me. What I desire, if I can say this… I desire intimacy with you. I'm not sure how to do that. I'm not sure how to balance my program and the profound draw I feel for you."

He closes his eyes and shakes his head. "I don't know what to do. When I'm with you there is an intense pull. Not animalistic. Tender. Gentle. Something I've not known."

He exhales and looks at her with tears in his eyes.

"I don't know how to do this, Zee… I don't…"

She reaches and grabs his face with both hands. "Look at me, Damian. You don't have to do anything right now. Let's just… just be… until you make a decision that works best for your life. Don't worry about me," she says gently.

He looks at her, tears wetting her hands. "Don't worry about you?" he says. "Is it wrong to want both? To do what's right and to want you, too?"

"I don't know, Damian. I don't know what to do with you either. You are something completely new to me, too. I have my own personal struggles with intimacy, but I agree there is something between us. I'm just not sure what it is or what to do with it, if anything at all."

They sit there in silence looking at one another. Hoping for clarity. Damian breaks the silence.

"Zee, I have to go out of town to cover Jenson again. Can I call you when I return on Sunday?"

She closed her eyes and tried to breathe. Chest tightening.

"I don't know… Maybe we need to do what your sponsor suggested. Maybe…we…"

He grabs her hands and holds them to his chest. "No, Zee… I don't think I can do that. You know how much I look forward to seeing you, calling you, being around you? I can't just go cold turkey. I know it's not right, but it's my truth… I can't… It has been more than 10 years since someone carried my heart outside of my chest and I long for that again. Program or not. I don't want to lose you, Zee."

She puts her fingers to his lips. "Don't stress, Damian. It will work out. Honor your program," she says gently.

"Besides, I'm in therapy for my own issues and I don't want to entangle you in those. It would be too much for you to handle. Trust me on that."

He gently kisses her hands one at a time. Eyes closed. Both embracing the moment.

He clears his throat to speak. "Zee, may I ask you a favor?"

"Sure, what is it?"

"Can I hold you… just hold you in my arms… in case this *is* the last time?"

She didn't like how that sounded. Could this be *the last* time they touch? Did she *really* mean that she wanted him to honor his program?

She held his glance. "Yes, Damian," she said as she starts to stand up.

Confused, Damian asks, "Where are you going?"

She pulls him from the couch. "Follow me…"

Unsure, he lets her lead. She walks him into the bedroom, a place where men have never been.

He hesitates, almost stopping.

"Zee… I can't…"

She hushes him without turning towards him. She leads him to the bed and kicks off her shoes. He does the same. She beckons him to lay down with her.

"Zee, this is not what I was asking… I was just…"

"Damian, stop talking… Lay next to me… Hold me… just hold me."

Together they lay on the queen-sized bed, his body curled against hers. He spoons her and she leans her body into his. He gently wraps her with his body and both exhales. In silence, they communicate without words. She can feel his heart beating against her back, his breath bathing her neck. He can feel the warmth of her against him; her scent enraptures his senses.

For the next couple of hours, the outside world disappears. They lay in one another's embrace. Silent. Questioning. Desiring. Curious. Scared.

Zora breaks their entanglement first. She slowly rolls over to face Damian. Their eyes locked. She kisses him. He kisses her back. Gently. Passionately, but nothing more. No pressure. No expectation. She lightly pulls back.

"What's the matter, Zee?" he asks confusion etched on his face.

"I'm sorry, Damian, but I have a 3 p.m. meeting. I need to get home. Call me whenever you want to talk. I'll try to answer."

The two of them rise from the bed. No words spoken. Struggle understood.

Outside, Damain walks to his car. Zora to hers.

Both turning back.

Both wanting to say more.

Both carrying something new they do not yet have language for.

Chapter Thirty-Two

The short ride home was painful. Unfamiliar. Uncertainty. Excitement. Confusion. Curiosity.

Zora parks and enters her home emotionally drained. This is so not her. Emotions are off limits. So many questions consuming her. No answers. No solutions. Not sure she even knows what to do with all that she heard.

She kicks off her shoes, drops her purse on the kitchen island and searches for something quick to eat for lunch. She's noticeably hungry since she didn't eat all of her muffin almost three hours ago.

She opts for a bowl of Mediterranean salad from yesterday and a bottle of water. She stands at the island and forks it into her mouth slowly. Almost robotic. Mindlessly. Too many other things taking up space within her.

She needs to focus. Her Zoom meeting is in 45 minutes. She needs to be sharp. This annual THRIVE Employment Empowerment program focuses on local employers hiring young people for the summer. It takes a great deal of trust, cooperation, and coordination to take on youth as employees, most of which are from underserved and marginalized communities.

Zora loves giving back and this is something she looks forward to every year. This is her baby. A vision she started about five years ago and it has proven to make a marked difference in the lives of both young people and businesses. It is a win-win all around.

She checks her watch. 2:48 p.m. She swallows the last of her salad and the final sip of her water and heads to her private office downstairs. Laptop powered up and logged into Zoom. She sits in silence.

Productive meeting. 4:20 p.m. Zora closes her laptop and leans back in her chair. No sound machine. No candle. Just space to absorb. She closes her eyes and exhales.

Now what?

She needs a distraction. She heads upstairs and calls her mother. It's been a week since they spoke.

Video call. She dials. Her mother answers on the third ring.

"My Zora," she says with joy filling her face. "How are you, my daughter?

Zora paints on a happy expression to disguise the turmoil raging withing. "Hi, Mommy. I was thinking about you. This has been a busy week, but I never want to neglect reaching out," she says with a bright smile.

"I'm doing good, daughter. Two new clients so Chae and I have been juggling all of the details of all our clients," she says with her palm on her face.

"But we are happy for the work. With everyone trying to DIY everything, it is wonderful to have people who trust us with their homes and businesses." She looks away briefly. She's in the interior design office.

"Sorry, my daughter. So how are you doing? You heard from Reese?"

Zora hesitated so that she could give the proper response. "I've been doing well. Just had a meeting for the THRIVE Employment Empowerment event that is taking place next Saturday," she says. "You and Daddy still coming? I hope you still want to hire another youth for your office," she says with a twinge of concern.

"Yes, of course, my Zora. We enjoyed participating over the last three years. Now that we have financial strength, we can afford to bring someone on for the summer."

"That's great. Thank you, Mommy."

She pauses before continuing. "Is Daddy still going to host a youth for the CAP program?"

"I believe so," she says. "Give him a call."

Zora avoided her suggestion and the Reese topic completely. Not even interested in her father's cold interaction or discussing Reese Parker.

Thankfully, Chae came into the office and interrupted, telling Mommy they need to get ready for their next design meeting.

"I have to run, my daughter," she says waving. "See you Sunday at dinner, right?"

"Yes, Mommy. I'll be there. Have a great meeting," she says with a warm smile.

The call ends. Crisis averted.

***

In Bowie, Damian is mindlessly moving through his home. He's hungry but doesn't have an appetite. He knows he needs to pack for his trip tomorrow. His chest is tight. His mind racing. So many feelings. Fear. Frustration. Curiosity. Recovery. Desire.

Where is the balance?

How does he find it for himself?

The ring of his phone interrupts his thoughts. Jenson.

He answers, hiding his anxiety. "Hey, man, what's up?"

"Just checking to see when you'll arrive in Richmond?" Jenson asks. "You flying or driving?"

Damian takes a deep breath to steady his voice. "I'm driving. It's less than three hours away."

"That's what's up," Jenson says. "We are booked at the Holiday Inn & Suites – West End. They have free breakfast," Jenson chuckles.

"Yeah," Damian says. "At least we don't have to rent a car." He hesitates. "Jenson, did you get us adjoining rooms?"

Jenson releases a deep sigh. "Yes, Damian… I know I need you near my room… I know…"

"Good, we don't need you to fall into any more folly. Right?"

"Right, Bruh" Jenson says with irritation in his voice.

"Let me start packing. I plan on hitting the road around 10 a.m. after traffic dies down a bit. I'll check in with you in the morning."

"Alright, man," Jenson says. He is clearly frustrated to need a chaperone, but he also knows the rules, which he struggles to keep.

The call ends.

Damian walks slowly to the back of the apartment to his bedroom. He pulls his large overnight bag from the closet and begins pulling clothes out of his dresser. Organizing the clothes on the bed, his mind reflects on earlier today. Laying on the bed, Zee wrapped in his arms. Her warmth. Her softness. Her scent. Blood rushes to his face. His chest tightens. He can't breathe.

I miss her already.

Will she push me away now that she knows?

I don't want to think of life without her.

His thoughts are interrupted again when his phone rings. Pastor Hayden.

Damian sighs and takes a deep breath before answering. The call connects.

"Hello, Pastor Hayden," he answers sounding somewhat grounded. He knows differently.

"Hello, Damian. I'm just checking in. You ready for your trip this weekend?"

"Yes, Sir. I just spoke with Jenson. Everything is lined up," he says sounding responsible.

"Good. Good," Pastor Hayden says. "How are you getting there?"

"I'm driving so we won't have to rent a car or catch an Uber. It also ensures that we are always together for accountability," Damian says.

"Smart thinking, son," he says. "Don't forget to call me and your sponsor when you arrive and provide your hotel and room numbers."

Damian rolls his eyes. He hates feeling like a little boy who is on punishment, being clocked for his every move.

"Absolutely, Sir," he says forcing a smile that he hopes can be felt although he is internally frustrated.

"Thank you for taking the lead, Damian. This is necessary. I'm sure you understand."

"Not a problem. I get it. It is for both of our good to run a clean and productive program."

"Exactly. Have a safe trip, Damian. I look forward to hearing from you. Have a good evening."

"Yes, Sir. You, too."

The call ends. Damian sits on the side of his bed, emotions rising. Jaws tightening.

Zee.

Chapter Thirty-Three

Zora turns off the lights to her office and slowly makes her ascent to the main level of her home. Her stomach is unsettled. Twisting. Maybe a cup of hot tea. Maybe a glass of wine. Maybe a fix.

Go ahead, Zora, Skyy taunts. *Make a call. You need this. It's been two days since Brandon bent you over.*

Zora tries to shake the voice booming in her head. *Be quiet.*

She knows Skyy is right. She is feeling a little antsy. She should do better, but physical pressure is building.

Damian does nothing to help the situation. What makes her think that lying next to him in the bed is harmless? His touch stirs her. Challenges her emotions and her flesh. She can't ignore that his presence alone moistens her. Hell, he can't even have sex. Why should she hold back from being satisfied?

She can't.

She won't.

That's right, Zora, Skyy's voice rumbles within. *You know you want to. You need to.*

Zora makes her way to the third floor. First slowly, then running. In her sanctuary, she showers and prepares for an encounter.

Now mid-June, the weather is ripe for a sexy sundress. She finds a floral, A-line, strappy sundress that meets her knees. Perfume. Smokey makeup. Beauty mark in place. Honey Blonde wig in a bag. It's still too light to leave out of the house that disguised. God bless Mrs. Fitzpatrick, she chuckles.

Sitting on the side of her bed, she reaches in the top drawer and thumbs through her fixer phone.

Shelton. It's been a while since she has enjoyed him. She hits the call button.

Two rings. He answers.

"Hello?"

"Hi, Shelton, this is Skyy," she says in a sultry tone. "Remember me?"

"Remember you? Of course. You're hard to forget," he says with a lift in his voice.

"You busy tonight? Thought maybe we can see each other."

Silence.

Did she offend him?

"Are you there, Shelton?" she asks more shyly.

"Yeah, I'm here." He pauses. "I'm supposed to meet a college buddy of mine for happy hour at his hotel. Can I meet you after?"

She sighs into the phone. “I really want to see you now, if you know what I mean.”

“I’d love to, Skyy, but I can’t leave my buddy hanging. We already made plans.”

She brightens up. “I have an idea,” she says playfully. “I can join you two for a drink and then afterwards we can…”

He laughs out loud. “Are you serious, Skyy? You suggesting a threesome with me and my buddy?”

She laughs. “Why not? Never done it before. Might be fun. You game?”

“Sounds interesting. Let me ask him…”

Skyy interrupts him. “Don’t tell him. Let it be a secret. A treat. A welcome to the city, so to speak.”

Shelton considered Zora’s offer. “Let’s do it. You are wild,” he says laughing.

“If you say so,” she says laughing. “Where is the hotel? I’ll meet you there.”

Shelton gives her the address and tells her to meet him in the lobby at 5:30 p.m.

“See you then,” she giggles. She grabs two condoms and makes her way to the hotel.

***

Zora enters the lobby of the hotel Shelton provided. He met her smiling from ear to ear.

“Hi, Skyy. You look great,” he says. “You changed your hair.”

Shit. She thought she wore this wig with him the last time. *Oh, well.*

She recovers. "The weather changed. It's too hot for long fluffy hair, ya know?"

He shakes his head in understanding. "I get it. 90-degree weather in the DMV is serious," he says with a chuckle.

While they chat, Shelton's phone rings. He answers within one ring.

"Hey, Luis, I'm downstairs. Can I come up first?"

Luis tells him Room 313. Shelton and Skyy take the elevator to the third floor and knock on the door.

Luis is surprised to see his friend with what he thought was a date.

"Hey, Shelton… You brought a date with you, man?"

"Well, not really," he says chuckling. "This is Skyy. She is here to make our evening more interesting."

Luis looks at Skyy and lifts and eyebrow along with a cheesy grin. "Really? That so? How interesting?" he says chuckling.

"You'll see," Shelton says as he looks at Skyy.

They all agree to go to the restaurant bar in the lobby.

"Nothing like wine and spirits to get things going," Shelton giggles.

Zora knows that Skyy doesn't need any assistance. Just knowing she's about to be fixed is enough for her.

At the bar, Skyy sits between Luis and Shelton ping ponging her attention between the two. At one point she spins herself towards Shelton, parts her legs slightly, and whispers in his ear. "Put your hand up my skirt" and he did.

Moist. His expression was enough for her. She spun herself around to face Luis and whispered the same thing, leaving him more curious about why she had joined them.

After about 90 minutes of conversation, indulgence, and teasing, the threesome makes their way back to Luis's room.

As Luis unlocks the door, Skyy thinks, *Oh, yeah, it's about to be epic.*

Once inside, Skyy provides some direction. She turns to Shelton and asks, "Shelton, what is Rule #1?"

"No talking," he says with a certainty.

"Rule #2, Shelton?"

"Skyy is in control," he says looking at Luis with a grin.

"Rule #3, Shelton?"

"Condom always."

"And Rule #4," Skyy says, "No violence whatsoever. No force. None. Period."

The men look at one another in agreement with wide grins.

Skyy drops her purse on the bed and commands Shelton to come to her. She then directs Luis to stand close, but not to touch her yet.

Shelton follows her instructions and she kisses him hungrily. Deep kisses that cause him to moan. Luis is getting aroused just watching. He can feel his penis responding, but he doesn't touch her.

Skyy then turns to Luis and kisses him in the same manner. Shelton standing by. Watching. Waiting his turn.

"Take of your pants, both of you," she commands with a smirk on her face. She's ecstatic. She's never had a threesome – her first Ménage à trois – and her vagina is perked for the experience, moisture forming on her lips and inner thighs.

Both men stand pantless with erect penises visible for all to see. Skyy can see that both men are comparable in size and this turns her on even more.

She instructs Luis to lay on the bed with his legs hanging off the end. "Shelton," she says breathy, "Take your position behind me."

Luis lays on the bed, penis at attention. Skyy lifts her dress, bearing her naked ass, and straddles him, but doesn't engage his penis. She starts kissing him deeply, causing him to groan against her mouth, tongues intertwined. She snaps her fingers towards Shelton and he comes behind her. She passes him a condom and he rolls it on. She stops kissing Luis long enough to tell Shelton to take her. "Give me what you got, Shelton… You know how I like it…"

As she returns to kissing Luis, she gasps as Shelton spreads her cheeks and enters her in one thrust. He is working her from behind just like she is used to. Deep thrusts. His penis hot, long, and thick. She is moaning against Luis' mouth with each stroke. She starts to stroke her clitoris on Luis' erect penis, and he grinds his hips beneath her creating the right amount of friction that engorges her. She can tell that he feels a little neglected, so she dislodges Shelton from her vagina and tells them to switch places. Shelton on the bed, Luis at the rear. She hands Luis a condom and he rolls it on. She looks back at him and says, "Now, Luis… Fill me…"

And he does beautifully. She is pleasantly surprised by his technique. She thrusts against him with fervor. His stroke reminds her so much of Milo. She's taking him all in. She stopped kissing Shelton to enjoy what Luis was doing to her. "Yes, Luis… Deeper… Deeper," she moans. Shelton is watching and enjoying the scene, his penis waiting to engage again.

Skyy instructs Luis to back up, but not to pull out. She brings her mouth to Shelton's penis and sucks him passionately. Licking. Stroking. Sucking. Shelton responds with groans that combine with hers and Luis'. The three are in an orchestrated dance that has Skyy vibrating all over. She's intoxicated by the experience.

She pulls Shelton out of her mouth and flips over to insert Shelton's penis in her throbbing vagina. He lifts his hips and engages her vagina. She is tingling all over. She pulls Luis closer and puts his penis in her mouth and sucks him in as deep as she can. He moans with the work of her mouth. She nibbles the head of his penis that he appears to enjoy before she deep throats him again. Nibble, tease, suck, stroke. Repeat. Groans, moans, wetness become music in Room 313. The heat is undeniable. She can feel both men stiffening – Shelton in her vagina, Luis in her mouth – so she stops and provides instructions.

"Shelton stay where you are, Luis come closer," she commands. "Shelton in my vagina as I straddle you. Luis in my anus." The men look at each other with widened eyes.

Skyy snaps her fingers, "Now, fellas, now…"

Everyone gets into position. As Skyy pushes herself back onto Shelton's penis, Luis pushes his penis into her anus. Perfect rhythm. Bodies working in tandem. The pressure builds for all three. The vibration is undeniable. Skyy can feel both men stiffen. She tells them both breathlessly, "C'mon fellas…" she says through clinched teeth… "give me what you got… go deeper… stroke me… stroke harder… I'm about to… I'm about…"

Every one of them feels the buildup and almost simultaneously, they explode. Each expressing their release through a moan, a groan, a grunt, a scream, whichever was appropriate for what they were feeling. Hips moving in after-effects. Penises slowly stroking down. Vagina and anus humming with pleasure.

Relief.

No words.

They collapse in a heap on top of one another. Chests heaving. Mouths dry. Body parts pulsating, sweating, and wet with release. The scent of sex filling the room.

After about 10 minutes, Skyy taps Luis on the thigh to dislodge. She pulls up and disengages Shelton's penis and rolls over on her back. Still breathing heavily. Luis is standing with his hands on his hips, still trying to recover. Shelton has his elbow folded over his face still breathing hard.

Skyy finally sits up and scoots off the end of the bed, pulling her dress down as she stands.

Shelton and Luis look at her in astonishment. She adjusts herself and looks at both men giggling.

"Get dressed, fellas," she chuckles. "You just going to stand around with your penises hanging out?"

Shelton and Luis look at one another, as if just realizing they can see one another's penis. They jump up and gather their pants and underwear, putting them on as if the hotel was on fire. Skyy looks on in amusement.

Everyone now properly dressed, Skyy says, "That was amazing, Fellas. Simply amazing," she smiles looking as if she is sealing the experience in her mind.

"Well, I have to go… Enjoy the rest of your evening," she says as she walks towards the door. She turns and says, "Shelton, I'll be in touch…"

He slowly nods his head and smiles.

"Nice to meet you, Luis," she says grinning. "Let us know when you're back in town," she says biting her bottom lip.

He slowly nods his head in amazement.

She lets herself out of the room and heads towards the elevator with a HUGE grin on her face.

Alone in the room, Luis looks at Shelton. "What in the hell was *that*?"

"I don't know… never did that with her before," Shelton responds still breathing heavy.

Luis puts his hand on his forehead still trying to understand what he just experienced.

"Skyy is her name? She should be called Storm," he says still unwinding.

"More like tornado," Shelton says.

Both men laugh in contemplation.

***

Back in her car, Zora looks at her reflection in the mirror. Body very much alive with pleasure.

Happy hour indeed.

Chapter Thirty-Four

Taking the steps to her sanctuary, Zora takes in the weight of her day. A happy ending to an emotionally heavy day. Damian's truth. THRIVE meeting. Happy hour that was out of this world. She smiles widely.

Thank. You. Skyy.

She peels off her clothes and takes a hot shower. Her body responds to the heat of the water, the flow of it rolling over her skin massaging her muscles with tenderness. She rests her hands on the wall in front of her and closes her eyes. Her mind drifts to Shelton and Luis. *WOW! WOW! WOW!*

Crawling under her covers, she checks both of her cell phones. The fixer phone. Three missed text messages. Two from Shelton expressing his feelings about the day, suggesting that they get together again soon. Another from Milo checking in. He's ready to see her again as well.

Never without a fixer, she smiles to herself as she puts the phone back in the drawer.

Her personal phone. A few texts. Group text from the Besties confirming the time for tomorrow. Zora responds "6:30 p.m."

Another text.

Damian.

"Hey, Zee… just checking in… I understand if you don't respond. I'll check back tomorrow from the road. Two emojis. Smiley face. Tearful face.

Zora leans against the headboard contemplating Damian's text. She checks the time. 10:23 p.m. She opts not to respond. She wants to rest in the pleasure she just experienced without thinking about emotions.

Ugh.

She clicks off the lamp and lays in the stillness of the dark, her body reminding her just how much she loves happy hour.

***

Friday comes in muggy. Zora can feel the humidity in the air. She rolls out of bed and jumps into her daily routine. Run. Shower. Breakfast. She has a full client schedule today. She braces herself for the heavy mental pull that each client will bring.

She navigates each client meeting with professional finesse and closes out her workday.

5:15 p.m. Zora ascends to the main level of her home and dials GrubHub to order dinner for her Besties. A variety of salads and dressing. The healthier option. She knows the Besties will bring less healthier choices.

She checks the bar to make sure there are clean glasses and a variety of drinks to satisfy her friends' thirsts.

The order arrives at 5:45 p.m. and she transfers the different salads and dressings into decorative bowls. She lets everything chill in the refrigerator.

She sets her Alexa to play smooth jazz softly then she lights a few sage and lavender candles.

She heads upstairs for a quick shower and puts on a comfortable lavender and purple tie-dyed jersey knit romper pant set and purple footies. A spritz of perfume. Light make-up. Lip gloss. Diamond stud earrings.

A final look in the mirror.

Nerves.

She anticipates an emotionally charged evening.

Breathe, Zora.

***

6:30 p.m. sharp, there is a knock on the door and Nico enters using his key. Right behind him is Rayven and Lai, all carrying individual bags of morsels for the dinner spread.

Zora calls down the stairs, "Be right there."

She joins them in the kitchen and pulls the salads and dressings out of the refrigerator and organizes everything on one end of the island along with plates, bowls, and flatware. The Besties unpack their bags and do the same, creating a buffet of delight.

Each one grabs a plate and they gather at the round dining table off the kitchen. They open up with the usual banter. Laughter. Jokes. Chiding one another in fun.

Dinner wraps up and they clear the table, stacking dishes in the sink. The Besties adjourn to the lounge near the bar. Four comfortable sherpa chairs surrounding a live edge wooden table. Each Bestie grabs a glass and pours their favorite libation from the bar car. Everyone seated, Zora speaks up.

"Thank you all for agreeing to a more intimate gathering with just us," she says warmly. "I thought it would be a better atmosphere for talking without competing with loud music and such."

Each Bestie looks at one another; concern etched on their faces.

Lai speaks first. "Zora, are you okay? Are you sick? Please tell me you're not sick," she says almost frantic.

Zora takes a seat next to Nico. She needs his support tonight.

"No, I'm not sick," she says. She looks at Nico for reassurance before continuing. "I'm not sick like that, but I need to share somethings with you all as my best friends. Things that I've been hiding. Afraid to talk about."

Nico gives her a nod. "This is a no judgment zone. We will all speak our truths tonight. This is about love, safety, and healing," he says reaching for Zora's hand.

Lai and Rayven look at each other then at Nico and Zora.

"Are you two dating? Is that what this is about?" Rayven asks.

"Yeah, you two always act weird around one another. Zora, are you pregnant?" Lai expresses.

"No, no, no…" Zora says holding her free hand up looking at Nico.

Nico chimes in. "We were involved years ago, in high school, but that didn't pan out," he says looking at Zora for confirmation.

Lai and Rayven look at them with wide eyes and mouths open.

"Let Zora tell it," he says warmly looking at Zora still holding her hand.

Everyone leans back in their chairs except for Zora. She takes a swallow of her white wine and leans forward. Nico turns in her direction, letting her know this is a safe place and that he has her back no matter what.

She takes a deep breath and closes her eyes.

"Z, what is it," Rayven says impatiently.

Nico rebukes her. "Ray, let her pace this out. We have nothing but time."

He looks at Zora. "Go ahead, Z. The floor is yours," he says squeezing her hand.

Zora clears her throat lightly. "I ummm… I have been hiding an addiction for over 16 years. Something I'm not proud of openly, but that I thrive off of in private." She looks at Lai and Rayven reading their emotions and continues.

"I… I…" she can feel her eyes brimming with tears. The girls lean forward in their chairs.

"I am addicted to… ummm… I'm addicted to sex," she says with her head down.

"We always knew you loved sex, Z, that's nothing new," Lai chimes in.

Nico shoots her a warning look and she holds her comments.

Zora continues, with tears traveling down her cheeks. "I dress up in a disguise, and I pick up random men wherever I can and I have untamed sex with them. Outside, in alleys, between dumpsters, parks, in cars… any and everywhere."

She reads the room, clears her throat and continues.

"My alter ego is Skyy. She has an insatiable appetite for sex. She doesn't feel emotion. She doesn't want love. She just wants sex. That's it." She dabs tears away with the back of her hand.

Zora inhales deeply. "Skyy pulls at me fiercely. She controls me daily. I seek casual sex every day of the week, sometimes two or three times a day. The pull is relentless."

Rayven gasps, "Zora… how?… when?"

"Be quiet, Rayven," Nico quips.

"Nico has known about this since I was in the 9th grade and he was in the 10th." She checks Nico's face for permission to continue.

"I was Nico's first. I took his virginity when one of my tilts – that's what happens when Skyy shows up – when one of my tilts happened. I all but raped him in the backyard of a party that we both attended. We were friends, but I was horny. He was the closest person to me that night, so I took his virginity."

Rayven and Lai look at each other and then at Nico. Hands to their mouths.

Zora continues. "Anyway, I had sex with Nico every day, sometimes more than once a day for almost a year. He wanted love. I wanted lust. He didn't just want sex. He wanted commitment. I wanted never-ending pleasure. My insatiable appetite nearly ended our friendship."

Nico nods in agreement, looking around the group.

"I'm grateful that he chose to stay in my life," she says smiling warmly at him. "He has covered for me all this time. Covering me when we are all out together. He knows when my appetite is about to boil over so he covers and protects me," she says wiping her face and Nico dabbing his own eyes.

Zora exhales. "A few weeks ago, Nico threatened to cut me off if I didn't get help. He let me have it after he caught me having sex in Anacostia Park." She clears her throat. "He warned me a few times too many because I've become reckless. Random sex in public because my appetite is so overwhelming."

Lai raises a finger. "I don't mean to interrupt… Why is that we didn't know about this? I mean, how did you hide it from us?" she says with tears in her eyes.

"I thought I could control it. No one knows except my "fixers" – the men who engage me sexually with no strings attached – and Nico, and now you."

She breaks down in tears. Nico moves his chair closer to her to comfort her.

She continues through tears. "I live a double life. I'm a therapist that lives out my trauma through a sex addiction. I feel like a hypocrite. Helping others but can't help myself."

Rayven gets up and drops on her knees in front of Zora, rubbing her shoulder.

"Z, you are not a hypocrite. We all know we can't take our own advice. That's what therapists are for. That's what friends are for," she says looking around the group.

"Yeah," Lai speaks up. "We all have our own things, right?" she says looking around for agreement. All nod their heads.

Zora sniffles and speaks again. "Thank you all for listening. It has been hard. Very hard. I hate the addiction and absolutely love it at the same time. A constant internal battle that fights me externally."

Rayven speaks up. "May I ask you something?" she looks in Zora's eyes. "When did all of this start?"

Zora looks at Nico, who nods for her to continue. She clears her throat. "It started when I was molested as a child and the craving was developed from there. I'm in therapy for all that's worth; and I even went to confession. I don't know how to get resolution alone."

Rayven nearly falls over in surprise but catches herself. She lifts herself back into her chair, hands covering her mouth. "Z, I'm so sorry… so, so sorry…"

"It's okay. Nothing you could do… any of you can do except support me." She looks at Nico again and he speaks.

"I hold her accountable by keeping in touch for accountability. If I don't hear from her, then I know that Skyy is on the move. By that time, it's too late."

Zora smiles through her tears. "Nico is relentless. He doesn't let me get away with anything. He just wants me to be better," she says holding up their clasped hands.

Nico acknowledges with a smile.

Zora takes a deep breath. "I don't want to get into the details of my innocence being taken at a young age but know that it has long lasting effects that I'm still trying to recover from."

"We understand, Z. Thank you for trusting us with this. We love you. We really do," Lai says tears wetting her face.

Each one takes a sip of their drinks. Needed after all that Zora revealed.

Nico puts his glass down and leans in. "My secret is that I am dyslexic. I've struggled with it all of my life. Even at 29 years old, I still have issues reading without jumbling things up."

The girls look at one another in shock. He continues.

"The only thing I don't jumble is musical notes. That's why music comes so easily for me. It is shapes, not words," he says a little embarrassed. "I made it through school and college because I had teachers who gave me recorded notes and oral exams."

Lai chimes in. "You do so well, Nico. You're an amazing musician. We are so proud of the man that you are. Successful. Talented. Passionate about others."

Nico offers a soft teary smile.

Lai continues, tears filling her eyes. "My secret is that my father has been in an out of prison most of my life and is currently serving his fourth sentence in Texas. He won't be released until 2036," she says through tears. "I work hard to make him proud, but he is never around to see what I've accomplished. My music is my refuge. It says what I can't always express. I just want him to live to experience who I am fully."

"Wow, Lai. Thank you for sharing that," Zora says wiping her eyes.

Rayven leans forward, palms on her knees. She takes in a deep breath and speaks.

"Since we are all sharing our secrets... Steps is in financial trouble." The group takes a collective sigh, looking at one another.

Rayven continues through a cracking voice. "Yeah, the grant didn't come through and I'm barely staying afloat. Most of my students can't afford the classes and I'm the most affordable in the city. I'm hoping to host an open house and a fundraiser next month to raise funds to carry the studio for the next few months until I can figure things out. If that doesn't pan out, I'll have to file for bankruptcy and may lose the studio altogether."

The Besties sit in silence absorbing. Secrets shared. Hearts lighter. More eager to be supportive of one another.

Nico speaks up, clearing his throat. "I love you ladies like sisters. Thank you for embracing me as the only male in our group, even when I'm off the chain. Thank you for seeing me... fully."

Lai speaks up. "Group hug... group hug."

Each rise from their chairs and enfolds one another weeping, smiling, grateful.

The embrace loosens and Rayven breaks the seriousness of the moment.

"Ya'll look like a bunch of blowfish with puffy eyes and cheeks," she says laughing.

"Go to hell," Lai says laughing.

Nico raises an eyebrow and says, "Come to think of it you all do look like…"

Before he can complete his sentence, Zora pops him on the back of his head.

The group bursts out in laughter.

Zora raises her glass. "To friendship. To Besties. To Family."

Glasses clank in agreement as each finishes their drinks.

At the close of the evening, they all work together to clean up the kitchen, so Zora doesn't have to do it alone.

Zora looks at all of her friends and says, "Heart-to heart, strength-to-strength, Besties for life."

In unison, they all ring out, "Besties for life."

Chapter Thirty-Five

At 9:15 p.m. the Besties are filing out of the front door. Before Nico leaves, he shuts the door and hugs Zora, telling her he is so very proud of her.

She hugs him back. They stand in an embrace for a while. Truth told. Tension finally released.

Zora pulls back and looks at Nico, who smiles back at her. He leans in and kisses her lips lightly. She smiles at the friendly gesture, thinking nothing of it until the kiss came again and again and they were in a full tongue kiss. She pulls back again. Palms on Nico's chest.

"Nico?" she questions.

Embarrassed, he says, "I'm sorry, Z. You've always been my weakness. I just wanted to kiss you again."

Zora thought about that and asked, "Is that all you want, Nico?"

He looks at her. "No."

He presses her against the front door and kisses her passionately. She doesn't resist him. She feels Skyy and so does Nico.

"No Skyy today. I want Zora," he says over her mouth. "No Skyy…"

"What about your girlfriend, Nico? I don't want commitment." she says against his lips still kissing him deeply.

He doesn't respond. He gently pulls at her clothes. She helps him, dropping her bottoms and panties to the floor, while pulling at his sweatpants.

He's breathy. She's boiling. Skyy is coming alive. Skyy doesn't care that they are Besties.

He breathes against her mouth. "Zora… I want you so much… I…"

"You have a condom?" she asks still kissing him.

He moans a 'no' to her. She breaks the kiss and heads towards the steps.

Surprised at the break, he asks, "Where are you going, Z?"

"We need a condom, Nico. You know the rules," she says walking half naked up the steps. He follows her, pulling at his sweatpants that were falling as he walked.

In her room, she grabs a condom out of her fixer drawer and hands it to Nico. He rolls it onto his penis. She pulls him into the guest bedroom.

No men in her bedroom.

He willingly follows.

Zora is squirming now, hips gyrating in intense heat. She puts both hands on the guest bed and bends over.

Nico walks up behind her and grabs her hips, spreads her cheeks, and gently slides his engorged penis into her dripping vagina.

"Ahhhhhh," he says upon entry. "Zora… Ohhhhh…"

"Shhhhh, Nico…" she reminds him.

He is stroking her good. Real good. She hasn't been with him in over 16 years. She's impressed. VERY impressed. His manly penis is amazing in comparison to his teenage penis. Zora is responding according to the pleasure he is giving her. She thrusts her hips against him with purpose, drive, intention.

Make him remember what he gave up she thinks to herself. *Prove to him that this is the best he's ever had.*

She pops her hips rhythmically driving him nuts. Over and over. Pop. Pop. Pop. She didn't know how to do that at 14 years old.

She has grown in technique.

He is moaning with each stroke and pop. He adds a scooping action with each thrust and it is driving Zora crazy. She is moaning so loudly, she puts her face into the mattress to muffle her sounds.

He can hear her muffled commands. "Deeper, Nico… Deeper… Ahhhhh…"

He responds and pushes himself in as far as he could. Deeper. She is trembling. He keeps pushing. She keeps popping. He keeps stroking. She keeps thrusting. He stiffens. She protests.

"No, Nico… Not yet… Not now…thrust me, please… stroke me…"

He bites his bottom lip trying to hold back his impending release. Zora crawls up on the bed on her knees, ass in the air.

"Stroke me, Nico… Deeper… Stroke me… Ahhhhh… Stroke… Me…"

He is giving her focused strokes.

"Zora… I can't…"

"Let's go, Nico… Let's… goooooooo…" she screams.

He let's go and releases with an intense guttural growl, gripping her hips with his fingertips hard enough to bruise her. She continues to thrust against him, tightening her muscles, pulling everything out of him, working with her vaginal shocks. Both moan as she works him down. He slowly stops moving even though she is still lightly gyrating against him. He dislodges his penis and folds himself over her back while she is resting on her elbows, her ass in his chest. Both panting.

Nico manages words. "Zora… Oh. My. God…"

"What's wrong?" she asks.

"Wrong? Wrong? Nothing is wrong," he says against her back. "Where in the hell did you learn to do all that?"

She chuckles. "I've had a lot of time to practice since you last bent me over."

He slides off of her back, pulls up his pants and sits on the bed. She rolls over and folds the bedspread over her lap, grinning.

"So, you liked it huh? You missed me, admit it," she laughs.

"Girl, you are dangerous. No wonder your fixer phone stays lit up. Damn," he says raising an eyebrow to her.

She just looks at him with a sheepish grin. "Now, what?"

Nico rubs his face with both hands, looking at her. "I don't know, Zora. That was… you are amazing. Addictive is an appropriate word," he says in amazement.

"No emotions, Nico. You know that. Nothing has changed with that," she says looking at him.

"I know, Z. I know. But, damn. I've been missing *all that?* Whew," he says rubbing his face again.

Zora laughs. "When you have an addiction like mine, your body does what it needs to do to get what it needs to get. Technique evolves as the addiction evolves," she says as she pats him on the knee.

"That's my reality, Nico. I can't compete with evolution."

Nico just looks at her and says, "YOU are a drug, Zora Leigh Holley… You are addictive without a doubt."

She smiles at him warmly. "I must say that you've gotten better with age as well," she giggles. "But seriously, it's getting late, Nico…"

He looks at her with hunger in his eyes. "Do you think we can…you know…"

She stands, naked from the waist down, hands on her hips. "I don't know, Nico. I'm not sure you can handle being in rotation with my fixer pool."

He leans back on his elbows, revealing a new bulge in his sweatpants.

"I don't know, Z. I may be willing to jump in that pool if *this* is what I get," he says laughing.

She pats his bulging crotch before turning towards the door. "We'll see, Nico…We will see," she says with a sultry grin.

She walks him to the front door, collects her clothes from the floor, and lets him out.

"Good night, Nico…," she laughs closing the door behind him.

***

On the porch, Nico rubs his erect penis trying to get it to deflate. Walking to his car, he is dumbfounded.

Damn it, Zora. I'm getting in that pool.

***

Inside, Zora heads to her bathroom and cleans up before she climbs into bed. She checks both of her phones. Three missed text messages on the fixer phone. Shelton. Milo. Brandon.

Fixer, fixer, come get me, Mister.

"So many options," she chuckles to herself.

Her personal phone had a missed call from Damian. She is mentally and physically drained. She will respond to him tomorrow.

A text from Nico. She reads Nico's message: "Please put me in the fixer pool…" with a wide grin emoji following.

She laughs out loud and shakes her head.

Nico is crazy. Dangerously delicious, but completely crazy.

Emails, including Libby from Dr. Hanson's office. Asking if she's ready for another appointment.

Zora responds. "Monday any time between 11:30 a.m. and 1:00 p.m. Send me a link, please."

She acknowledges one thing: *The line between Zora and Skyy is blurring by the moment.*

Lights out.

Chapter Thirty-Six

Saturday comes in like a whisper. Zora slept hard last night. The weight of Friday – the pain of her clients, the release of truth with her Besties, and a satisfying romp with Nico – all lulled her into a deep sleep. She didn't even wake up to go to the restroom in the middle of the night.

She yawns deeply, rolling onto her side to face the window. A gray June day. Nothing on her schedule for the day. No rush to rise. It wouldn't bother her one bit if the world moved about without her participation.

She closes her eyes and inhales, then exhales, as she remembers her fixer session with Nico. She would be crazy to add him as a fixer; she'd be crazy not to add him.

He's my Bestie. I can't afford to blur that boundary. But who would know?

Zora shakes off the thought!

About 10 minutes pass before she sits up in the middle of her bed to consider how she should spend her day. No obligations to speak of. She knows what that means for her.

She can't afford to be idle. Boredom is just another reason to call a fixer.

No, Zora. It is not even noon yet.

Skyy, please go away.

A shower and a light breakfast help to push away the urge. At least for now.

She makes a cup of tea, plops on her chaise, and sends a text to the Besties:

"Happy Saturday, Besties. Thank you so much for your support last night. I rested well knowing that I was able to lay my secret bare. Thank you for sharing yours as well. I love you all."

Lai chimes in first: "Our family is tighter than ever. Thank you all for the love," with a row of heart-faced emojis.

Rayven was next: "I'm so full from the love and the bond we share." Three emojis: hugs, heart, kisses.

Nico followed: "Best night for the Besties. We will never be the same." Three red heart emojis.

Zora read into Nico's text and felt a bit flushed as she reflected on his "service."

Zora closes her eyes and sips her tea held in two hands. Her phone pings.

A text.

Nico.

Oh, God... Here we go.

"Z, you busy today? I want to talk," he texted.

"Not busy. What's up?"

No response.

Her phone rings.

Nico.

Zora answers on the first ring. "Nico, what are you doing?" she asks laughing.

"Z, I need to see you. Today, if possible," he says sounding serious.

Zora stops laughing. "What's wrong? You okay?"

"Yeah. Just need to talk to you in person," he says.

"Okay. What time? Where?"

"Are you available in 30 minutes? Your place?"

She places her teacup on the side table. "Sure, Nico. You're scaring me," she says. "Let me get dressed. See you in 30. Use your key."

"Alright," he says. "See you soon."

The call ends.

Zora sits in contemplation, wondering what this talk will be about. She sips her tea and waits. Nerves. Thoughts. Possible heat that she needs to ignore.

Keys and the door opens.

She yells towards the front door. "I'm in the living room."

Nico finds his way into the room and sits on the edge of the chaise as if he lived there.

She takes note but doesn't say anything about it.

"What's up, Nico?"

He inhales deeply before speaking.

"Zora," he clears his throat. "Yesterday was amaaaaazing."

"Okay," she says raising her eyebrows with curiosity.

He looks in her eyes. "I know you don't think it is a good idea for me to be part of your fixer pool, and I get that since I'm your Bestie," he pauses. "But I have to be honest. I never stopped having feelings for you, even when you rejected me."

She looks at him in surprise, putting a hand to her mouth. He continues.

"Yes, I've been in relationships – and I know you don't want a relationship – but I always compared them to you." He covers his forehead then runs his fingers through his hair.

"Nico, I…"

"Let me finish, please," he says. "You know why I get so angry when you "get fixed" – why I act the way that I do?"

"No," she says softly.

"It's because I don't want other men to have what I've longed for all this time. And last night just proved that to me." He exhales and continues. "If I can't have you emotionally, I would settle for being close to you as a fixer over nothing at all."

Zora puts her face in her hands and shakes her head. "Nico, I don't know what to say. I enjoyed you thoroughly last night. And I mean thoroughly. WOW! But, how wise do you think it would be for you, for us to keep being physical and you settle for that?" She checks his face.

He looks like a lost puppy, eyes welling with tears. "Zora… I…"

She interrupts him. "Nico, think about it. You wouldn't accept just being friends with benefits before. Why now?

Besides, how can you have a girlfriend or want to get married, but want to settle with just sex with me? Never fully having me. How does that even work?"

He pats tears from his face. "I know, Z… I know. I have no rational response. I just know that I'll do anything to stay close to you."

"Nico, I would love nothing more than to have you bend me over regularly, but is that really fair to you?"

He looks her straight in the eyes. "Zora, I will take whatever I can get. I will handle my own emotions and feelings. I just want to be close to you."

Zora throws her head back and grunts. "Nico, that makes absolutely no sense to me…"

"Oh, but you screwing random men does?" he says without thinking.

Before she could stop herself, she slapped him across the face.

"How dare you, Nico! You KNOW why I'm like this. You KNOW what happened to me and you throw that in my face?"

She tries to force herself around him to get off the chaise. He blocks her gently.

"Z, I'm sorry. That wasn't fair. I'm… I'm just frustrated. I…"

Tears start to form in Zora's eyes. She closes her eyes and folds her arms across her chest, symbolizing she's now guarded.

"Z, don't shut me out, please. I'm sorry. I shouldn't have said that. I know better," he says trying to get her to hear him. "Z, look at me…please."

Slowly, she opens her eyes, tears now running down her face. She just stares at him. No softness. Just pain. Betrayal. No words.

"I messed up, Z. I don't mean to put my insecurities on you. You don't deserve that. Forgive me. Please."

She clears her throat and says, "I think you should leave, Nico. I don't want to talk about this right now."

He placed a hand softly on her thigh. "I understand, Z. I do. I'm an ass and I know it. I never want to hurt you. Never."

"Please leave," she says in a cracked voice.

He rises from the chaise and stands in front of her, wishing he could erase the last 30 minutes.

"I love you, Z. I always have. I always will. I'm here when you're ready."

He turns to leave and she stops him.

"Leave your key," she says with pain in her voice.

"Zora, you can't mean… I'm your emergency contact… You really want…"

"Nico, leave your key and leave now, please."

He placed his key on the entry table and lets himself out.

For the next 30 minutes or so, Zora regrets last night's romp. She regrets allowing her heat to cross the Bestie boundary. She just regrets everything.

Tears flow unhindered. Vision blurred just like her twisted desire.

***

An hour later, Zora's phone rings. Video call coming in. Damian.

Damn it. Should she answer it?

She knows she looks like she has been in a fight with her puffy eyes.

What the hell, she settles as she wipes her face and connects the call.

Damian's face fills the screen with a smile that instantly fades. Concern now evident.

"Zee, you've been crying. Are you okay?"

She shuffles herself to sit upright on the chaise before responding.

"I'm okay, Damian. Rough couple of days. I'm alright," she says trying to convince both of them.

"I don't like it when you cry. You want to talk about it?" he gently asks.

"No, I'm good," she says warmly. "How is your trip going?"

"We don't need to stay until Sunday afternoon, so I'll be leaving after the afternoon session. I just have to get Jenson to the airport. Besides, it is less than three hours' drive," he says checking her face again.

"I'm sure the young men were enriched," she encourages. "Any incidents with Jenson?"

"The young men are enjoying the event. Jenson. Well, nothing I couldn't handle. He almost got into something again," he said rolling his eyes. "That dude."

"I'm sorry. I'm glad you're there with him and for him. We all need a good friend," she says remembering his words to her a few weeks ago.

"Yeah, we do." He hesitates. "Zee, can I see you tomorrow around noon?"

She puts on a sheepish grin. "I don't know. Can you or *may* you?" she asks laughing.

He chuckled. "Always fixing me, Zee."

He has no idea what it means to be fixed.

"Not fixing you; refining you," she says warmly.

He smiles wide. "Well, *may* I see you tomorrow around noon?" he asks correctly.

She tilted her head slightly. "Why do you want to see me, Damian," she said smiling lightly.

"Zee, I don't *want* to see you. I *need* to see you. Is that okay? I'll understand if you say no."

She could feel her face growing warm. Blushing. "*Need* to see me, Damian? Not sure how I feel about that," she said shyly.

"Don't think too much into it, Zee. Don't act like you don't want to see me, too," he says giggling.

She rolled her eyes and laughed. "Okay, Damian. Where?"

He hesitated and raised an eyebrow. "The condo?"

She smirked at him. "You know Kira will be moving in within 10 days. We can't keep meeting there."

He grinned wide. "Oh, she got the place? That's great," he said with excitement. He then paused. "So, where should we meet – that is if you *want* to see me after tomorrow?"

"Let's cross that bridge if or when we get there," she says with a smile.

"Understood," he said distracted. "Gotta run. Jenson is waving me over. I'll talk to you later, if you like. If not, I'll just see you tomorrow around noon. Condo."

"Your call," she says with a smile.

The call ended.

She needs to shake off all these emotions. Nico. Damian. Emotions are not allowed.

She needs Skyy to distract her.

She rises from the chaise. Pours her cold tea into the sink and heads upstairs.

Bedside table drawer open. Fixer phone in hand. Milo is what she needs today.

She texts. He responds quickly.

"Hey, Skyy, I'm game. This is kinda early for you, isn't it? Where do you want to meet?"

"I'm humming, Milo. Where are you? You got a place?"

"Give me about 10 and I'll hit you back."

Zora paces her room then goes into her hidden room and pulls out a shorter brunette wig. It's too hot for the long one Milo is used to.

Her phone pings. Milo.

He gives her the rendezvous spot. The old gym locker room at the Y. He works there during the day when he's not working at the bistro at night. It is closed on Saturdays, but he has a key.

She takes down the address and gets dressed for the occasion. The thought of getting "Milo-ed" turns the heat up between her thighs.

***

Within 40 minutes, Zora was bent over in the old gym locker room. She didn't care that it smelled like sweaty socks, jock straps, and musty mold. She was on fire. Pressure built up in her that needed to be released.

Damian be damned.

Milo knew just what she needed and he gave it to her just like she liked it. Deep. Strong. Purposeful. Committed to knocking the bottom out without apology. Holding her ankles, her hair in her face, Milo pounded her with promised pleasure. Successfully, filling her to capacity, making her screams echo throughout the facility.

The perfect distraction.

The perfect refuge.

The perfect medicine.

The whole Nico thing. Damian stirring unwanted emotions. She needed to protect herself and Milo did that for her. Every. Single. Time.

Consistent.

Skilled.

He calmed the vibration within, pushing the shadows aside. He hushed the confusion in her head. He commanded her vagina like a master, and she was eternally grateful.

After 30 minutes of relentless pleasure, Zora was back in her car and headed home with a million-dollar smile on her face.

He never disappoints.

She never regrets a Milo fix.

Chapter Thirty-Seven

Lazy Sunday. She checks the time. 10:37 a.m. She throws her covers off and flings her legs on top.

"Whew. It's so hot already," Zora mumbles. Laying there looking at the ceiling for about 10 minutes, she rolls out of bed and slowly pads across her bedroom to the bathroom. Although her sheer curtains are closed, the sun is baking her bedroom like a batch of chocolate cookies.

She can feel the stickiness on her skin. Hair clinging to her face and neck. Pajamas clinging to her body.

"If it feels like this in the middle of June, what will it be like in August?" she says wiping her forehead with the back of her hand. "Is the A/C working at all?" she wonders.

In the bathroom, she washes her face, brushes her teeth and takes a warm shower, washing her hair twice to remove the musty smell that sweatiness brings to a full head of thick, wavy hair. She couldn't stand a hot shower even if she wanted to. Too hot.

She dresses in a linen peach and cream stiped tank dress with white flat slide-on sandals. Light make-up. She pulls her hair up into a loose bun. Hair on her neck in this weather is unbearable.

In the kitchen she makes herself a hearty breakfast. She is famished. She didn't each much yesterday. Oatmeal sprinkled with blueberries, strawberry pieces, and a swirl of honey. Warm Chai tea.

"I must be crazy drinking tea in this heat," she whispers over her cup.

She takes a seat at the kitchen island and thumbs through social media as she eats. Nothing new to read. Nothing she wants to post. Too much going on in her own life to focus on what's going on in other people's manufactured online lives.

A notification cuts across her screen. She swipes down to read it. Damian.

"Hey, Zee, I'm just confirming 12 noon at the condo," followed by a huge grin emoji.

She smiled despite herself. She typed in her response. "Confirmed. See you soon," followed by a huge grin emoji as well.

It is 11:41 a.m. She finishes her breakfast and runs upstairs to spray a little perfume to hide any sweaty scents that may arise from the heat. She checks her face in the bathroom mirror and heads downstairs.

In her car, she is fighting knots in her stomach. A tightening throat.

Why are you so nervous? It's just Damian. Pull yourself together.

***

She arrives at the condo at 11:54 a.m., opening the blinds to let some light in and sprays air freshener just in case it smells closed up.

A knock on the door.

"It's open," she yells.

Damian comes in holding a caddy with smoothies.

Zora comes around the corner from the back hall to greet him. He has a big smile on his face as he extends his arm.

"I brought treats," he says giggling.

She reaches for the drink caddy, inspecting it as she walks to the kitchen. "Treats? How sweet of you," she says with a smile.

He stands in the kitchen and leans against the counter with his hands in his pants pockets. Zora notices his attire.

"Why are you in dress slacks and a collared shirt," she asks with her arms folded for effect.

He looks down at himself and looks at her. "I went to church," he says shyly.

She raised an eyebrow and tilts her head to the side. "Church? You never told me you went to church. Now, I KNOW I better keep my distance," she says laughing.

"Yes, I go to church, Zee," he says. "Part of my program, you can say."

"Oh, I'm sorry. Didn't mean to minimize your faith," she says gently. "I went to church myself a few weeks ago."

He folds his arms across his chest and raises an eyebrow. "Church? You never told me you went to church," he says jokingly.

They both laugh.

"Yeah, well, I'm trying to get myself together. I went to confession for the first time in 14 years."

"Really? That's a step in the right direction," he says warmly.

She interrupts him to shift the conversation. "So, I know you didn't come bearing smoothies to talk about church," she says looking at the flavors in the clear cups.

He shrugs his shoulders. "You're right, again," he says shyly. He moves towards the island where Zora is resting her elbows, bent at the waist. He's just looking at her softly.

She notices. "What are you looking at? You've seen me before," she chuckles.

"I have," he acknowledges, "I like your dress. It looks cool. Comfortable."

"It is," she says standing and leaning on the island with one hand. She looks at the smoothies to change the conversation.

"What are the flavors?"

He walks over and pulls the two cups from the caddy, holding them up one at a time. "We have Strawberry Kiwi and Mango. You choose," he says with a smile.

She reaches for the Strawberry Kiwi and sips from the straw. She nods her head at the taste. Then she reaches for the Mango and sips. "They're both really good. Choices, choices," she says giggling.

He steps closer and says, "We can share," looking her in the eyes.

She clears her throat and grabs the Mango and sips it. "You want to taste it?" she asks.

He reaches for the cup, but she hides it behind her back teasing him. "Come get it."

He laughs. "Oh, so you want to play with me, huh?" he says lunging for the cup, as she moves around the island.

He catches her on the second round in the opposite direction. She runs right into him. She is giggling and he is smiling hard. "Gotcha," he says.

She puts the cup down on the counter. "Yes, you do," she says shyly looking at him.

She's not sure where that response comes from, but she didn't correct it. He is holding her in his arms leaning her back against the island. Silence. Just looking at one another. Communicating. Breathing. Knowing. Understanding.

Damian kisses her on the forehead. She doesn't move. Bodies pressed together. Warmth evident. Messages transmitting. He reaches around her and picks up the Strawberry Kiwi and takes a sip. He doesn't swallow. Instead, he places his mouth on her hers. She opens and he transfers the liquid to her slowly. She moves it back to him. A kiss emerges between the flavors. Soft. Gentle. Tender. Telling.

Without breaking the kiss, Damian puts the cup down on the counter, reaches around Zora, and lifts her onto the counter so that her face is level to his. She parts her legs so that he can stand comfortably between. To get closer to her.

She scoots her hips forward so that she is crotch to crotch with him. He senses what she did and he breaks the kiss.

"Zee…"

She interrupts him. "Just rest in the moment, Damian. No pressure," she says as she reengages the kiss and he willingly participates. The kiss feels like a dance. A song without words. They are intentional with the movement of their mouths. Their hands rub one another lightly. Passion without pushing. Natural.

Zora can feel herself burning, but she is fighting not to scare him off.

Back off, Skyy.

Not him. Never with him.

Her breathing gets ragged and hunger starts to rise. Damian can feel her pressing against his crotch and his body responds against his will and better judgment. Mild grinding. Not animalistic. Communicative movement that says" I feel you. I want you. I need you," even though they both know they cannot cross that line.

Damian steps back. Hands on each side of Zora's hips. Chest heaving. Head down. In his head he is counting to 1-2-3-4-5-6-7-8-9-10. Slow breathing. And repeat.

Don't do this, Damian. Don't. Do. This.

Zora can see he is struggling with himself. She's got her own struggle in pursuit. Her panties are moist and she can feel her own heat.

"Damian," she says lightly. He is despondent. Still counting in his head. Still breathing.

He is unaware that she slowly removed her panties and lays them on the counter.

She takes his hand and kisses his palm. "Close your eyes, Damian."

"Zee, please…"

"Shhhhh… trust me. I won't hurt you. Close your eyes for me. Please."

He closes his eyes reluctantly.

She parts her legs, takes his hand and puts it so that he can feel her moisture. He gasps when he realizes what she is doing. He opens his eyes wide looking at her face and then at his hand.

"Zee, we can't… I can't…"

"I'm not asking you to do anything. I'm not asking for you to enter me," she says. She looks him in the eyes warmly and says, "Just touch me… touch me, please."

He looks at her with fear, confusion, desire, guilt in his eyes.

"Please," she pleads softly.

He takes the hand that she has between her legs and he massages her gently, her wetness coating his fingers. Breathing against his urges. He can feel himself getting stiff in his pants. "Oh, God… Oh, God… Zee…"

"Yes, Damian…?" she says in a breathy voice.

He continues to stroke her until she leans back on her elbows, and he slides his finger inside her dripping vagina. Then another finger. He works his fingers as if he was making love to her. Slowly. Purposefully. She responds moving her hips with his hand. She is moaning. He is fighting, but he doesn't stop. His engorged penis is starting to hurt.

She lays flat on the counter and slides to the edge. "Taste me, Damian…"

"Zee," he says through staggered breaths. Clearly aroused by the bulge in his pants and the look on his face. "I haven't done that in over 10 years… I am not sure…I…"

"Damian, taste me… I want you to taste what you do to me…"

He slides her away from the edge of the counter, hesitates, then loosens the top button of his shirt, before he gently plants his face between her legs. She gasps at his touch. His tongue is hot. Slick. Powerful and gentle. Teasing her. He may not have done it in 10 years, but he hasn't forgotten how to do it. He masterfully tantalizes her clitoris, labia, and inserts his tongue into her vagina. Tasting her. Lapping her juices. Her hips are meeting his mouth as he feeds his tongue like a penis into her wetness. She reaches down and rubs her hands over his head, moaning, groaning, soaring.

He sucks her clitoris in a soft rhythmic motion that drives her crazy.

He stops and pulls away. He unbuckles his pants and pulls out his penis. He slides her to edge of the counter and touches the tip of his penis to her lips. He just wants to feel her. Her wetness. He throws his head back and grunts in protest with himself.

"Zee… I want you… Oh, my God… I want you…" he pants. "Control yourself, Damian… Control yourself,

Damian…" he repeats over and over aloud, but doesn't move from the counter.

He slowly rubs the head of his penis across her labia… up and down strokes without entry… enjoying the wetness, her scent, the possibility. Stroking his head. Stroking her labia. She is responding. Moaning, but not forcing him inside her.

"You feel so good, Zee… I want to… I want to…" He's panting harder.

Zora realizes she can't allow him to compromise himself. She slides off the counter and drops to her knees. She takes him in her mouth and works him. He's thick. Chocolate. Long. Hot. The smell of his pubic hair excites her even more.

She licks him. Strokes him. Sucks him. He is going crazy. He is holding her head, fingers through her hair. He hasn't been touched that way in so long. His hips respond in rhythm to her strokes. She moans against his shaft and he groans back. She continues to stroke him until he is about to release. He is leaning against the opposite counter head tossed back. Chest heaving. Gripping the counter with enough strength to crack it. Explosive nectar. She drinks him in and swallows.

She has only done that with one person in her entire life.

She stands up and stands across from him. After a few moments, he comes to himself realizing that his pants are at his ankles, penis exposed. He's embarrassed. He pulls his pants up facing away from Zora.

She stands looking at him, hands resting on the island counter behind her.

"Damian, you want to talk about it?" she says softly.

He's despondent. His face etched in emotion. Is it anger? Is it fear? Is it guilt? Is it pleasure?

He clears his throat. "Zee, I…" he hesitates. "I haven't had… I'm sorry… I…"

She steps closer to him, hands on his face. "Damian, you didn't have sex. I promised you I wouldn't be the one to ruin your program." She tilted his face towards hers. "I just wanted to… needed to feel you… to know you… and for you to do the same… no guilt."

He places his forehead on hers. "Zee, I don't understand what you are doing to me. I thought I was stronger. Better. I can't control my thoughts. My emotions are all over the place. I can't focus. I'm irritable when I'm not with you. I…"

She lifts her head to look at him. "I know… I get it. I don't do emotions. At. All," she says shaking her head. "But you bring something out in me. Something I've been running from. Afraid of. Something outside my boundaries. Things I don't want to feel or acknowledge. When I'm with you, I don't want sex, which is crazy. You're not like my fixers… you're… more."

He interrupts her. "Fixers? What is that?" he asks curiously.

She sighs lightly. "Remember the last time we were together, and I told you that I had intimacy issues?" He shakes his head 'yes.'

She speaks softly. "Well, I have a sex addiction. I really do. It is like a drug that I can't get enough of, but when I'm with you, I don't feel the pull of addition. It's a different kind of pull. Being with you doesn't feel cold or disconnected or transactional. It doesn't feel like I'm being fixed. Serviced. And all that scares me."

She checks his face. He is looking at her in confusion without judgment.

"What does that mean, Zee," he asks looking more serious.

"It is a long story that I promise to tell you one day really soon. Just not today," she says looking away.

He pulls her face back to him and looks at her. He exhales deeply. "Zee, I don't know what to do about all that I'm feeling. What you're doing to me… How my world is completely upside down… utterly wrecked, but I want to know everything. I want to know *all* of you…"

She leans against his chest and puts her arms around his waist, body pressed against him. "I can't believe I'm even admitting this… But I want to know more of you… everything. You are disrupting my normal. Going against my grain. Scrambling my code. You are making me break my own rules."

He dips his head and kisses her softly. Tenderly. Longingly. He speaks against her mouth between kisses "No emotions? What is *this* then, Zee?"

She looks at him. "I don't know… I don't want emotions. I can't have emotions," she says with her eyes filling. She lightly clears her throat. "Emotions mean commitment.

Commitment just means expectations, obligation, disappointment, and ultimately pain.

He holds her face. "Are you sure that's not what you want because that's what you're giving me. You're giving me emotion. Emotion is what we experience every time we are together."

She steps away, but he pulls her back to him. "Don't run from me, from us, Zee. Don't."

She dabs tears from her cheeks. "Living within my addiction eliminates the possibility of pain. Emotions are too painful. Emotions create responsibility. Something I can't do. Addiction is sheer pleasure. Emotions don't exist in addiction. Addiction is my sanctuary. Emotions are a cave. I'll choose temporary pleasure over permanent emotions any day."

He holds her tighter. "Look at me, Zee," he says gently. "Like it or not, there *is* something between us. Something stronger than us. Emotions. You can't deny that. You feel it, whether you want to admit it or not. You feel me. You feel us. You feel emotions, Zee. You do."

"Damian, I don't like that reality. What are we doing?" she says, eyes pleading for answers. "I'm not ready for this."

"We'll figure it out," he says looking over her head. "I have about 18 months left of my program, unless I'm released early." He looks at her again. "Maybe I can find a way to get out of it without having to go to prison. I need to find a way to be with you, Zee. I must…"

She puts her fingers to his lips. "I don't know how to do this. I just don't want to be the blame for any of it…"

"Zee, you're not to blame for any of it. I'm a grown man. I knew that I wanted… *needed* to see you today. I needed any excuse to be close to you," he says smiling warmly and rubbing her cheek. "One day, one moment away from you is too long. I need you, Zee."

She leans into his hand and closes her eyes. He pulls her close and she rests in the warmth of his arms. His safety.

"Sorry to say, but I need you, too," she whispers.

He chuckles softly with his lips in her hair. "You're not sorry."

Time slipped away from them. By the time they break their embrace, it is after 2 p.m.

They look at one another. Clearly lost in the moment not wanting it to end.

"What about our smoothies," she says joking, knowing they've melted by now.

"I'll drink mine. Strawberry Kiwi?" He says with a grin.

"Sure."

She checks the time and almost panics. "Oh, my God," she exclaims.

Concern on his face, he asks, "What's wrong?"

"I have family dinner at 4 p.m. in Arlington," she exhales. "Sorry, but I need to get home and change."

"Oh, okay," he says grabbing his drink.

She reaches for her panties now on the kitchen floor. She picks them up and puts them in his shirt pocket.

"Zee, what are you…"

She pats his chest pocket. "A little keepsake for you to remember me…" she says giggling.

"I don't have a keepsake for you... besides a watered-down smoothie," he says chuckling.

She offers him a wide smile. "You left me a beautiful keepsake."

She pauses.

"I swallowed it."

If he could turn a shade of red, he would. "Oh, that..." he says embarrassingly.

"I had great time, Damian," she says warmly as she looks for her sandals in the kitchen.

"Me, too," he says with a smile.

She reaches up and kisses him softly and he returns the tenderness.

"Emotions... Yuck," she says laughing. He joins her with a hearty laugh of his own.

They walk out to the street together.

He hesitates. "Call you later?" he asks.

"Yes," she smiles. "I'd like that," she says as she rushes to her car.

What a day.

Damian. Damian. Damian.

What am I going to do with you?

As Damian walks in the opposite direction to his car, he smells his fingers and remembers her with a smile, taking a sip of his watered-down smoothie.

Zee, what am I going to do with you?

Chapter Thirty-Eight

Driving to family dinner, Zora's mind is consumed with her time with Damian. Emotions frighten her, but she can't deny them.

He does something to me I can't describe.

Once inside her parents' home, she's distracted. Nothing has changed about the routine. Mommy cooked amazing meals. Dad still distant. Marcus, Amri, and Chae adding their special flare to the conversation. She sat there taking it all in but longing to get home to talk to Damian.

Her mother interrupts her thoughts. "Zora daughter, Reese called and said that you missed his award recognition," she said while wiping her mouth with a napkin.

Zora exhales lightly. "Mommy, I told him I would think about it. I didn't obligate myself," she said a little edge in her tone. "I'm sorry, Mommy. I don't like to be forced into something I don't want. I don't want Reese," she said as a matter of fact.

Everyone at the table held their breath. Didn't take another bite. Unsure of her mother's response.

"Zora, you are almost 30. When are we going to get grandchildren? When are you…?"

Zora interrupts the inquisition. "Mommy, I'm not interested in getting married or having children," she says taking a small bite. "I love you, Mommy, but please stop pushing. Please."

Silence around the table. Chae speaks up to ease the tension.

"So, Zora, how are the plans coming for the THRIVE event coming up next weekend?"

Zora is grateful for the strategic redirection of the conversation.

Zora fills them all in and shares her excitement that they have about 40 employers who want to hire youth for the summer months of July – August. Everyone shares how proud they are and promise to be in attendance. Even her dad agrees to attend. She was surprised, but grateful.

Dinner ended on a lighter note, at least for Zora. She is not entertaining anything that pressures her. She hugs her parents, squeezing her mother for reassurance, and the others and heads home.

In the car, she exhales mentally and physically. She's looking forward to an easy-going conversation with Damian.

***

Back home and relaxing on her chaise, Zora reflected on her day with Damian. She doesn't know what's happening with her. She doesn't like it. Maybe a little bit. She smiles. Her phone interrupts her thoughts.

Video call. Damian. Her smile widened so much her cheeks hurt. She composes herself to answer.

"Well, hello, long time no see," she says with a smile.

"I know, right," he says smiling back.

She talks about the family dinner and pressure. He talks about a call with his sponsor, feeling like an imposter while explaining the events of his weekend chaperoning Jenson.

They laugh about everything and Zora's face changes slightly as she prepares to ask him a question. Concern is etched on his face as he braces himself for whatever she is about to say.

"Damian…" she hesitates. "Ummm… I have a weird question for you."

He leans back on his sofa. "What is it? No secrets. I want you to know all of me," he says with a warm smile.

"Here goes: Where did you learn to "taste" like that… like you did to me today," she says shyly.

He closes his eyes, unsure how to start. He inhales and opens his eyes, staring at her directly through the camera.

"Zee, it's a long story. A painful story to be honest." He pauses. "You sure you want to know?"

"Yes, Damian. I do. In fairness, I shared my addiction with you – at least in part. I just want to know because you drove me absolutely mad and I couldn't respond how I typically would."

He holds up a hand in surrender and clears his throat.

"When I was about 7 years old, my mother died of cancer, and I was left to live with my dad who was addicted to drugs and alcohol. He had a terrible habit, one that often left him in debt to suppliers." He paused and took a deep breath.

"Well, my dad started bringing me to these "parties," where people were doing drugs and other things. Introducing me to things that I was too young to see or understand." He paused again, swallowing.

"Anyway, one weekend there was a "party" at this high-rise building. Fifteen floors or so. We would board the elevator and ride to the 10th floor. Me and my dad. He was often high and he held my shoulders with a grip that instilled a fear in me." His eyes started to water. Zora noticed.

"Damian, you are safe. I won't let you fall. I am not here to judge you. You can stop whenever you want to. I'll understand."

He smiled gently, appreciating her gentle approach and allowing him to drive the conversation. He dabs at his eyes.

"So, he would do this initially to get the people to know me as his son. Little did I know that he was…" he choked a bit. Throat tightening.

"Damian, you don't have to continue. We can stop." He shook his head 'no' and continued.

"Well, about the fourth or fifth visit, my dad introduced me to this woman. She was thin and scantily dressed. She called me to her and took my hand. My dad told me to "go on" as he sat drinking and smoking a cigarette." He closes his eyes and swallows, tears running down his cheeks."

"Damian… you don't have to…"

He holds up a hand to stop her and continues.

"This woman took me into a bedroom that had purple lights against dark walls. She pulled me to her and asked if I liked treats. I didn't know what she meant, but I soon found out. She put her finger in her vagina and then told me to lick her finger. I didn't want to and I started to cry. She put her finger to my lips and said, "Shhhhhh." When I didn't respond how she wanted, she called for my dad, who burst into the room, roughed me up and told me to do what I was told. She kept making me do that – lick her wet fingers – for about 20 minutes, while my dad watched. I was so sick. Scared. Then the unexpected." Damian held his head down in shame and covered his eyes with the palms of his hands.

Zora sat in silence. Giving him space to decide if he wanted to continue. Her counseling techniques overriding her emotions.

After about 5-minutes, Damian clears his throat to continue.

"She lifted her mini skirt and laid back on the bed with her legs open. My dad told me to kiss her "there" until he said to stop. I was crying uncontrollably by then. He yelled at me to shut up. The woman was getting frustrated with me, looking at my dad and saying, "You told me he would do it. You promised me.

She pulled me between her legs. My dad coached me and she moaned. He shouted, "Lick her. Suck her. Use your tongue, boy." The woman was pulling my face deeper into her crotch as I did what I was told. She let out a scream and clinched my head between her thighs tight. My dad "congratulated me" for making a woman cum. Called me 'a man.' I had no idea what any of that meant."

Damian hesitated, held his face and rubbed at his eyes. Zora waited.

"From that day on, my dad would take me to those parties. Up the elevator. Tenth floor. The same scene every weekend, some weekdays. Forcing me into unpleasant situations. My face planted between some woman's legs. The more I did it, the more I learned what the women liked. My dad continued to watch. This was sort of an "agreement" for whatever debt he owed. Or maybe he was too high or drunk to 'get it up' for them, so he promised me to the women as an option. In the beginning, I hated it, but I learned to enjoy it when I felt my body responding. I was well-endowed even at a young age. Eventually, I was introduced to having sex with grown women who were always drunk or high. Eight years old having sex. Sharpening my skills, so to speak."

His voice cracked. Emotion taking over.

"Zee… I was just a little boy. My father prostituted me for his addictions. This happened until I was fifteen or sixteen. By this time, I was sexually active and now desiring sex more frequently, but on my own terms. I was sleeping with girls, women, anything with a vagina. It didn't matter what they looked like. I just wanted sex. My sex drive was built in those dark rooms until they were on full display in my real life. Until I couldn't control my urges and ultimately ignored one girl's 'no.'"

He started sobbing.

"I was a little boy, Zee… My, God… I was just a little boy!"

She gives him time to settle himself as best he can. When he did, his face was wet with tears, eyes red and puffy.

"I'm sorry, Zee," he says. "I haven't told that story since I was assigned to the program. I'm so embarrassed," he says shyly.

"No need to be embarrassed, Damian," she said warmly. "Trust me, I understand more than you think." She pauses.

"Damian, is that why you don't like elevators?" she asks cautiously.

He looks into the camera, tears still brimming his eyes. "Yes… It is a trigger. Elevator rides remind me of the abuse and how it shaped me and my elicit behavior," he says with a trembling voice as he hung his head.

"You were brave tonight, Damian. Really brave. I'm proud of you. I didn't know my question would spawn all of this, but I'm glad you told me." She gently says, "Look at me, please…"

Damian looks at her wiping his face.

"Hear me clearly. You didn't do this to yourself. Your dad, those women, *they* did this to you. Our childhood experiences often shape our adult behaviors, but that doesn't mean you asked for or deserved those experiences. You participated because you were lured into something your body and mind weren't ready for. Adults lured you. Abused you. The shame you feel is theirs, not yours. I know that doesn't sound right because you endured it. It doesn't make it right, but you are not your trauma. Do you believe that, Damian?" she asks.

He shakes his head slowly. Eyes closed. He clears his throat lightly.

"What are you feeling?" she asks in full counselor mode.

He looks up at her. "For so long… so long… I felt like a freak. Like it *was* my fault. And when I started enjoying it and engaging others in my sexual exploits, it only deepened the shame, even if my sexual activities didn't stop. I grew to need that feeling, that release, that experience daily. As you said earlier, it became an addiction. Even at 8, 9, 10 years old. I wanted it. I needed it and it followed me into my teenage years, affecting my adult years."

He exhaled deeply.

Tears welling up in his eyes again, "Thank you, Zee, for listening, you know… without judgment. For letting me release a secret that only The Anchor Project knows."

She smiles at him warmly. "You're welcome, Damian. You're secrets are safe with me. Trust that. It is part of the ethical code that I hold as a licensed clinician."

He shifts his eyes up at his screen. Incoming call. Pastor Hayden.

"Hey, Zee, I gotta take this call. It's my mentor," he says with a gentle smile. "I'll call you tomorrow?

"Yes, I'll talk with you tomorrow."

The call ends. Zora sits in Damian's truth even as she is preparing to tell hers fully in therapy tomorrow.

She retreats to her sanctuary early carrying the weight of the day.

Damian's touch.

Emotions.

Family.

Truth.

Sleep comes more easily than she anticipated. She slept through the notifications coming from the top drawer of her bedside table.

Skyy has to wait.

***

Monday morning hits like a wave. Zora wakes knowing that today is the day she will reveal the second layer of her story to Dr. Hanson.

She takes her run a little earlier than usual because her first client is at 8 a.m. rather than the usual 9 a.m. This will allow her to see three clients before her 12:15 p.m. session with Dr. Hanson. She opted for face-to-face this time because she knows she will need in-person support as she tells her story.

***

Client three session is over. Zora puts her laptop in sleep mode and heads to the kitchen to grab something light to eat. She doesn't want nausea to take over.

She checks the time and heads to Dr. Hanson's office.

Nerves.

Head spinning.

Mind racing.

She wants to retreat but doesn't. She has to go so that she can grow through this.

Up the elevator and into the counseling office. Libby greets Zora with her usual bubbly personality. After a five-minute wait, Libby lets her know Dr. Hanson is ready to see her.

Zora clutches her purse to her chest, as if it will shield her. As if it will hide the cracks in her soul. She walks slowly down the hall and knocks lightly on the door.

"Come on in," Dr. Hanson says warmly.

Zora enters the office and takes in the atmosphere. It has been over a month since she was there. A few changes, but the same for the most part. Dr. Hanson motions her to a chair and then joins her in the chair beside her.

"How have you been, Zora?" she asks with a gentle smile.

Zora releases a nervous breath. "I've been okay. Moving through everything. Navigating as best I can, but I'm good."

Dr. Hanson gives her a look that says, "I await the truth whenever you're ready…"

Zora notices it and adjusts in her seat, still clutching her purse with a death grip.

"Relax, Zora," Dr. Hanson says placing a hand lightly on her hand.

Zora closes her eyes and takes in a few deep breaths then exhales in counts of five. Repeat.

"When we spoke last, you shared your story about your father, and you mentioned there was another layer to your story. Are you ready to tell me about that, Zora?" Dr. Hanson asks softly.

Zora shakes her head 'yes,' although her stomach is screaming *hell no*.

She starts slowly. "Well, my parents were always so busy. I often had to entertain myself as an only child. Stay out of the way. Out of my dad's way. As a little girl, I longed for attention as I told you. But my dad wasn't wired like that. At least not for a daughter." She coughed lightly.

"As I mentioned before, my dad enjoyed coaching and mentoring the young boys on the football team or anyone who needed a fatherly presence." She inhales deeply.

"He would have young boys in and out of our home, wherever we moved, they were always there. One boy in particular was there regularly. Every other weekend. Sometimes for the summer. He was nice to me. He was my friend. He made me laugh." Zora pauses.

"I remember one night it was storming outside and I was afraid. I went to my parents' room, but my dad told me to go back to bed. Our house had a split-floor plan, and our rooms were on opposite ends of the house. Anyway, on this particular night, the little boy who was staying the weekend heard me crying and he came in and held me. Told me that storms didn't hurt. I believed him and he held me until I fell asleep. When I woke up the next morning, I was in my bed alone. The next day he smiled at me and told me it was okay. We became fast friends despite our age difference. He was about 8 years old, and I was five years old. Whenever he visited, he was nice enough to play with me in our living room. He would show me how to build Legos, how to use my imagination making up stories. He felt like part of the family. Like a brother." Zora cleared her throat lightly and continued.

"Anyway, he started visiting my room to help me fall asleep when he was there. He knew I was afraid of the dark so he would tell me stories to relax me. One night, he told me that kissing makes everything better. I didn't know what he meant. He kissed my cheek and I kissed his cheek. We did this every night that he stayed. He always told me, "it was our secret" and I trusted him. Eventually, he would kiss me through my pajamas, placing his mouth on my chest, my stomach, my private area. He would tell me everything was okay and that I was his best friend. So, I trusted him." Her voice cracked a bit, but she continued.

"With each visit, he introduced me to my body. He would touch me under my pajamas softly, talking to me the entire time, holding my glance for security. If ever I wanted to talk, he would say, "Shhhhhhhhh… no talking," and I followed his instructions. After about six months of "light touching," he started kissing me with my pajamas off. I liked how his kisses felt so I didn't stop him. By the time I was turned six, he introduced me to oral sex and I loved it. I couldn't wait for him to visit me again. He would do oral sex on me and then taught me to do it on him. We had tenderness with one another, even as little children."

Zora paused and asked Dr. Hanson for some water. Dr. Hanson passed her a bottle from her mini fridge. Zora took a big gulp and continued.

"Well, my new best friend – his name was D.J. – then introduced me to intercourse. I had never felt anything like that. It hurt, but I knew not to say anything. To remain quiet. He would put his fingers to my lips with a whispered "Shhhhhhhh." He would then softly kiss the pain away down there and then kiss me on the mouth to soothe me more. I eventually got used to how it felt. How *he* felt. I enjoyed it. A lot. He did, too. We enjoyed each other. It became a beautiful secret.

Over the years, we continued to engage in our secret sexual relationship, which matured with each encounter. He knew what I liked and I knew what he liked. We knew how to ground one another. He was hurting. I was hurting. We bonded for comfort, but it grew into something deeper. By the time I was 12 years old, we were pros at pleasing one another. I grew to love him. I considered him to be my boyfriend. Stockholm syndrome. Falling in love with my abuser. But back then I didn't see it as abuse. He wasn't rough. He didn't hurt me. He talked to me and walked me through each experience tenderly. I loved him, even if the way that love came to be, wasn't right or normal."

Zora takes another gulp of her water, as tears brimmed her eyes.

"Then a time came when he didn't show up like usual. He didn't come to our house. Weeks passed. Months passed. Years passed. I was devastated. Where was he? Why did he leave me? Didn't he love me anymore? Did he still want to make me feel good and I make him feel good? Where did he go? … Where did he go?" she said through flowing tears.

She looks at Dr. Hanson with confusion on her face, face wet, makeup running. She covers her face and wails in her hands.

Dr. Hanson waits for her to settle. "Zora, do you want to continue?" she asks.

Zora starts panting, grabbing her chest. Anxiety. Panic. Shame. Guilt.

"I… I… I need some… air…" Zora says in staggered breaths, sweat forming on her face.

Dr. Hanson stands and brings a fan and waves it around Zora's head, face, and neck. Zora was crying harder. Dr. Hanson cautiously places a cold cloth on Zora's neck. It helped.

After about 10 minutes, Zora recovers and is ready to continue. She takes the last gulp of her water and looks at Dr. Hanson with watery eyes.

"Why did he leave me? Why did he abandon me?" she asks through trembling lips.

Dr. Hanson considers her response carefully. "Zora, sometimes we don't know why people do what they do. He was young just like you. Maybe something happened. Maybe he didn't intend to abandon you," she says gently.

Zora looks at her, never realizing that perhaps that could be true. The D.J. she knew was gentle. Kindhearted. He would never *just* leave her.

Zora clears her throat and dabs her face. "Perhaps… perhaps you're right. D.J. wouldn't just leave me without saying goodbye. He just wouldn't. Not *my* D.J.," she said as she wiped at her face resolutely.

She turns to Dr. Hanson to finish her story.

"When he left me, he left me with intense urges. A sex addiction that I fight with every single day of my life. He opened me up to a world of intimacy and when he left, I didn't know what to do when I became aroused and he couldn't soothe me. Since then, I vowed I would *never* allow intimacy or emotions to be part of anything involvement with a man. I started sleeping with the other boys who came to our house. It simply became another secret that benefited each of us equally." She sighs deeply.

"I have sex every day, several times a day with random men, but also with regulars. I can't get enough sex. I fill my days and nights with sex. If I'm not working… sex. If I'm bored… sex. I know it is a coping mechanism, but it is a safe place. Emotions aren't invited. Only pleasure. Immense pleasure. That's it," she says as her voice trails off.

Dr. Hanson leans towards her and puts her hand gently on Zora's shoulder.

"Zora, how is this process working for you as a person? Not as someone with an addiction, but as a person who deserves love. Love from your father. Love from a man eventually? Real love that is not based on sex alone?"

Zora gives herself a moment to consider Dr. Hanson's questions. "I don't know. I'm afraid of emotions. Getting close to someone. No. Sex is transactional for me. No talking. No feelings. No expectations. No pain. That's all I'm used to. Ever since D.J. left, I have used sex to soothe myself – even as a 12-year-old girl – I would have sex with any boy who was interested or willing. They wanted sex. I needed sex. Today, my sex drive is still very intense, and I just let it happen. I crave it. Whoever will give it to me. No strings attached. No commitment."

"I see," Dr. Hanson says. "So, have you ever considered trying to temper the desire, the drive. Have a normal relationship with just one man that you can be sexually active with all the time rather than random partners?"

"No, I haven't. I don't know how to be monogamous. I enjoy the variety. Variety is a barrier to feelings. No time to concentrate on one person. I guess for me to consider monogamy, he would have to be one hell of a man to pull me out of my addictive lifestyle," she says as a matter of fact. "I wish him luck with that," she chuckles.

Dr. Hanson checks the time and gently reminds Zora, "Our time is coming to a close. I'd like to see you again in another week. Can we schedule that, Zora? I think we need to dig more into how to work through your coping mechanisms. Figure out some alternatives?"

Zora looks at Dr. Hanson, understanding her point of view. "This is one of the hardest things I've had to do… telling my truth… Dr. Hanson, and then to be charged to release my addiction… now that? That is quite the challenge."

She puts her hands on her forehead and exhales deeply. "Alright, I'll let Libby know my availability," she says.

"Thank you, Dr. Hanson, for listening. I've only told that to one person in the world. One."

"You're welcome. That was brave. Real progress today," she says warmly. "Take care, Zora. See you next week?"

"Yes, Ma'am... Next week," she says rising from the chair.

***

Back in her car, Zora reflects upon Dr. Hanson's suggestion. Mind wandering, considering the possibility of recovery.

She's not ready to quit.

Recovery starts with an individual's determination to do better. To be better. Recovery cannot be forced. It must be chosen.

She'll think about it.

Maybe.

Chapter Thirty-Nine

Another day, another level of stress. Zora is fighting with her rising desire spawned by her time with Damian the day before. Telling her story to Dr. Hanson only served as a reminder that her need for pleasure is her mainstay. Something she can count on. Trust.

After closing up her office for the day, she makes herself a quick dinner. Chopped cucumbers in a vinaigrette with chopped chicken in it. She needed something stronger tonight. She opts for a glass of white wine.

After she eats, she is antsy. She doesn't really want to talk to anyone. Well, maybe Damian, but she thinks better than to call him. She goes to her bedroom and checks her fixer phone.

Ahhhhhh, multiple texts. So many choices. Should she even engage them? Should she try to be a one-man woman?

I don't think so.

She texts Shelton back and prepares to meet him. He suggests that they meet at his home office. She dresses in an easy-access sundress and heads to the location. She needs to shake off the last couple of days. Shelton is just what she needs. Easy. Uncommitted. Suitable and capable.

***

In his home office, he greets her with a wide grin. He knows the rules, so he didn't bother with the pleasantries. He was enjoying the drive by booty calls just as much as she was. He wasn't looking for a relationship either, but free sex is always on par.

In ritualistic form, they start with the typical kissing. Strong. Hungry. Skyy is brewing and Shelton is familiar with her "burn." She hands him a condom, and he rolls it onto his swollen penis. He spins her around as she lifts her dress. She spreads her legs and bends for entry. She is dripping wet. It has been a whole day since she was touched. Today she needs to be filled.

Shelton slaps her on her butt cheek and slid himself inside her with precision. He moans upon entry. She gasps as she receives him. "Give it to me, Shelton… Fill me…" she pleads.

Shelton makes it his duty to please her. He thrusts her with all his power. His hips slapping against her ass with each one. She is holding onto the edge of his desk, which shakes with each thrust. She is almost howling with pleasure. She pushes against him so hard, he almost loses his balance. They continue in this rhythm. No words. Just pleasure. Her vagina begging for more with each thrust. Shelton is groaning deeply, biting his bottom lip, gripping her hips with all he has. He's thinking, "She gets better every time... Oooooooh..."

It's like Zora can read his thoughts. "You like that? You like that, huh? Give it to me harder... power, Shelton... more power."

He almost knocks her over with his next thrust. She yelps in response but keeps pushing against him. Over and over. He looks at himself entering in and out of her vagina and gets even more aroused. He is feeding her all of his length. Stroking. Pumping. He feels like he is about to split her, but she doesn't stop him. His penis starts to stiffen. She can feel it but doesn't stop him. She throws her hips back and gives him a pop and another pop of her hips. A new move he hasn't experienced. They both explode and release individual groans and moans.

Heavy breathing, pulsating genitals, they just hold their positions. About five minutes later, Zora dislodges his penis from her vagina, and she pulls her dress down. She turns to him and smiles shyly. He smiles back, clearly satisfied and stunned at the new move she put on him.

She kisses him lightly. "Thank you, Shelton. I needed that. I really needed that," she says smiling wide.

Removing the condom and pulling up his pants, he returns the sentiment. "No, thank YOU, Skyy. You're better than fine wine," he says chuckling and shaking his head.

"Gotta go," she whispers. "Next time?"

He nods his head, "Next time, for sure."

***

Zora arrives home a little after 7 p.m. Ms. Fitzpatrick waves as she parks. Zora lightly waves and heads into the house. At this point, she could care less what Ms. Fitzpatrick or anyone else thinks. She has needs.

She grabs another glass of white wine and heads to the bathroom and runs herself a hot bath. She grabs her phone to catch up on socials. Once in the bath, she appreciates how the hot water soothes her throbbing vagina. She sips her wine and rests her head back on the bath pillow.

Her phone rings.

Without thinking, she answers. Damian. Video call.

"Ummmm, did I catch you at a bad time," he asks laughing.

She scoots down into the water, bubbles covering her chest. "I don't usually take video calls, but since it is you, I figured it was okay," she says chuckling.

"Oh, so I get to see you soaking, huh?" he asks with a raised eyebrow.

"I guess so… Here you are looking at me surrounded by bubbles," she raises an eyebrow back at him.

They both laugh.

"May I call you back when I get out?" she asks to which he said, "That's fine. I'll be up."

***

An hour later and dressed in a lounger, Zora texts Damian back letting him know that she is "presentable" and ready for him to call her back. A laughing emoji follows.

Her phone rings immediately and Damian appears on video, smiling brightly.

"Hey, you," he says. "You enjoy your soak?"

She smiles wide back at him. "I sure did. Did you enjoy the peep show?" she asks laughing.

He just shakes his head in response. That's all she needed to know.

They exchange playful banter and fill one another in on their days. Damian shares how he feels weird when she's not around him. He thanked her for listening to his story and for not avoiding him because of it. She told him that she finally told her therapist her full story.

"When do I get to hear your full story, Zee?" He asks softly.

"I'm not ready for you to hear all the sorted details yet. Maybe in a couple of days," she says gently. "I'm still processing the fact that I said it aloud for only the second time in my life."

He nods in acknowledgement. "I understand. I'm here when you're ready," he said looking in her eyes. "By the way, why were you in the tub so early"

She hesitated. Unsure of what to say. She opted for the truth.

"To be honest, I just got fixed and I needed a shower," she said looking at him.

He didn't know what to say right off. He swallowed and approached cautiously. "Just got fixed… you mean you just had sex? Is that what you mean, Zee?" he asked trying not to sound jealous.

"That's what I mean, Damian. You're off limits and I had to release the sexual tension you created yesterday," she says trying to make light of it.

Damian didn't laugh. He just stared at her. Silent.

She sighs. "What, Damian? I told you I have a sex addiction. Why are you surprised? Why do you appear to be bothered?" she asks sitting up more straight on the chaise.

He pauses in reflection. "I know what you told me, but that doesn't mean that I like it, Zee. You *know* how much I want you. To be with you. You also know the consequences if I follow through with how much I want you. If I allow myself to make love to you… You know that…" He inhales and exhales deeply.

"Well, Damian, I'm not…"

He interrupts her. "Zee, I'm not going to act like your addiction doesn't affect me. It does. I'm not going to act like I'm okay knowing that some other man is doing to you what I long deeply to do myself. I'm not. I'm not going to act like I don't see you as mine. I do."

He sighs and tries not to allow his emotions to show. It didn't work. His eyes begin to fill. He shakes it off, but not before Zora caught it.

"Damian, I'm sorry, but you…"

He interjects again. "Zee, do you think it is easy for me to know that some other man is putting his penis inside you?

I know it may not bother you if I was having sex with other women, but I am a realist. It bothers me. Understand me, I get the addiction, but I want to know if there will be a time where you will just want me. Nobody else?" he says slightly frustrated.

He wipes his face with both hands and waits.

Zora speaks up softly. "Damian, I know what you're saying and I understand. I do. I want to be with you, but I can't. I want to feel you inside me, but I can't. How do you expect me to just stop cold turkey with no option to follow?"

He looks sternly into the screen. "I guess I can't expect that from you. I'm just sharing how I feel, Zee." He clears his throat and pauses before continuing.

"Well, if I'm being honest… and I am… I'm falling in love with you, Zee. I won't apologize for it. I'm not going to deny it nor will I invalidate my feelings," he checks her face. "I know you don't *do* emotions, but I can't hide mine. I won't hide mine," he says as he leans back on his sofa. Eyes closed. Lips tight.

Zora is silent for a moment. She takes in everything he says to her.

"Damian, I'm not sure what to say. Your feelings are valid and I receive them. I just need you to give me space to process what you said… what I'm feeling, even if it is not what I want… at least what I thought I didn't want." She closes her eyes and breathes slowly.

"I am afraid to admit what you do to me. Who you are to me. I am afraid of allowing emotions to rule me… my heart.

I never considered being with anyone with commitment. Never."

Her eyes start to fill. She quickly wipes them.

"Damian, I don't know how to handle you… the presence that you bring to me… to my life. I've not known that in over 16 years. I've avoided it. Emotions hurt too much. I don't trust them. They hollow you out."

He looks at her directly. "Zee, they only hollow you out if you let them. Emotions are really a gift to fill you… to fill your life, but you have to welcome them. Embrace them, not fight them."

Tears flowing down her face, Zora attempts to respond. "Damian, I don't know how to navigate emotions. The last person I gave those to left me. No words. No warning. Never heard from him again. That cracked my soul. I was devastated. I don't know if I want to be that vulnerable again, putting my heart on the chopping block. I just can't."

Damian whispered to her. "Zee, I'm not here to crack your soul, to leave you. I want to love you, even with the challenges of your addiction. I just want to love you. That's all."

She is sobbing lightly. He tries to pull her into him.

"Zee, look at me, please," he pleads. "Please let me love you. I need to love you, and I need you to love me back, even if it takes time… Let me fill that void. Let my love fill you. Please."

Zora looks at him softly. "How, Damian? How can you accept me how I am? I'm a mess…"

He smiles gently. "I'm a mess, too, Zee. You heard my story. You know about my program. You know my limitations, but I will never believe that I'm not worthy of love because of my past. I will never deny you love because of your past or your present."

She holds his stare. She can see that he is sincere. She shrugs her shoulders and wipes her eyes.

"Why do you want me? Why do you want to love me? I don't know how to be faithful to one man… I…" she says through her tears.

"We will figure it out. If you let me… if you let love come, we will figure it out… What do you say, Zee? You want to try? We can go slowly. I just don't want my life without you in it… in my heart."

She clears her throat and looks at him through wet eyes. "Damian… I need time to process this. I'm not saying 'no,' but I'm not giving a definitive 'yes.' I do realize that we have something, but I don't know how to do this," she says wiping her eyes. "Give me some time?"

He nods slowly. "I'll give you time, Zee… I'm not going anywhere," he says softly.

She mumbles a soft, "Thank you" to him.

"Zee, I need to get ready for a virtual group meeting at 8 p.m. May I see you tomorrow? You can pick the place," he says with a smile.

She sniffs and wipes at her cheek. "Yes, I'd like to see you tomorrow. I have an open schedule. Just call me and we can make time."

He thanks her and says with decisiveness, "I love you, Zee. Don't forget that." The call disconnects.

Mentally drained, Zora heads to her bedroom. She curls under the covers and holds her breath hoping the thoughts will be suffocated for lack of oxygen. This kind of spiraling is different. She's used to spiraling to be sexually pleased. Tonight, she is spiraling from emotional overload.

Who can she call?

Without a thought she dials Rayven.

Zora shares how Damian came into her life and how they have become close without sex involved. Rayven was so proud of her. Zora tells her that she's catching feelings and doesn't know how to navigate that space. She hasn't felt love in so long and she doesn't trust herself. She doesn't know what to do with it.

Being the level-headed voice of reason, Rayven offers that Zora just sees how it goes and if it grows. She encourages Zora to take a leap outside of her fears. She may be surprised at what happens when she takes the shackles off her heart. She reminds Zora that everyone is not out to hurt her and it is okay to open the door – even if just a little crack – to trusting someone with her. With her heart.

After being on the phone for over an hour, Zora thanked her friend and hung up the phone and turned off the bedside lamp.

Laying on her back in the darkness of her room, Zora combs through her conversations with Damian, Dr. Hanson, and Rayven. She's scared. She needs to consider all her options. There may be another side of life and love. One that needs to be explored.

As long I don't talk myself out of it.

Chapter Forty

Sunshine peeking through the drapes rouses Zora from a deep sleep. She opens one eye to survey the room. She rolls over slowly and looks at the clock. 8:09 a.m. She slept past her run time. Her body feels like it has been dragged through a field. She ponders if it was her fix with Shelton or the emotional exercise she experienced over the last couple of days. In truth, it was both.

She sits up in the middle of the bed, folding her knees to her chest, resting her chin on her knees and closing her eyes. Feeling spent after being fixed is nothing new to her. But the emotional weight that has crashed through her world is more than she bargained for. She wants black and white. Simple. Uncomplicated. Emotions are too much of a rainbow blinding her with all the variations that are possible. Layered. Complex. Rife with joy, pain, disappointment, expectation, responsibility, pleasure…love… the whole rainbow. She shutters at the thought of activating her emotions again. It's a gamble she's not sure she can risk, let alone win.

Throwing her legs over the side of the bed, she heads into the bathroom and splashes water on her face. She captures her reflection in the mirror. Messy hair. No makeup. Eyes heavy with uncertainty and fear.

Stop pondering so much. Chances offer change. Give yourself a chance for something different.

She turns on the shower and gets ready to start her day. Breakfast. Tea. Checked email and messages. She chooses her chaise to cradle her. To settle anxiety that is rising in her chest. To distract herself, she calls her mother.

"Hi, Mommy, how are you?"

"I'm well, Zora daughter," she ways warmly. "I'm getting ready for an early meeting to discuss the details of our summer youth employee. How are you?"

"That's great, Mommy. I'm excited. THRIVE is going to be more successful this year than last year. Thank you, again, for taking on a youth," she says trying to remain in avoidance mode. "But, I'm good. Have a final meeting on Thursday to close all the loose ends for Saturday."

"I'm happy for you daughter," her mother says smiling. "I have to run, Zora dear. Meeting in 10 minutes. I love you."

"I love you, too, Mommy."

Ending the call, Zora sits in silence. Her heart starts to race. She can feel herself getting agitated but was interrupted when her phone rang.

Damian.

She adjusts herself mentally and connects the video.

"Hey, you," he says smiling wide. He checks Zora's face, never missing anything when it comes to her.

"You okay, Zee? What's going on?" he says gently.

She sighs lightly. "I'm okay. Feeling a little anxious. Not sure why," she says softly.

"I'm free now, you want to meet?" he says warmly.

"Yes, that would be nice… Where are you now?" she asks.

"I'm near Dupont Circle. We can meet at one of the spots around there if you want."

She pauses. "I just sent you an address to meet me."

He checked his phone and notes that it is less than two miles away.

"Got it. See you soon," he says smiling. "You need anything before I come?"

"No, I'm good. See you soon."

***

Within 10 minutes, Damian rings the doorbell. Zora answers dressed in a sleeveless lemon-yellow romper with bedroom slippers.

Zora opens the door and lets him in. He looks around.

"This your office?" he asks. "Nice."

"Yes, it is. My home is upstairs," she says smiling gently.

He takes in the surroundings of her office as she shows him around. She meticulously removed any markings that would give away her full identity. He only knows her as Zee, not Zora.

They head up the back stairs to her personal home. She could have let him in the front door, but thought it was important for him to see her in her element as a clinical therapist.

He follows in silence. Into the kitchen they emerge and he looks around with his hands in his pockets. "Wow, Zee, this is beautiful," he says warmly. "This looks like you," he says looking at her smiling.

"Me, huh?" she says chuckling. "It's simple, but mine," she smiles as she leans against the island.

He pauses and grabs her hand. "Zee, why did you invite me to your home?"

She smiles at him. "I wanted you to know me… all of me. What better way than to invite you into my sanctuary," she says squeezing his hand lightly. "Believe it or not, you're only the second man that has been in my house. The first was my bestie, Nico."

Eyes wide, he says, "Really? Why me?"

"I told you. I want you to know me. So, I need to show you *all* of me."

She continued to hold his hand as she gave him a tour of the main level: the living room with her beloved chaise, the lounge with the bar, the kitchen, the dining room, which she rarely uses, and powder room. He quietly takes in the environment.

She looks at him softly and says, "Follow me," as she takes the stairs to her private floor.

Concern fills his face and she calms him. "Just a tour, Damian. I won't try anything. I promise," she said chuckling. "Just trust me."

He nods and follows.

On the private floor, Zora shows him the guest room and restroom and then looks back at him as she leads him into her bedroom. He hesitates.

"Come on, Damian. I need to show you something," she says gently. "You are the first man I've had in my bedroom, believe it or not," she said with a warm smile.

"Really?" he exclaimed. "I thought for sure…"

"No, Damian… My bedroom is where I can separate addiction from reality. No "getting fixed" in my bedroom. Ever."

She gently pulls him into her bedroom and turns to him. She looks at him through eyes that are scared and brave at the same time. She grabs him with both hands.

"Damian… No one and I mean NO ONE has ever seen what I'm about to show you. I just need you to see me… all of me. I'm scared, but I need you to know," she said with her eyes welling with tears.

He reached up and touched her cheek to catch a tear that started a path from the corner of her eye. She closed her eyes against his touch.

He whispered, "Show me, Zee… I want to know you."

She slowly pulled him into her closet and then opened a section of clothes to reveal a hidden door. She pushed it open and entered. He followed. They stood in the middle of the small room. Dark. Sultry. Scented. Damian looked around.

Shelves of different wigs – about 15. Clothes that looked nothing like the Zee he knows. Mini skirts, leather thigh-high boots, see-through bustiers and corsets, fishnet stockings, boxes of condoms, and many other risqué outfits. He just takes it all in. No words.

Zora is standing out of his way, tears running down her face. Shame rumbling through her. He hears her sobs and turns to her.

Taking her hand and wiping her face. "Baby, don't cry. Thank you for letting me see you. For letting me into this part of your world," he said as gently as he could.

Her voice tightened as she tried to speak. "Damian… This is my secret. This is where I become her… where I become… Skyy," she said hanging her head.

He pulled her to him and wrapped his arms around him. He holds her securely. Safely. She sobs into his chest. He lets her. He didn't try to stop her. He didn't question what he saw. He just accepted it. All of it. All of her.

Moments pass and then she pulls away from him slightly tilting her eyes up to his. He just looks at her in resolution.

"I still love you, Zee. I do," he says as he kisses her forehead. "What do you want to tell me now?"

She wipes her face and leads him out of the inner sanctum and asks him to have a seat on the bed while she goes into the bathroom to wipe her face better. He sits quietly and waits.

When she comes out of the bathroom, she stands in front of him and pulls open the top drawer of her bedside table.

He looks at her softly, allowing her to invite him into whatever she wants him to know.

She removes the fixer phone and hands it to him. He looks at her curiously. "What's this, Baby?"

She wipes her nose with the back of her hand and clears her throat. "It's my fixer phone… The one that I use when Skyy emerges… when Skyy needs a sexual fix." She swallows looking at him in the eye.

"Only fixers are on that phone. I text them or they text me. No videos. No phone calls. None of them have my personal cell phone."

She turns away briefly. He holds his stare, focusing on her face. "I'm here, Zee… I'm here," he says tenderly.

"Check the phone," she tells him.

He's cautious. Not sure if he wants to see what is on the screen. He looks at her, almost with fear in his eyes.

"Please, Damian. Check it for me," she whispers as she wrings her hands in nervous anticipation.

Damian clicks the side button. The screen comes alive with light. Multiple text messages. So many text messages. He swallows and looks at her. She permits him to read them. She asks that he read them aloud. He does. She stands in her truth. Skyy fully on display in the presence of something she's never had. Love.

After all messages have been read, Zora sits next to Damian on the bed, leaning over resting her head on his shoulder as tears begin to flow again. He gently wraps his arms around her. They sat in silence for what seemed to be an eternity.

Zora finally speaks. "Say something, Damian… say anything… please…"

He unlocks his arms from around her and turns his body on the bed to face her, holding her hands gently. He looks her in her eyes, tears forming slowly. He brushes a lock of her hair from her face and holds his stare. He is breathing deeply. Heart racing. Not from arousal. From an impenetrable love.

He clears his throat lightly. "Zee… you have… you have only deepened my love for you because you trusted me with what you've never shared with anyone. That speaks volumes. That tells me that you know that I won't hurt you."

A tear falls down his cheek.

"It tells me that you love me, even if you never utter those words. I know that you do."

She leans into him and whispers into his chest. "I… I think… maybe I do…"

He smiles warmly into her hair and pulls her face to his. He kisses her with a tenderness he never knew he could express. Different from the other times. Deeper. With resolve. She responds and kisses him back equally. A kiss that echoed what her heart feared to speak.

She gently pulls him down to lay on the bed as they continue to kiss. She whispers, "Lay next to me, please."

He rests up on his elbow and says, "Before I lay next to you, Zee, is there anything else I need to know? Your story?" he says wiping her face and then his own.

She stands. He thinks she's leaving. "Zee, where are you going. Don't…"

She started pacing. Hands on her hips. Tears streaming again. "I'm not leaving, Damian. You want to know the truth? Do you…?" she said through a strained voice.

"Yes, Baby… I do," he says gently.

"When I was a little girl, I was molested. Without all of the dicey details – because I cannot fall into that emotional abyss today – it happened for years and I fell in love with my abuser. He wasn't a predator. He was always gentle. Then one day he was gone. Never heard from him again. From that day on, Skyy became my refuge, my coping mechanism. A place where I bury emotion, any feelings. Skyy is the drug that numbs me. And as you can see from my inner closet, she is very much alive and well. She shows up when I'm stressed, anxious, lonely, discouraged… for whatever… whenever… Daily."

She stopped and covered her face with her hands. Sobbing more intensely. "WHY. DO. YOU. WANT. TO. BE. WITH. SOMEONE. LIKE. ME, Damian? WHY????"

He stands and goes to her and gently pulls her back to the bed. He lays her down and nestles himself against her, letting her express what she's feeling, but not letting her go. She can feel the safety of his body. The strength of his arms. The security of his love. Eventually, she allows herself to melt into his embrace. Her sobs soften until they stop altogether. He just holds her in silence. No questions. No judgment. Just love and acceptance.

He whispers into her ear, "Because I love you. That's why."

She lets that settle in. She didn't fight it. She didn't fight him. She rested.

Her fixer phone pings breaking into the silence and Zora moves, but Damian protects her, holding her closer.

"Not today, Zee. Skyy is not invited today. Just you. Just me. Just us."

What could she say to that?

Nothing. Absolutely nothing.

She nestled closer to him, and both dozed off in a peaceful midday nap.

***

After about an hour of peaceful rest, Damian's phone rang. Work. He kisses Zora on the cheek hoping to slip out without bothering her. It didn't work.

"Where are you going," she asks rising up on her elbow.

"Work is calling. I need to get to a 2:15 p.m. meeting," he says looking guilty. "May I call you later? Will you be home later, Zee?" he asks hoping she will give him a definitive answer.

"I should be home. Not sure," she says looking at him shyly. "I'll try. Maybe if you come back, I won't need to go anywhere else," she says with a light smile.

"I'll strongly consider it, if it means I can protect you from Skyy," he says with a serious look on his face. She caught it and understood.

She slides to the edge of the bed and stands so she can walk him to the door. At the front door, he gives her a gentle hug and kisses her as a reminder. "No Skyy today, Baby. Please," he says softly.

She reaches up and kisses him again. "No Skyy," she says trying to convince herself.

***

To keep her promise, Zora settles into her day and into the night on the phone with Rayven, then Lai, then Nico. She apologized to him and he did the same. She is not about to say that fighting Skyy was easy. It was not. She kept her promise to Damian. *Her* Damian.

Did she just say that?

Yep, she did.

***

The rest of the week was a repeat of the same. Clients. THRIVE meetings. Besties check-ins. Quasi dates with Damian. Her house. The park. The coffee shop. The bakery. Finalizing the lease for Kira and the condo and scheduling the deep cleaning.

A full week indeed.

Her fixer phone was blowing up all week. She fought as much as she could. Skyy still won a few days. She allowed herself to get bent over, but Damian was present each time. She could hear his voice, "No Skyy, Baby," but her urges were too strong to ignore. Damian knew when Skyy showed up because he could feel it when they spoke. He called her out lovingly and she promised to do better. He just reminded her: "I love you, Zee."

In her last conversation, Zora reminded Damian of the THRIVE event tomorrow. He agreed to be there to support. She lovingly thanked him with the warmest smile she could conjure up. Damian returned the warmth. He is determined to let his love destroy Skyy's pull if it's the last thing he does.

***

Today is the day! The THRIVE Event. Zora arrives at the Blackburn Center on Howard University campus. She buzzes around finalizing tables for employees, vendors, signage that provide direction to smaller rooms for interviews, etc. She is overjoyed. In just one and a half hours, the place will be swarming with youth, and their families and employers seeking to hire them for the two-month session.

Zora is dressed cool, but still professional in a pair of hot pink wide-legged slacks and bold printed blouse that compliments her slacks. She has on gold strappy sandals and jewelry that accessorize perfectly. She has her hair pulled up into a loose bun with whisps of hair framing her face.

The room begins to fill up, and she is walking through, clipboard in hand, with a smile as she extends her hand to greet everyone. She has her assistants show employers to their assigned tables to set up.

Zora waves to Lai and Rayven as they spot her across the room. Nico isn't far behind walking aimlessly from table to table taking in the scene.

"Glad you could make it," she exclaimed, hugging her friends. "Thank you for your support. I mean it. All of you." She notes someone trying to get her attention and she excuses herself.

It's time. She mounts the podium and gives the statement of the occasion. She gives some directions – where lunch will be held, where the restrooms are located, timing of interviews for time efficiency, etc. – and lets the event do what it was built to do. Network. Community. Empowerment.

She sees Damian and stops herself from running to him.

Be cool, Zora. Don't look desperate.

He walks up to her and admires her, taking her hand and giving her a spin. She laughs.

"You look amazing, Zee. Absolutely, amazing," he says smiling broadly.

"Thank you, Damian," she says with a warm smile and a twinkle in her eye. "You don't look to shabby yourself," she chuckles. He thanks her with a bow and a chuckle.

They walk around the venue and chat as she explains what each section is around the room, pointing to certain employers, etc. She walks him to the interview rooms and back to the main room, introducing him to colleagues as her "friend," and an inconspicuous wink to him, which he acknowledges, noting that discretion is in order.

Her mother gives her a wave from across the room, and she heads that way with Damian. Before she reaches her mother's table, she runs into her father.

She hugs him and whispers, "Thank you for coming" in his ear and smiles at him. He turns to Damian and extends his hand.

"Young man," he says shaking his hand with strength. Damian returns the gesture with a smile.

"It's been a long time," Mr. Holley said looking at Damian. Damian holds a look of confusion on his face.

"Do I know you, Sir?" he asks politely.

"You look just like your father," Mr. Holley says patting him on the back. "Spitting image, if I must say." Damian looks at Zora and shrugs lightly.

Mr. Holley turns to Zora and says, "You remember him… You *have to* remember him. That's D.J.… D.J. Lucas. He used to come…"

Zora heard nothing else after she heard, "That's D.J. …"

She shot a look at Damian and tried to force a smile. "D.J.? You're… You're D.J.? Nice to see you again," she said feeling bile building in her throat, panic rising.

Damian parts his lips and looks at Mr. Holley and then back to Zora, placing his hand on his stomach and says, "Zo-Zo? You're Zo-Zo?" He instantly feels sick.

Zora tries to collect herself and smiles and points. "Ummm, excuse me," she says quickly. "Mommy is calling me over. Daddy I'll talk to you soon." She looks over at Damian as she walks away. "D.J., we must catch up."

He clears his throat. "Yes, that would be nice."

In a flash, Zora went one way. Damian the other.

What the hell?

After Zora speaks with her mother, she spots Nico and drags him across the room.

Nico is alarmed at the urgency. "Zora, what is the matter with you? I was talking to someone… What do…"

"Shut up, Nico! I need to speak with you… NOW!" she says through clenched teeth.

Chapter Forty-One

Through the wireless communication device in her ear, Zora gives directions to her team to cover the event, be vigilant, present, and helpful. She must take care of an emergency and will be back on the floor shortly.

In a closed room, Zora is in a full on anxiety attack. She is perspiring. Shaking. The room is spinning and she passes out in the nearest chair. Nico stands nearby calling to her.

"Zora… Zora…" he says fanning her. He opens the bottle of water he was holding, pours some into his hand and places it on her face and neck. She responds to the chill of the water. Almost screaming as her body jolts alive.

"Zora… talk to me," Nico pleads.

She coughs and bends over in the chair, head between her knees, gasping for air, and trying to speak.

"…trashcan… I need… a trashcan…"

Nico grabs the one next to the door and brings it to her just in time for her to vomit violently into it. She has buried her head so deeply into the can, only her shoulders could be seen.

Nico is pacing. Unsure of what is wrong. What is happening. He speaks lightly.

"Zora, what is happening, sweetie? Talk to me, please. You're scaring me," he says in a panicked voice.

After a few minutes of emptying her stomach contents into the trashcan, she throws herself backward into the chair, wiping her mouth with the back of her hand. She is clearly distraught. Hair now out of its neat style, water spots on her slacks. She doesn't care. She is devastated.

She looks at Nico, tears filling her eyes, followed by deep sobs. Nico just looks at her. Not sure how to help.

"Z, how can I help? What do you need?" he says clearly concerned.

Zora collects herself enough to utter, "He's here... He's... here..."

"Who's here, Z? Who's here?" Nico says kneeling beside the chair. "Talk to me, sweetie..."

Zora clears her throat and in a strained voice says, "D.J. is here... the one who... who molested me... the one who had... had sex with me for seven years... the one who I... I fell in love with... the one who opened the door... to Skyy... my addiction to sex... the one who I've been seeing a lot of lately. I... I didn't know it was him, Nico... he's... here... Oh. My. God... Nico, he's here..."

She's sobbing uncontrollably now. Inconsolable. Nico leans back on his heels, eyes wide, a hand now covering his mouth trying to make sense of it all.

"What do you need me to do? You need me to seek him out and kick him out? Tell me what you want me to do, Z. Tell me and I'll do it," he says with fervor in his voice. He is now in protective mode.

Zora tries to open her eyes, but the tears won't let her. She speaks in a whisper.

"I've been seeing Damian for months now; first as friends… then more than friends, but without benefits. No sex. Just hanging out… Just talking… Just intimacy. Emotional intimacy that I never expected, but I've been receiving. But… I… I didn't know… I didn't know it was him… Nico… I didn't know he was D.J. … Why didn't I know?… Why didn't I…"

She couldn't finish. She was overcome with emotion. Nico places a gentle hand on her arm.

"Z, I don't know what to say. What does all of this mean?" he asks curiously. Almost with jealousy.

She sniffles and wipes her face. She looks at Nico, mascara running. Lipstick smudged.

"It just happened, Nico. We met in Atlanta, but he just happened to be from Bowie. He was the one who rescued me from that near rape situation." She clears her throat. "We kept in touch. We laugh a lot. Talk a lot. He got me the applicant for my condo from his colleague connections." She puts her hands on her cheeks and groans deeply.

"I started falling for him. I started to feel… emotions… and you *know* that is not something that I do. Never." She sighs deeply. "He was always gentle, tender, kind. Never imposing. Never asking or expecting anything from me, even though he knows my story. He…"

Nico is getting agitated. "You mean to tell me you let this stranger into your world and you're catching feelings for him, Zora?"

"Nico, this is not the time for jealousy. I've been spending time with the one who stole my innocence and didn't know it. I don't know what to do. How to move forward. How to face him."

"You're thinking about seeing him again, Zora?" he questioned. "Are you serious right now?"

Zora sits up straight in the chair and looks Nico squarely in the eyes.

"Nico, I don't know what I'm going to do. If it means closure, then yes, but for now, I just need to process it. Damn it… Can you just let me process it?"

Nico lifts his hands in surrender and stands with his hands in his pockets. Zora stands as well and tries to make herself as presentable as she can, given her devastation. She asks Nico to find Rayven and have her come to her as quickly as possible and bring her purse and a bottle of water. Nico sighed heavily and went to locate Rayven after he grabs the liner from the trashcan to discard in an outside bin.

Rayven comes into the room where Zora is and gets filled in on the details, but Zora needs her to help pull her look back together. She can't go back into the event looking like a raccoon that just lost a fight. Zora is grateful that her friend always has makeup in her purse, just in case. For emergencies like this.

Rayven touches up Zora's face and fixes her hair as best she can. She gives her the bottle of water and a stick of gum to calm the vomit scent that is lingering on her breath. She smiles warmly at her friend.

"You ready, Z? I'm here if you need me, Sis," she says with a reassuring smile.

Zora embraces Rayven for what felt like an eternity and she exhaled. The two Besties stood there together in silence so that Zora could get settled enough to reemerge back into the event.

"I'm ready, Ray," she says forming a smile. "Stay close, please," she says with eyes fighting back tears.

***

Back on the event floor, Zora carries herself as if nothing had happened. She is a pro at putting up a facade. She checks in with her team on the wireless earpiece and mingles, being careful of her surroundings, so she doesn't run into Damian. Well…D.J. … Damian.

Whoever the hell he is.

Nico comes and checks on her. Asking if she has seen D.J. again. Zora just nods 'no' and continues to make her way around to the various employers and venders. Smiling for the world while her insides are imploding.

What she thought was safety now poses a threat. A threat to her emotions. Her spirit. Her security. Dare she admit. Her heart.

The person who abandoned her 16 years ago after taking her innocence has been in her personal sphere all this time. So unsettling. Uncomfortable. It only confirms why she never wanted intimacy. Her deepest wound has been ripped open without warning.

She smiles over the internal screams.

***

The event wraps up a success. Fifty youth hired for the summer session. Zora anticipates next year's THRIVE event will be even more successful. She orchestrates the clear out of the venue, ensuring that it is left better than how she received it. Interview rooms straightened up. Tables and chairs stacked to one side. Floors swept. Trash pulled and stacked neatly for pickup.

She hugs her team and thanks them for a job well done. She couldn't do it without them she tells them with warm gratitude.

In her car, Zora reflected on the day. The joy. The excitement. The sense of accomplishment. Empowerment. The revelation. The crash. The wound.

The ride home, although short, seemed to stretch on for too long. The drive on autopilot, the road hummed beneath the tires as the streets were alive with people living their lives. Stoplights. Street signs. Crosswalks. All hindering her escape. Tears welling in her eyes, Zora wonders how many of them had their chest cracked open today.

How many of them are reeling from the weight of unexpected, devastating news?

How many of them have had their innocence stolen?

How many of them have stolen someone's innocence?

How many of them have come face to face with their past like a wrecking ball hitting a brick building with unbelievable force?

She can't breathe, but she needs to make it home safely. She wipes the falling tears from her face. She inhales slowly. She exhales slowly. She can feel panic rising again.

Hold it together, Zora.

Hold. It. Together.

In her driveway, she grips the steering wheel to stabilize the earthquake that is rising within her. Tears are burning her eyes again. She quickly opens the door and finds her way into the house where she collapses in a heap on the kitchen floor. Briefcase, purse, and keys landing wherever. She doesn't care. She is heaving for air. Everything is trembling. She is numb and in excruciating pain at the same time. The room is blurry. Her throat is tightening against the bile fighting to flood her mouth.

"Help me! Help me," she pleads into the air as she crawls frantically towards the powder room.

This scene is all too familiar.

Her head in the toilet, she vomited for the second time today. Dry heaves cause her stomach to ache with such intense pain as she lowers herself onto the floor. She lay there on her back. Tears running into her ears, muffling her hearing.

Maybe they will make her deaf so she can't hear anymore lies.

Maybe she'll go blind, so she won't have to watch her life crumble before her eyes.

She hears her phone ringing in the other room. She's too exhausted to care who it is. She lets it ring.

She lies there another 10 minutes or so and her phone rings again, for the third time. She just ignores it.

She is jolted back to reality.

BANG…BANG…BANG!

Someone is knocking on her door as if it were on fire. She slowly lifts herself to her knees, flushes the toilet, and stands. She heads to the door curiously. She's not up for company. She didn't invite anyone over.

"Who is it?" she asked in frustration.

"Z, it's Nico…"

She exhales in a deep sigh and opens the door. He takes in her appearance as he comes in.

"Z, you look like hell…" he says as a matter of fact.

She rolls her eyes at him. "Whatever, Nico. Not my best day. So… What's up?"

He heads into the living room and sits on the edge of the chaise.

"I was concerned about you, Zora. You were dealt a heavy blow today. You alright?"

Zora joins him on the chaise. She leans back and lets the chaise nestle her. She folds her arms across her chest, chin resting. She knows she looks a mess. Breath smells of vomit, but she doesn't care. Her world just got wrecked.

She looks at him and whispers, "How did I not recognize him, Nico? How?"

Nico scoots closer to her and places a hand on her knee. "Z, it has been 16 years. How were you expected to know what he looked like after all that time? Don't beat yourself up." He wiped her cheek to catch a tear that formed.

"Did he act like he knew you? Did he recognize you?" he asked cautiously.

She looks at him. "Not that I know of. I never told him my real name. He just knew me as Zee, with two e's. That's what he called me. When he came here to my office, I had hidden anything that had my name on it because I didn't want to tell him my real name yet."

Nico widened his eyes and leaned forward. "He was here, Zora? In your house…? Why would you…?"

She quickly interrupted him. "Nico, he… Damian… and I were sharing ourselves slowly… sharing our personal stories, and I wanted him to know about Skyy. I showed him everything. He didn't judge me. He accepts me. He just wants to love me. Despite knowing about my addiction. He was different. Never met anyone like him," she says shyly.

Nico considered everything she said. Jealousy brewing.

"Z, you let a strange man into your house? Emotions, Zora?" He runs his hand across his forehead. "Wow!"

Zora just sits quietly. She doesn't owe him any explanation. Silence becomes a presence hoovering between them. Nico wants to comfort her, but he can tell she won't agree to that.

Nico rises slowly as he prepares to leave. “Zora, I’m here… I’ll always be here.”

She looks up through wet eyes. “I know, Nico. I appreciate you.”

Nico lets himself out. He stands on the front steps and looks back. He knows she’s hurting. If only she understood how much he is hurting, too, as the truth settles. She has opened her heart up to another man.

***

Zora takes a long hot shower hoping to wash away the pressures of the day. The beauty of it. The betrayal of it. She steps out of the shower and stands in the mirror. She’s still in shock. It’s too much. She broke her own rules, and it backfired.

Her phone pings. She steps out of the bathroom with a towel wrapped around her moist skin. She checks her phone.

Nothing.

She opens her bedside drawer. The fixer phone. A message. She hesitates then clicks the side button. The screen lights up.

Milo.

She holds the phone to her chest, remembering the day she showed it to Damian. She felt tears trying to come. She shook them off. Inhaled and exhaled. She reads the message and responds. She agrees to meet Milo behind the bistro in 40 minutes.

Skyy is back.

Zora welcomes her back.

She needs her back.

Zora dresses in a thin short dress with flat sandals. She has no time for beauty today. A short wig, minimal makeup, including the beauty mark. She needs to numb the pain. Milo is just what she needs.

It's only about 5 p.m. They are both being a bit reckless. It's still daylight. Who cares.

She meets Milo at the spot and he's ready. Belt already loosened. Leaning against the wall with a grin from ear to ear. He can tell by the look in her eyes that she's not up for anything more than a fix. No jokes. No smiles. Just sex.

He grabs her and pulls her into a hungry kiss that she welcomes. She's pulling at his clothes and moaning against him with renewed energy. She pulls a condom out of her bra, and he rolls it onto his ever-ready penis. She talks against his lips. "Take me, Milo… I need you to hurt me… hurt me now…"

He spins her in one movement, and she lifts her dress and bends over. He slides inside her with purpose. He thrusts her until she is yelping with each pump. He is gripping her hips tight so that she doesn't fall forward. She is taking him all in.

In her mind, she is fighting Damian's face. His voice. His kisses. His touch.

He can't do this to me.

I don't need him.

He doesn't matter.

With every thought she fights, she pushes herself against Milo as if to break his hips. Each thrust is meant to crush every emotion she is feeling.

No emotions.

Feel nothing.

Each thrust is meant to erase anything that Damian is trying to do to her, to be to her.

He did this to me.

He made me like this.

She wants to hate him. With each thrust of her hips, she is trying to convince herself that Damian is a predator. An abuser. *Her* abuser.

Milo is bracing every thrust, moans and takes it. She is animal tonight. She hears a sound. Footsteps. Milo tries to dislodge his penis, but she doesn't stop.

Milo looks up and his friend, Gil, is standing there watching. Zora turns her head towards Gil, hair hanging in her face.

"You want some? You want some of this?" she says while still thrusting against Milo.

Gil looks at Milo in confusion. Milo just smiles and waves him over.

"You got a condom?" Zora asks through staggered breaths.

Gil looks at her and then at Milo and says, "Yeah, I got one…"

"Get over here, then," Zora commands.

Milo smirks as he continues to pummel her vagina. After Gil rolls on his condom, Zora reaches for him and dislodges

Milo. She spins and pulls Gil closer so he can plant his penis inside her soaked vagina, while she kisses Milo. Gil is slowly grinding Zora's vagina. She stops kissing Milo long enough to correct his action. "No, bang me… Hurt me, man…"

Gil follows her command and bangs her out, pumping her so hard she has to hold onto Milo while kissing him. Zora then stops kissing Milo and bends over and takes Milo in her mouth while Gil is doing her good. "Deeper," she tells Gil and he obeys. She gasps at his stroke and moans as she puts her mouth over Milo's penis.

After about 10 minutes, Gil is ready to release, but Zora flips and pushes her vagina back onto Milo's penis, taking Gil into her mouth. This activity continues another 10 minutes until she can feel both men stiffen. She can feel her own release looming. She is thrusting her mouth and her vagina. A masterpiece of sexual pleasure. Gil releases first. Zora is grateful he has a condom on. She has only swallowed one man. Her mind goes to last week with Damian. She shakes it off. She commands Milo to push her harder. He does and she releases in a squeal.

The three let the moment ride until the high subsides. Eventually, Zora releases Milo's penis. He and Gil both pull up their pants. Milo just leans against the wall. His usual expression of satisfaction on his face. Gil is still taking in what he just experienced. Clearly, not something he is used to. He looks at Milo, smiles, and gives a thumbs up as he is allowing his breathing to slow.

Milo, ever the gentleman, introduces the two.

"Gil, meet Skyy… Skyy, meet Gil," he says laughing.

The group start laughing and then quietening so no one will know they are out there in broad daylight.

Zora kisses Gil lightly on the lips. She turns and kisses Milo deeply.

"It's been fun, fellas," she says as she turns towards the street where she is parked.

Gil waves, like a little boy who just got his favorite toy. He just watches Zora as she sashays away.

"What the…"

Milo slaps him on the back, laughing, "There, there, Gil… That's not what she's here for. Enjoy what you experienced and that's it."

***

Zora arrives home and cleans up. She exhales deeply. Her fixer phone pings again.

Should she respond?

Why the hell not?

The day is still young.

She lines up two more fixes that take her well into the night.

Vagina screaming loudly with the residue of pleasure.

Damian who?

CHAPTER FORTY-TWO

While Zora exits the uncomfortable situation, Mr. Holley asks for Damian's contact information, which he provided through the haze of emotions that kept gut punching him over and over.

The news that Zee was Zo-Zo came like a shipwreck in the middle of nowhere. He felt as if he had been thrown overboard without a life preserver. No land in sight. He's taking in water fast. He was drowning. He can't breathe.

Damian smiled his way through the crowd at the Blackburn Center. Waving cordially as he tried to steady the ground beneath his feet. He was sinking. Sinking into what felt like an abyss, water covering his head as he sank 200 feet below the surface, unable to come up for air.

Out in his car, he loses it! He erupts in a wave of emotion. Emotion that felt like grief. His chest was tight. His stomach in knots. His body quivering uncontrollably. He feels like his eyes were about to roll out of their sockets. Pain at the back of his neck felt like he was about to have a stroke.

He covers his face with both of his hands and screams. Screams loudly. He doesn't care if anyone can hear him. "No, no, no, no," he shouts into his hands.

The tears begin to burn his eyes. He cannot fathom what he just heard himself say.

"You're…You're Zo-Zo?"

It can't be. She's not… How can she be…?

Unable to hold it in, he quickly opens his car door and vomits in the parking lot. Assured that he fully emptied his stomach, he slams the door shut and bangs on the steering wheel with all his strength as tears continued to flow.

He wipes his face as he mumbles under his breath… "Zo-Zo…? Zo-Zo…?"

He pushes the ignition button and drives. He's not sure where, but he drives. Nothing around him makes sense. He's almost sure he's driving below the speed limit when he hears multiple beeps coming from behind him, while other cars speed around him holding their horns and yelling out of their windows.

He doesn't care. He gathers himself enough to make a call. He hits the button on the steering wheel that allows him to call out who to call.

"Dial Pastor Hayden," he says through trembling lips.

The phone rings three times and Damian is about to disconnect the call when he hears a voice.

"Hey, Damian," he says warmly. "Great to hear from you. What are you up to?"

Damian can't speak. He just clears his throat several times, fighting back tears.

"Damian, you there?" Pastor Hayden asks. "Are you okay, Son?"

Damian musters as whispered, "No..." he coughs. "No, Sir... I'm not."

Pastor Hayden is concerned. "Where are you, Son? Where are you...?"

Damian can only eek out, "I'm not sure... I don't know..."

Pastor Hayden gently asks engages him. "Damian, look around. What do you see? Anything look familiar?"

Damian blinks several times to clear the haze from his eyes. He looks around and tells Pastor Hayden he thinks he's on 295, but he isn't sure which direction he is driving.

Pastor Hayden softly asks, "Damian, do you have your sponsor phone with you, Son? Is it where you can reach it?"

"Yes... Yes, Sir, I have it..." he whispers through tears.

"Good, Son... Turn it on for me... Can you do that safely?"

Damian reaches into the center console and pulls out the phone and clicks it on.

"I have it on now, Sir..." he says as tears start to flow more freely.

"Okay... Let me check your location."

Pastor turns on the locator. All of the men in the Anchor Program have phones with locators in case they are "in trouble" and need help.

A bleep shows Pastor Hayden that Damian is headed south on 295, but his home is north on 295. Pastor Hayden provides some direction.

"Okay, Son, I see where you are. You're headed away from home. Can you get to my church? It's about 10 minutes from where you are now."

Damian chokes back tears. "Okay. Yes, Sir I can meet you there."

"Okay, Son, I'm on my way there now. Stay on the phone with me, please," Pastor Hayden says with tenderness.

Pastor Hayden took Damian under his wing when he got into trouble and landed in juvenile detention the first time at 13. He has been mentoring him consistently – which is what Damian needed – for almost 20 years. Damian's sponsor is one thing, but Pastor Hayden is that father he always longed for and needed as a Black boy.

***

In the church, Pastor Hayden guides Damian to his office at the rear of the sanctuary. Damian is very familiar with being there. When he was younger, that's where he would escape the abuse of his father. Pastor was the first person that Damian told his story to when he felt comfortable enough to do so. Damian was about 21 years old when he told Pastor what he endured as a child. That's why Pastor Hayden is tender, yet firm. He was building him into a man, especially after his father died.

The two sit in silence for quite a while. Damian is clearly distraught, but Pastor doesn't interrupt his process. He gives him space to start whenever he's ready. Pastor works on his message for tomorrow but periodically checks in with Damian without words.

Finally, Damian clears his throat to speak. "Do you have any water, Pastor," he asks shyly.

Pastor hands him a bottle from the mini fridge and comes around the desk to sit in the chair next to Damian.

"You ready to talk, Son," he says placing a hand on his shoulder.

Damian shakes his head in a soft 'yes,' and speaks.

"I don't know where to start… I'm just… I am so…" he says through a cracked voice.

"Take your time, Son," Pastor offers with grace.

Damian fills him in on his blossoming friendship with Zee, to which Pastor raises an eyebrow, but doesn't speak. Damian assures him that it is not a physical friendship, but one that is emotionally intelligent and intimate because they share their lives, their past, their fears, their trauma openly without judgment. That he had no intention of jeopardizing his program.

Damian begins to weep. "Pastor, I didn't mean to fall in love with her. I promise you I didn't. She was different. Real. Funny. Warm. All the things," he says wiping his face.

"What happened, Damian? Did you slip, Son?" he asks cautiously.

Damian looks him in the eye. "No, Sir… I mean we took a nap, but that was because she needed comfort – not sex," he says checking Pastor's expression and continuing.

"Anyway, today I went to her event at Howard University. She sponsors it every year, so she invited me to see how it is run in case I want to hire a youth next year. So, she and I are talking and sharing a laugh when this man walks up who says he recognizes me."

Damian choked back a sob he felt building in his throat.

"So, this man tells me I look just like my father. Needless to say, he reveals to both Zee and me that *I'm* D.J. and then I realize *she* is Zo-Zo… the little girl that I molested for seven years."

Damian couldn't hold it any longer. He bent over to his knees and sobbed uncontrollably.

Pastor Hayden doesn't display his shock. He just lets that truth rest in the room. For both of them. He knows Damian's story. He knows how Damian came to be sexually active as a young boy and how he engaged in sexual intercourse with a little girl who he grew to love even at a young age.

Through muffled sobs, Damian cries… "I didn't know it was her… I didn't know… what have I done? Pastor, what have I done…?"

Pastor Hayden tries to console him as best he could, but realizes this is something that Damian has to resolve internally. Alone.

After about an hour of divulging his truth, Damian looks at Pastor Hayden with a puffy face, lips still trembling. Chest heaving for a clean breath.

Pastor Hayden speaks up softly. "You say you love her. What do you think this means for you? What did you think this would lead to, Damian?"

Damian just shrugs his shoulders and wipes his face as the tears had begun to flow again.

"I don't know, Pastor. She's in my soul. It's like she never left." He sniffs. "What are my options? Like, with the Anchor Program?"

Pastor leans back in the chair and puts his two index fingers to his lips to consider Damian's predicament and question. He takes about five minutes to ponder while Damian sits in silence, legs shaking and wringing his hands.

"How long have you been in the program, Damian?" he asks purposefully.

Damian thinks about it. "Almost 12 years, I think. I came in at 21."

Pastor hesitates. "Let me talk to your sponsor for your options. I believe you have to be in the program for 10 years and then you can be released on probation. But let me confirm."

Damian sat up in his chair, hope washing over his face. "Would you do that, please, Sir?"

"I'll do that for you, Son. You've put in the work on so many levels but let me make sure before we come up with a plan. That fair?"

"Yes, Sir… that's fair," Damian said almost smiling, but still wiping tears from his face.

They both rise and embrace. Mentor and mentee. Father and son. Encouragement. Strength. Comfort. Possibilities.

Damian is able to drive home, but he still has to face the reality that he is in love with the little girl he damaged so long ago.

He doesn't know how to reconcile that, but he must. Somehow.

Can I love her and heal her wounds at the same time?
I'm going to try with all that I am.

Chapter Forty-Three

Zora rolls over and winces at the rise of a new day. She feels like she has a hangover although she didn't drink anything yesterday. *Maybe I should have had a drink.*

Can this day bring her any comfort? Anything that can erase the earthquake that happened yesterday? She wishes she could discard it and the weight that came with it. Too much to carry. Too much to accept. Just too much of everything.

Uggggh!

She needs a run! She leaps out of the bed and prepares herself for the day to smack her alive. Out of the door and onto the street, Zora takes her usual route, hoping to clear her head. She is in a mental fog. An emotional crash. She needs to regroup. Recover. Somehow, she lost confidence in everything she thought she knew about herself. About her judgment. About her clarity and discernment of all things true. She can't quiet the sentence that blew everything out of the water for her: *"This is D.J."* What is she supposed to do with that?

She runs harder to fight against the reality that slapped her life into a tornadic spin. She feels tightness in her chest. Her mind is starting to race along with her heartbeat. As she makes her final turn towards home, The Cathedral of St. Matthew comes into view. She slows her pace then jogs in place before she heads towards the church and up the steps. Before she realizes, she has entered the church and requested an on-the-spot confession session. The staff member led her to the vacant confessional where she waited for the priest who is available at the moment.

The little door opens, the priest obscured, he speaks:

"May God, who has enlightened every heart, help you to know your sins and trust in his mercy. May the Lord be in your heart and on your lips, that you may rightly confess your sins."

Zora clears her throat and speaks in her Korean accent:

"Bless me, Father, for I have sinned. It has been 5 weeks since my last confession. These are my sins: I have fallen consistently into my addiction, especially over this last weekend. I am harboring resentment and shame, not just for my sin, but for coming face-to-face with someone who hurt me in my past."

The priest walks Zora through the regular steps of confession and the assignment of a number of Hail Mary's – although Zora hasn't been consistent with the last set of assigned Hail Mary's. *I think I only did the last set once.*

She leaves the confessional without looking back.

***

Back home, she showers and dresses in something light. A lime green two-piece terry shorts set. It's going to be a hot day. Not to mention Family Dinner is at 4 p.m. today.

She opts to stay in the house, at least until dinner. She needs refuge. She needs comfort. She needs closure.

She makes herself a piece of avocado toast and a sliced peach and eats it standing at the kitchen island. She makes a cup of Chai tea and settles onto her chaise and sips slowly. Her mind is all over the place. She no longer felt safe. Betrayal announced by exposure she didn't ask for. Betrayal she didn't need.

She rests her tea on her lap and closed her eyes. Processing. That's all she can do. Process. What does all this mean? She's exhausted just considering everything. Her phone rings, but she ignores it. She doesn't want to talk to anyone. Not right now. The phone rang again and then a third call came in.

Notifications. Voicemail. Text message.

Another call interrupts her peace. She reaches for the phone and tries to hide her frustration.

"Hello?"

"Hi, Zora daughter," her mother says. "Are you okay? I called you earlier."

"I'm sorry, Mommy, I was resting. The event took a lot out of me, but I'm good."

"Just making sure you're coming to dinner," she says warmly. "I need you to bring some dessert. I'm thinking Soboro-ppang… you know I love that soft bun with the crunchy, peanut butter topping," she says with a chuckle.

Zora smiles at the memory of that bread. "Yes, Mommy, I'll stop and pick some up on the way. See you soon. Love you," she says hurriedly.

The call ended, and Zora checked her voicemail and text messages.

Voicemail from Mom. Texts from the Besties. She sends a quick response to the group text letting them know that she is just laying low today. She doesn't feel much like talking. The Besties text back "We understand… Rest, Sis… We're here if you need anything… We love you…" She smiled at the warm sentiments but just needed some space.

She checks the time. She needs to get dressed so that she has time to get to the Korean market before heading to her parents' house.

She dresses in a powder blue romper with flat silver sandals. Nothing fancy. Not even close to the "family ready" image she typically presents. *Oh, well, this will have to do.* She's not up to pretense today. This is what they get.

***

Zora arrives at her parents' house and falls into the regular routine of smelling what her mother is stirring. Greeting her father. Asking if there's anything she can do as she puts the Soboro-ppang down on the island. Her mood is subdued. Quiet.

The doorbell rings and in flows Marcus, Amri, and Chae. The usual suspects for family dinner. The host that brings balance to the undercurrent of tension that is ever-present between Zora and her father as well as her mother who doesn't do much to address it. Everyone is greeted with a hug, smiles, and pleasantries. True to form, each one grabs something to bring to the table, each one chattering about this or that with a chuckle or a lilt of interest.

Seated at the table, everyone is about to serve themselves when the doorbell rings again. Mr. Holley offers to answer the door. When he returns to the dining room, company is with him. Unexpected company. Damian.

Zora nearly faints at the table, but she pinches herself under the table as a distraction tactic creating physical pain to avoid the emotional pain that just flooded her system.

She forces a smile as the others echo their greetings around the table. Damian catches her eye and tries not to react.

Mr. Holley speaks up. "This is D.J. one of my former mentees from way back in the day," he says with a face-wide grin.

Zora feels the pangs of that same reality she had as a child. Her father would have preferred a son. But *this* son? D.J.? Oh, he has no idea.

Damian takes a seat next to Mr. Holley. He's uncomfortable and Zora catches it. Conversation is easy flowing among the group, but Zora remains reserved. Not much to say. Chae notices.

"So, Zora, how many youths were hired yesterday?" she asks warmly.

Zora places her fork on her plate and shares that 50 were hired and that it would have been more if she had more employers at the event. She is hopeful for next year's event to bring in more.

That is all she had to offer. She's fighting the need to scream. Fighting internal panic. Fighting the need to fold herself under the table.

Then her mother chimes in.

"Zora, daughter, did you ask Reese to participate? He hasn't heard from you, and you missed his ceremony," she says with a bit of disappointment.

Zora inhaled and exhaled deeply and slowly. Damian takes note but says nothing. He's already proven that he is good at staying in the background.

"Mommy, we've already had the discussion about Reese," she says through clenched teeth and a smile. The group can feel the tension. She puts her fork down again with resolve.

"I love you, Mommy, but this is the last time I'm going to say this… I am not interested in Reese. I do not want a relationship. I do not want to get married. I do not want children," she says tears welling in her eyes.

Her mother responds. "I just don't understand why, Zora. I just…"

Zora interrupts her as respectfully as she can. "You want to know why, Mommy? Do you really want to know?" She takes a deep breath before speaking again.

"I don't want children because I don't want them to feel unseen and unprotected. I don't want children because I don't want them to be touched inappropriately like I was. I don't want…"

Marcus chimes in. "Maybe we should go. This is something perhaps you need to discuss as a family…"

Zora cuts in. "No, Uncle Marcus. You all are family and all of you need to know," she says with tears now flowing down her cheeks.

"I was molested from age five until I was 12 years old by the boys you brought into our home, Daddy. I was sexually active and enjoying it at the age of six. I was…"

"No, no… Stop it, Zora… Stop it… Don't say that," her mother says hysterically her hand covering her mouth.

"No, Mommy… It is true. I had to fight for Daddy's attention. I always felt he wanted a boy, but he had to settle for a daughter. I dealt with it, but those boys? Those boys gave me something Daddy didn't. They gave me attention…"

Mr. Holley speaks up. "Zora, I…"

"No, Daddy… I practically begged you to show me attention, affection, to love me like you did those boys on those teams, but I was always in the way… clearly not what you wanted…"

"That's not true, Zora… I always wanted you, I just…" he insisted through a trembling voice.

"You just what, Daddy… No, you preferred a son. I watched how you interacted with those boys. The joy on your face. The energy you gave to them. Energy I *never* received no matter how hard I tried to get you to see me, to love me like you loved them. Yes, you provided a home and the necessities. But the one thing I asked for… the *one thing* I begged for was love and attention that *never* came."

She wiped her face with her napkin. She had a captivated audience. All stunned but couldn't move or speak.

Zora is sobbing now. "I was left unprotected, Daddy. I was a little girl in a house with a bunch of strange boys, one in particular had sex with me regularly to the point that I fell in love with him… then I just had sex with any boy who let me coax him into it…"

Marcus reaches out to touch her shoulder, but she gently shakes him off. She looks at him lovingly, but her eyes also said, "let me finish." He understood the sign.

She choked back the tightness in her chest. "Imagine that… a little girl… enjoying sex… asking for sex…hoping for sex in the darkness… desiring sex before she knows what it meant… so now your grown daughter, the licensed clinical therapist, has been fighting through a sex addiction since she was 12. I'm a therapist who can't help myself."

Multiple gasps fill the room along with weeping, but she continued.

"That's right. I have sex every day, sometimes multiple times a day with different people that I meet. Some have become regulars. And, no, I'm not a prostitute, but my sex drive is insatiable. I crave sex all day. It rules me. I live within the pleasure of sex. Strange as it sounds, sex is safety for me. It has become a haven without commitment, without emotions. How does that happen? It happens when a little girl is introduced to sex when she just wanted the love of her father and the support of her mother, instead of the comment 'that's just how your father is. He loves you, daughter'." She quickly wipes her nose with her napkin and continues.

"Yes, I believe that my father loved me, but I needed more than provision and directives. I needed protection. I need acknowledgement. I needed to know that emotion was okay. That I was seen and that love was okay."

Mr. Holley covers his face with his hands and sobs, "I'm sorry… I'm so sorry… I didn't know… I didn't…"

Zora's mother appears to be in shock. Chae tries to comfort her with little response. Marcus and Amri just lean on one another with tears wetting their faces. Damian sits quietly like a fly on the wall, his own tears flowing, stomach churning, experiencing every emotion that Zora is emitting because *he knows* that he is the cause of all her pain. Reality hits differently. *I did this to her.*

Zora continues. "So, I live with an addiction that was bred from emotional abandonment and neglect. When I danced around longing for attention, I was told to sit down and be quiet. When I was afraid of the dark or storms, you told me to go back to bed or to get over it. When I wanted to be held, I was pushed away because you were busy. When I was crying, you told me no to, that emotion gained me nothing."

She takes in a trembling breath, closing her eyes. "Abandonment, neglect, dismissal, rejection – all of those things created a recipe for a yearning exposed too soon through molestation. They all culminated in unrelenting desire that seeks attention through reckless bouts of unquenchable desire, void of connection. Void of love. That's who I have become. That is my reality."

Zora turned her attention to her father and spoke from the depth of her pain.

"So, Daddy *all those sons*, the ones you loved so much… they stole your little girl's innocence. Their touch stole her trust. Her ability to understand love and intimacy. The sons you longed for created an appetite for the unimaginable life that I now live. A life of addiction and disconnection. A life of emotional fear. A fear of being wanted. A fear of abandonment and rejection."

She turns to her mother with loving eyes that leaked tears.

"So, Mommy… No, I don't want children that I don't know how to protect… that I don't know how to love… that I may inevitably abandon emotionally, scarring them with trauma they didn't ask for or deserve."

Zora wiped her face a final time, pushed her chair back, and stood slowly.

"I need to be excused. Please don't try to stop me. I need to be alone. I'm done talking."

Damian speaks up. "Zee, I can…"

Zora stops him with a raised hand. "D.J. don't…"

She called me D.J. instead of Damian.

He felt the sting in her words and accepted it knowing he deserved it… all of it.

Painful silence hovered. No words left to be said. Only weeping around the room.

Zora leaves without protest from the group. She drives home fighting every emotion that she has just released but also feeling lighter that her secret has been told to the one who was the cause of it all. Daddy issues led to addictive behavior that has disrupted everything she could have had, including love.

***

The Holley household was hollowed out by Zora's truth. Seth Holley expressing the weight of regret spawned by his emotional absence that shaped Zora's experience. Nun Holley devastated for not being more vocal about Zora's constant cry for her father's attention, making excuses rather than demanding adjustment. Marcus and Amri try to shed some light on what happened and let them know they are available to talk if needed. Chae hugs Nun and holds her as she weeps uncontrollably on her shoulder.

Eventually, the Holley house was empty. Just Seth and Nun sitting in the reality of human frailty and failure. They just hold one another and agree that they will need to accept what they allowed, but not without the pain of it. They also agree to go to counseling because they recognize they will need it to move forward as a couple and as parents.

***

Damian drives home on autopilot, Zora's words screaming within. The woman he loves is the *same* little girl he wounded all those years ago. He is deeply troubled by the impact of that truth. His mind is shrouded in guilt and shame. His spirit is in knots. He needs to talk with Zee, but he understands that she needs space right now. When she's ready, he will be ready. He just hopes she doesn't shut him out.

In the meantime, he needs to process everything. He presses the button on his steering wheel to call with Pastor Hayden. After two rings, the call connects. The two agree to meet within an hour to discuss Damian's options for release from the program. He must be able to love Zora freely. It is imperative.

After his meeting with Pastor Hayden, Damian does something risky. He sends Zora a text:

"Zee, we need to talk. It cannot wait. Please don't shut me out. Love, Damian."

Chapter Forty-Four

Driving home, Zora can feel the effects of a whirlwind of a day. She can barely feel the steering wheel in her hands or hear the city moving around her. Her head is still spinning from her decision to divulge her trauma during the family dinner. It may not have been the best time or place; or perhaps it *was* the perfect time or place. Either way, it had to be said. She has been carrying the weight of that wound far too long.

Ironically, she felt conflicted hoovering between feeling lighter – relieved – and carrying the weight of the world. It may not make sense to the average person, but to Zora it is as real as it gets. "My entire life hurts right now," she says in a whisper.

She exhales deeply and pushes the call button on her steering wheel. Dr. Hanson answers. Zora shares with her the events of the last two days – the revelation that D.J. is Damian and that she shared her secret life with her family. Dr. Hanson walks her through it so that Zora can process it before it gets too deeply embedded and she compartmentalizes it. She presents some thought-provoking scenarios and questions to which Zora acknowledges needs some consideration. They agree to an unscheduled video call in the morning before Zora's first client arrives. The call ends.

A text lights her dashboard. Damian. She doesn't have the strength to read it right now. Later. Much later. Zora stares at the road ahead of her as the rest of the world swirls around her. She feels like she's been living outside of herself for two days. She needs something to ground her.

When Zora arrives home, she heads upstairs to take a quick shower before reaching for her fixer phone. *I deserve this after the day I've had* she thinks to herself. She texts Shelton. They make plans and meet up for him to bend her over and thump away the noise in her head and her heart. He did his job well. VERY well. At least in that moment, he was successful, but afterwards, Zora can still feel the void of her reality while her vagina reminded her of what she needs to address. The questions that need to be answered. Clarity that must be provided for herself, not for anyone else.

Back home, she showers and puts on her lounger but remains in her bedroom. After about 15 minutes of silence, contending with her thoughts, she enters her inner closet once again. Not to become Skyy. But to stand in the presence of Skyy and ask herself if she can live without this part of her life. Can she truly live a monogamous life with a man? Can one man satisfy the hunger that constantly burns within her. Can one man quiet the addiction that has ruled her life for so long?

As she looks – turning slowly taking everything in – looking around at the rows of wigs perched on Styrofoam heads, the sexy clothes, the makeup, the shoes, all the things, she doesn't have the answers. She can feel the fear rising within. She slowly crumbles to the floor, covers her face, and weeps. *Is this all I'll ever be?*

After about an hour in the inner closet, she climbs into bed, pulls the covers to her chin, stares at the ceiling, and lets the tears run into her ears.

In the darkness, she whispers within herself. *Am I capable of being normal?*

Only time will tell.

***

Out of the door earlier than usual, Zora takes her run and returns home to get ready for her video session with Dr. Hanson. She really needs some guidance. Her world is tipping. Her existence feels foreign and she is not sure how to navigate all the truth, reality, emotions and everything that comes along with it.

After a 1-hour session with Dr. Hanson, Zora has some inner work to do to stand in who she was, who she is, and who she is becoming. Each individually indiscernible, but in desperate need of addressing.

The rest of her day goes as well as it could. Client issues, woes, trauma, all which Zora handles with care considering she's the same as they are. She is a wounded healer doing the best she can to help her clients to arrive at their best selves.

At the close of the workday, Zora retreats to her private home and orders dinner. While she waits on its delivery, she sends a group text to the Besties. Each is showing her love and expressing they are there for her and that they can't wait for their meet up this Friday. Nico's turn to pick the place. They share a few harmless jabs and jokes, each closing the conversation with an emoji relating to their last statement. Zora appreciates her circle of friends. She realizes that she would be an utter mess without them.

She notices the unread text from Damian and finally decides to read it: "Zee, we need to talk. It cannot wait. Please don't shut me out. Love, Damian."

She holds the phone to her chest and closes her eyes. She's not sure what to feel. She shakes her head trying to raddle her own thoughts.

She misses him. She's mad at him.

She wants to see him. She can't stand the sight of him.

She wants to touch him. She wants to slap him.

She wants to hate him. Dare she try to love him.

Thank God the doorbell rings pulling her out of her thoughts. In the kitchen she dips the Mediterranean dish into a separate bowl and grabs a glass of wine. Settled on her chaise, she slowly eats every bite and sips wine in between. She considers everything Dr. Hanson said. Everything she's afraid of. Everything beautiful. Everything devastating.

Everything that feels good. Everything that hurts. Everything dangerous. Everything safe. Everything that is uncertain. Everything that is comfortable and those things that are not. Old things. New things. All the things.

Her phone pings. She doesn't rush to check it. She doesn't want to be bothered. She keeps eating.

Ping. Ping.

She sighs heavily and reaches for her phone on the table next to her. A text. Damian. Again. She lays the phone face down and continues to eat. She's not sure she's ready to face Damian. She needs to, just not today!

The rest of the evening, she scrolls on social media, checks emails, and cleans up her dishes. She stands at the kitchen island, both hands planted in front of her, her head hanging between her shoulders, her eyes welling up with tears. She doesn't recognize herself and she's scared. After five minutes of unexpected tears, she wipes off the counter and wipes her face, then heads upstairs.

In her room she reaches for the fixer phone hoping to quiet the unfamiliar, but the phone in her hand rings.

Video call.

Damian.

Damn it.

She composes herself and connects the call as she plops on the bed. Damian's face comes into view and her stomach knots. Her throat tightens. He speaks.

"Hi, Zee," he says softly while his eyes search her face. "Why are you crying, sweetie?"

She just closes her eyes and shakes her head slowly, unable to speak.

"I know it's late and I know you've been avoiding me, but I really need to talk to you. We really need to talk, please," he says as gently as possible. "I understand how fragile the both of us are at the moment, but I need a way forward whatever that looks like."

Zora opens her eyes that are now wet from tears that have started to form. She wipes them with the back of her hand and clears her throat.

"Dami… D.J. … I…" she stammers.

"Zee, I'm still Damian. I'm still him…" he says in a whisper.

"Damian," she chokes out "I don't know what to say. I'm not sure what to…"

"Sweetie, we need to meet tomorrow. This can't wait another day. It will help both of us to move on, whatever that means." He pauses and takes in a deep breath.

"Can we meet tomorrow around 11 a.m.? We can meet somewhere neutral, but private. I just need to know if you want to do this. I know that I *need* to do this."

She looks at him with watery eyes. "Fine, Damian, we can meet but I make no promises."

"I'm not looking for any. I just need to clear things for myself and for you. That's it, Zee."

She clears her throat and speaks. "Let me check around for a place and I'll text you the address tomorrow. That fair?" she asks softly.

"That's fair," he says with a soft smile.

She felt the power of his smile, but she struggled to let it land internally. She wanted to fight against the nagging prompt to lean into his warmth.

The call ended. Both sit in silence in their individual locations. Zora makes a call to line up a meeting place.

Tomorrow will be here before they know it.

***

A later start than usual. 8:10 a.m. Zora wakes with her stomach doing flips like she just took the first drop on a mile-high roller coaster. The sun is shining outside, but it feels like a storm brewing within. Anxiety. Fear. Uncertainty. All make for a recipe for her wanting to back out of the meeting with Damian, but she knows it is necessary. Despite how she feels, she will persevere.

To untangle some of those feelings and to clear her mind, Zora takes her morning run. No podcast in her ear this time. She needs to listen to her thoughts. No one's suggestions. Not what is trending. Just her thoughts. Something she rarely engages fully. She often swallows her thoughts and cares for the needs of others. Not today. She needs to listen to what she needs for a change.

What do I want?
What do I need?
What is real and what isn't?
What makes me happy?
Where do I find joy, not just pleasure?

Is recovery a real option?
Is love possible?

These and other questions swim through her mind as she ponders each one to the degree that a 3-mile run can offer. More time will be required, but this is a starting point.

***

Back home and showered, Zora ate her breakfast more slowly than usual. Maple Brown Sugar oatmeal topped with granola and a side of chopped strawberries. Each bite an opportunity to consider her life. She ate so slowly her oatmeal had to be reheated.

Dishes washed, she heads upstairs to get dressed. A cream wide-legged capri duo, printed with pink and yellow accents. Cream Sketcher sneakers and gold jewelry. Light makeup and a bronze lipstick. It is 92 degrees today, so she opts for a high loose ponytail to keep her hair off her neck.

10:15 a.m. she texts Damian the address. Nico offered his studio office since he won't be there until the evening.

Zora heads inside and paces nervously until she hears the doorbell chime. She adjusts her composure and steps out to greet Damian, who is holding two smoothies: Strawberry Kiwi and Mango. She smiled despite herself as she welcomed him in. They settle into the small office and close the door. They sit on the office couch and sit in silence for a moment, both taking a nervous sip of their smoothies. Damian clears his throat and speaks first.

"You look beautiful, Zee," he says with a warm smile. "Thank you for agreeing to see me. I know this is awkward, but it bares attention so that we can better understand how to move forward, whatever that means."

Zora looks at him warmly but doesn't speak. Damian continues.

"Without rehashing what we already know, I need you to know that I didn't abandon you, Zee. At least not intentionally. You were my best friend. My first girlfriend, if you will. My father died when I was 15 and social services pulled me into foster care because I was still a minor. I had no living parents and no other relatives wanted to take me in. So, what you deemed abandonment was really me being forced to live with people I didn't know. I bounced from one foster family to the next because I was angry. I was a menace to others and myself. I was drowning in my own sexual addiction, and most people didn't want me in their homes. That spawned me constantly getting into trouble and I ended up in juvenile detention more times than I can remember.

Pastor Hayden, who became my mentor at 16 and who is still my mentor today, was there through it all. When I was facing prison time for the sexual assault, it was Pastor Hayden that offered the Anchor Project. That project forced me to look at myself, my history, my trauma. It made me accountable and responsible for my actions. Consequently, I had to commit to the 10-year process, which included being assigned to a sponsor and a priest, who I had to partner with at a local church. That partnership fostered me going to seminary and eventually growing my faith. Don't get me wrong, that part of the program centered me, but it is not my intention to remain an adjunct priest…"

Zora gasped. "You're… you're a priest? OMG…Were you part of confession?"

Damian reached for her hand. "Yes and no. I went through the process like a priest as part of the program, but I know that's not my calling so to speak." He checks her face, which softened a bit before he continued. "I did perform confession, but we don't know who the penitent is. Everything is anonymous."

She sighed. "I've gone to confession a few times this summer. I hope you weren't *my* priest," she says with a giggle. Damian chuckles back but returns to the conversation at hand.

"Zee, I need you to know I'm not that little boy. I'm not D.J. anymore. I don't think like him. I don't act like him or respond like him. I don't even desire like him. I was a little boy, and I unknowingly, unintentionally pulled you into my personal pain and trauma without understanding how that would affect you. I've carried that all my adult life, not knowing what happened to you as a result of what happened."

He tried to choke back his emotions, but not without his eyes welling with tears.

"Sweetheart, I need you to know… please hear my heart… I need you to know that I've grown into a man. A real man. A responsible man. An accountable man. A man who is more aware, tender, and emotionally intelligent than I ever imagined was possible for a guy like me. A man who is clear on who he is despite my past mistakes. It took me years to forgive myself for acting out of what was done to me and how I transferred that to you. My experience… our experience has made me vulnerable on so many levels; empathetic and more grounded. Zee, I've grown so much… I've grown into the man you met at Spelman, the man that has come to cherish what we have been curating the last several months. The man who has fallen in love with the woman you are today. All of that woman. The woman I fell in love with before I knew you were the little girl from my past. The beautiful woman you have become and who has spent her life using the wound I created to help others. Zee, I've become a man who owns everything he has done and is extremely careful with what he does now. A man who leans more into wisdom than reacting or acting out of self-preservation."

He acknowledges that Zora has been crying while he was talking. He tenderly wipes her face with the back of his hand. She doesn't stop him but rests her face against his hand. She looks at him with tender eyes.

"I am not here to ask you for anything you're not ready for. I want to respect where you are. Your boundaries. Your truth. But I am here to let you know that I am desperately in love with you and no matter what happens from here, I need you to know that. To feel that."

He lifts her hands and kisses them softly, his tears dripping onto her knuckles. He looks at her with a half-smile. "Your turn…"

They are both silent for a while. Sipping their smoothies to fill the moment. Zora shifts on the couch and leans in to speak after lightly clearing her throat.

"Damian… I… What happened then… what you did to me back then… I won't lie; it scarred me deeply. I loved you, and as unusual as most would consider it, I really did. You were my first everything. You were my everything. When you left, I thought you didn't love me anymore. I thought I did something to make you mad at me. I didn't know where to put those feelings so I just turned to pleasure from others hoping you would find out and come back to me. But when you didn't, I was already addicted to sex and I still am, as you know.

No amount of sex can change what happened to me. I am who I am now because of that experience. Because of you. I didn't know you did what you did because you were living with trauma. How was I to know that? I wouldn't know that."

Zora wipes her tears.

"You crashed into my world, Damian. You did something I never thought possible. You hijacked a part of me. You pulled me into your sphere, into your heart without me knowing you were D.J. *That* D.J."

She begins to sob and Damian reaches for her, but she gently pulls away.

"I can't deny what we started since meeting at Spelman. I can't deny how we care for one another, how we move around one another. I can't deny what my heart is whispering while the rest of me is screaming 'don't do it… don't fall for it' despite the truth. I can't do anything about D.J., but I can do something about you, Damian. The more we engaged in one another's lives, I hate to admit it, but I fell in love with the man who showed up without knowing who I was. The man who wants to love me knowing who I am now. A sex addict."

She touches his face softly.

"Damian, I honestly don't know how to do this – whatever *this* is – but I'm open to considering it. I'm not promising you that Skyy won't invade our space. I am not promising you that I won't want to quit or flake out on you because of fear. I do promise that I will continue going to therapy to work on me. Just know that I have to do it at my pace, so it will require patience on your part. I can't promise you the end of Skyy, when she will disappear, if at all."

She chokes back a sob. "I don't know the future, Damian, but I won't deny myself the opportunity to see what that looks like for me. Possibly for us."

Damian pulls her hands to his chest and closes his eyes as they flow with tears. They sit in silence that feels like agreement. Accepting one another without concrete answers. Without pressure. They can feel progressive trust formulating sustainable choices whatever that looks like. In the quiet of the room, just the sound of the mini-split air conditioner humming in the background, they just look at one another, saying everything without saying anything.

After about two hours, Damian walks Zora to her car. He gently brushes a lock of hair from her face with a warm smile. He leans down and kisses her softly on her cheek. She turns and sweetly kisses him on the lips. He doesn't force anything more. He rests his forehead on hers and both close their eyes.

He whispers, "Whenever you're ready, Zee, I'm here. I'll always be here."

She whispers back, "Thank you, Damian. Thank you."

They part ways, both soaking in what they discussed and holding it as hope, possibility, but only time will tell.

Chapter Forty-Five

Friday 4:35 p.m. Zora exhales deeply. It has been an arduous week. An emotionally and mentally draining week taking care of clients and herself. She is still combing through her conversation with Dr. Hanson, herself, and Damian. All carry their own weight and the need for review, consideration, adjustment, and action by Zora. She's uncomfortable. Skyy has been on the move almost every day. But today, she gets to relax with her Besties. Nico's choice.

Nico opted for movie night at his house, which was a welcome change from them being in the thick of DMV nightlife. The four friends watched a comedy, ate popcorn, drank light libations, talked and just chilled. It was restorative. They all needed it with each of their lives in constant motion. The night ended with the usual hugs and giggles.

***

Saturday brings relief from being able to sleep in late. Zora stared at the ceiling as the sun peeked through her drapes. Nothing much on her calendar except to meet Lai to get some shopping done in preparation for a Korean celebration in two and a half weeks. She jerks herself out of the bed and heads for the bathroom for a shower. She then texts Lai to confirm they will meet in China Town at 11:30 a.m.

Dressed as cool as they can, the two women stroll through the streets of China Town visiting small shops to collect decorations, trinkets, and such. The two enjoyed the day, something they both needed to take away some of the pressure both have been enduring of late. Zora packed all of the items in her car and the two went to lunch. As they walked, Lai notices a group of clergymen seated at an outside restaurant patio. She acknowledges them.

"Father Luca, it's great to see you," she says excitedly. "My mother was asking about you the other day. She didn't see you in Mass last week."

The three men greet her, and Zora's eyes meet those of Father Luca. Damian. She doesn't react openly, but it was weird to see him dressed in a priest's collar. She smiles lightly and composes herself as Lai chats with the men. Neither Zora nor Damian let on that they know one another. One priest speaks up exuberantly.

"We're here celebrating Father Luca. He has finally completed his program with us and will be moving on to other life's passions," he says as he slaps Damian lightly on his back.

Congratulations are exchanged and the ladies make their way to their lunch destination. Zora is noticeably quiet and Lai notices.

"Z, you okay?" she says looking over her menu.

Zora swallows slightly. "I guess the heat is getting to me and I'm famished," she offers to cover for herself and not to put Father Luca, i.e., Damian, on blast. Lai and the Besties know about D.J. being Damian. They have no idea he's also a priest. She's only learned about that part of Damian's life earlier this week and she is still trying to reconcile it with the man who has exposed something she never dreamed. Emotions.

The ladies finish their lunch and part ways with a hug and a wave. Tomorrow is family dinner and Zora needs to process how that will be since her emotional admission a week ago.

The rest of the evening, Zora mindlessly scrolls on social media, texts with her Besties and has a video call with Damian, which has become one of her favorite things these days. He was just checking in on her since their talk earlier in the week. They didn't talk long, but it was long enough to make an impression.

Zora went to bed with a smile and tears at the same time.

Conflicted and processing. Comforted and scared. Considering and uncertain.

***

Sunday shows up with rain showers. Zora lays in the bed listening to the sound of rain hitting her windows. It's rhythmic. Soothing. She's not sure how long she was laying there, but it was cathartic. Each drop gave way to easier breathing. Lower anxiety. Some level of safety. Clarity.

She eats a light breakfast. A favorite go-to. Two pieces of avocado toast and green grapes. She tops it off with the infamous cup of Chai tea as she catches up on the news on CNN. She notes "Same ole same ole."

To fill her day until dinner, Zora goes to her private office to get a little work done. She turns on the sound machine, which pairs well with the rain outside, and lights her sage and lavender candles. She takes her time and sorts through client files and organizes those who have progressed from those who are stuck and those who are new to her practice. She compiles her statistical data from the year up to the end of July. She loses herself in her work for hours. She was in her happy place. Helping others. She felt productive. Accomplished. She checks the time and shuts down her laptop and heads upstairs to shower.

It's 2:15 p.m. Zora dresses in a lightweight denim-looking sundress with silver sequin detailing sprinkled on the upper bodice. She pairs it with silver flat sandals, silver hoop earrings, and light makeup.

***

The drive to her parents' house has her nauseous. She's not good with confrontation even if she started it. She knows that there may be questions. Ready or not, she will face them head on.

She pulls into their driveway and sits in the car for a moment. She can feel her mouth getting dry. Her heart is racing and she can feel perspiration forming down her back despite her car A/C being on full blast.

Slow breathing. In 1-2-3-4-5. Out 5-4-3-2-1. Repeat.

She gets up the nerve to ring the doorbell but uses her key to enter. The house smells delicious as always. Just her parents are in the kitchen at the moment. She walks into the kitchen and her parents pause. Zora smiles lightly and approaches her mother, embracing her with a hug that says, "It's okay." She can feel her mother's shoulders shutter as she begins to weep against her chest. Zora leaves space for her mother to do what she needs to do. After a while, her mother looks at her with a wet face.

"I love you, daughter, and I'm sorry… I…" she says as he voice cracks.

"I love you, too, Mommy… I really do."

Her father leaned against the counter with his hands in his pockets and tears streaming down his face. Zora understands how difficult emotion is for her father. She got that trait from him. But she walks over to him, and he folds her into his chest. He sobs into her head, and she just gives him the time he needs. He has pinned up his emotions so long, she doesn't stop him.

When he felt safe enough to release her, he whispers against her hair, "I'm sorry, baby girl. I'm so, so sorry…"

She looks at him warmly. "I know Daddy… I know…"

The doorbell interrupts the family moment. Marcus and Amri come through with Chae in toe, each carrying something for the meal. They each greet Zora lovingly as they pass their wares to Nun and Seth.

Everyone gathers around the dining room table, seated in their usual chairs. The room is quiet, but it is saying so much. It feels like quiet courage forging healing. Zora pushes her chair back, stands and speaks up warmly.

"First and foremost, I want to apologize for last week's emotional dump. I'm not apologizing for what I said, but how things came to light. I could have timed it better, but it happened the way that it did because it needed to. I wasn't in control and that is what made it more real for all of us."

She looked around the table. "I never want to hurt anyone that I love, but I've been hurting myself all these years and I needed to let you all into my world so you could better understand why marriage and family are not at the top of my list. Who stole my innocence is irrelevant. I'm not fully healed but I'm growing in that direction. I'm taking my personal therapy more seriously." She fights back tears but can see that everyone else isn't.

"I just ask that you love me for who I am. Flaws and all. I don't want pity. What happened, happened. I understand – and we each much realize – that trauma has fractured all of us in varying degrees, but love and acceptance are the healing properties going forward."

She wipes a tear that escaped her eye. "That's all I have to say other than I love each of you so very much." She quietly takes her seat and looks at her father with a warm smile.

Everyone around the room shared their love and support for Zora one by one. It was an emotional family moment. Dinner was delicious as usual. Dessert was devoured with joy. Laughter rose again around the table. Conversation was rich with wisdom and encouragement.

Family dinner ended on a much lighter note. Zora drove home feeling more loved than she could imagine.

***

Two weeks have passed since Zora and Damian talked about everything. Life has been a little unrecognizable to Zora. She's not as frantic or anxious as usual. She notices that she is more present. More aware of herself, her surroundings, her truth. She continues to struggle with her pain and addiction. Skyy is still alive and active, but Zora is trying to better navigate her constant sexual urges. Some days she wins. Other days she is sold out to sexual pleasure – often more than once a day.

One particular day, Zora transforms into Skyy and is headed out of the door when her doorbell rings.

"Who can be ringing my door without an invitation?" She huffs as she pouts heading towards the door.

She swings the door open. She gasps.

Damian is standing on her front steps with a gift basket in his hands. He's smiling at her, but he is also taking in her attire. He can clearly see that she is headed out on a fix. Zora feels embarrassed but asks him to come in quickly as she looks up and down her street for nosey neighbors.

She leans against the door and looks at Damian expecting him to judge her. He doesn't.

"What are you doing here, Damian? I was on my way out…" she says timidly.

He kisses her cheek softly. "I can see that," he says softly not breaking his stare with her eyes.

He extends his arms and hands her the gift basket full of some of her favorite things.

"What's this, Damian?" she says as she admires it like a child in a candy store.

She heads into the kitchen and Damian follows. She places the beautiful basket on the kitchen island and begins to unwrap the gold cellophane and ribbon. She's giddy as she peels it open to find a bunch of grapes, a couple of avocados, Chai tea boxes, Ferro Roche candy, a single-serve bottle of white wine, jellybeans, and small paper hearts sprinkled throughout.

She looks at Damian with watery eyes. "Why did you do this? I didn't do anything to…"

He interrupts her. "Zee, you don't have to *do anything* for me to think about you, for me to shower you with love on all levels."

"This is beautiful, Damian. You're too good to me," she says as she reaches up and gives him a gentle kiss and patting at her face careful not to smear her makeup.

He watches her carefully. She looks at him as if ashamed. He reassures her.

"I'm not here to stop you, Baby. If you have to go, then go. But if you want to stay, I'm here. I want you to always know that I see you and I love you. You don't have to disappear into the person of Skyy." He touches her face tenderly. "Call me when you get back in so that I'll know you're safe."

Zora stands there dumbfounded. "You mean to tell me you know I'm going to get fixed, and you are not going to fight me on it? Who does that? Why do you love me so much," she says tears welling in her eyes.

He puts his finger to her lips. "Shhhh… Don't ruin your makeup. Do whatever you have to do. I love you." He kisses her lips softly and lets himself out the front door.

If it weren't for the sexual furnace edging her on, she would not go, but her fixer is waiting for her.

Zora drives to the rendezvous place to meet Milo, who is what she needs today. At least that is what she *thinks* she needs. The entire time Milo has her bent over and is thrusting her so good and she is thoroughly enjoying him – as always – her mind flashes to Damian's face over and over and over. She almost stops Milo mid-thrust, but she is not about to leave without being fully pleased herself. When the fix was over, she thanked Milo and was on her way.

***

The ride home was different. Zora was more confused. She is usually smiling ear to ear after being with Milo, but not today. She is deep in thought. She had an "aha" moment.

Milo doesn't see her and it was never an issue until now. She was content with her fixers just "doing her," not seeing her.

Why is this bothering me now?

Skyy doesn't care if they see me or not.

In the silence of the ride, Zora recalls something Dr. Hanson said at her last session:

"Your addiction has been a survival tactic that has kept anything that resembles love and commitment away. For you, love equates pain, abandonment. Commitment equates to something clean and tidy, existing inside a perfect place. Consider the fact that love doesn't need or demand perfection. As terrifying and as real as love is and can be, it just wants to be chosen and accepted. Give yourself a chance to see what love looks like for you. Meaning experience love living outside performance or hiding behind surface desire. Think about that, Zora. Give yourself the gift of love."

Zora filters Dr. Hanson's words and processes them carefully.

Does she really deserve love?

Is she even capable of receiving or giving love?

***

Back home and after taking a shower, Zora makes herself a cup of tea and takes her usual place on the chaise. Holding the cup with both hands, she allows the steam to lap at her skin. It was soothing. Her senses engaged. Her emotions bubbling to the surface. She weeps into her tea as she sips it slowly. Her thoughts drift to Damian.

Shoot. I forgot to call him.

She wipes her face and composes herself before she dials him. The call connects and she puts on a smile she hopes will camouflage the fact that she had been crying.

His face comes on screen. "Hi, Damian… I made it home," she says with a smile that would cause a flower to bloom in the middle of a storm.

He looks at her. "Glad you made it home. Why have you been crying, Zee? Talk to me…"

Damn it. He doesn't miss a thing.

"I'm fine," she responds, but he's not convinced.

"Sweetheart, you know I see through you. You can't hide from me. I see you, remember," he says warmly.

"Yes, you do… I don't like it, but you do," she says with a chuckle to lighten the moment.

He chuckles back. "Well, I'm glad you're home safe. Lock up tight. I'd like to see you in a day or so. Is that possible? At your house, perhaps?" he asks holding his stare.

Zora sighs lightly. "Sure, Damian, that's possible. How about Thursday around 6 p.m.? I'll have dinner for us."

"Perfect," he says with a smile. "Have a good night, Zee. See you soon."

The call ended, leaving Zora to her thoughts. She doesn't fight them. She embraces them and then engages them. She needs internal acceptance of everything so she can have a clearer path forward for her own sake.

***

Thursday, 5:00 p.m. Zora puts the turkey steaks in the oven for 40-minutes. "It is too hot for oven food," she thinks to herself. She rinses the vegetables in preparation for them to be steamed and she puts the red Russet potatoes on boil. She chuckles aloud. "When did I ever cook for a man? Never."

She heads upstairs and takes a quick shower and dresses in a sunflower maxi sundress and yellow flipflops. Her makeup light, and a bronze lip gloss. A dash of her favorite lavender body spray and her hair hanging in soft curls over her shoulders.

Back in the kitchen, she puts the vegetables in the bamboo steamer. She puts the Russet potatoes in a bowl and garnishes them with rosemary, garlic, and complimentary spices.

The doorbell rings. Damian.

She adjusts herself, conscious that she is nervous more than she's ever been with him before. She opens the door and invites him in.

"WOW!" he says with a wide smile. He leans in and kisses her cheek. "You look beautiful and something smells amazing," he says peering in the direction of the kitchen.

She giggles. "It's almost ready. Five more minutes," she says stirring the vegetables and pulling the turkey steaks from the oven so they can rest, keeping the juices intact.

"You thirsty? Help yourself to the bar or the refrigerator. I have juice, lemonade, water…"

He comes into the kitchen taking it in and seeing her imprint through the décor. Classy, but understated. He reaches for the refrigerator and pulls out bottled water.

Dinner is served and they settle in at the dining room table; a place Zora hardly ever uses. They talked about what's been happening over the last two weeks, they laughed and made jabs at one another. It felt so natural. Familiar. Safe. Scary. All at the same time.

They clear the table and Damian helps her load the dishwasher and put away the food. Standing so close to him Zora can feel his heat, but not in a sensual way. The warmth of his presence. The way she would feel when they were together at the condo before she rented it out. She liked the way they moved around one another. A dance of sorts. Coordinated just by them, for them.

He felt it, too, but he just let it ride internally. He doesn't want to force his presence on her although he would rather be with her than anywhere else. Throughout the evening, they exchange tender looks, shy eyes, blushing moments.

They retreated to the living room with a light dessert; chocolate pudding parfait topped with whipped cream and granola. Zora sits on her chaise, but Damian shifts her preference. He takes her by her hand and guides her to the sofa to sit with him. She rarely sits there. The perspective is different.

Damian pulls Zora close to him, and he wraps his arms around her. No words. Just security. No expectations. Just living in the moment. She leans against him and he rests his chin on her shoulder breathing her in. Her scent. Her presence. Her touch. She breaks the silence first.

"Damian…" she says softly. "Thank you for joining me for dinner… for being here with me tonight. I…"

He gently lifts her from behind and turns her towards him. "Zee," he says cupping her face, "there is no place I want to be tonight… or ever, if I'm honest," he says lightly kissing her cheek.

She looks at him differently than before. She almost looks into him and he can feel it. She is boring into his soul, searching, seeking for something to be wrong with him.

"Who you see… This is who I am, Zee… This is the man you get, if you want me," he says whispering.

She leans in and kisses him softly on the lips. He accepts it. They allow the kiss to be what it is, to do what it can do. It ignites. Zora turns around to him fully and wraps her arms around his neck and pulls herself into him. He soaks her in until she shifts and stops kissing him. He didn't question her. He didn't fight her to continue. He wants Zora to be in control of what they are slowly becoming.

She rises and reaches out her hand to him. He looks at her curiously but gives her his hand and he rises to his feet. She leads him towards the stairs. He pauses.

"Zee… Where are you going?"

She turns and puts her finger to his lips. "Shhhhhh… Just follow me," she says with a warm smile.

She leads him into her bedroom and she kisses him tenderly, pulling him into her in a way she's never done before. He breaks the kiss and looks into her eyes.

"Make love to me, Damian," she asks with tears in her eyes. "I want to know what it is like to make love again."

He kisses her softly and rests his forehead on hers. He pulls away and consents. "If that is what you want, Zee…"

"I do…" she says softly as she begins to peel the straps of her sundress off her shoulders. Damian takes over and begins to undress her like a delicate flower. She has never experienced this type of care and attention, so she is letting him take the lead.

He kisses each of her shoulders and down her arms and she inhales with each touch of his lips on her skin. Her dress falls to the floor and he removes her bra, leaning in to kiss her collar bone and her chest, careful not to touch her breasts yet. Zora can feel herself shuttering. Damian notices.

"You okay, Baby? You want me to stop?"

"No, I'm okay. This is just new. Don't stop…" she whispers.

Eventually, she is standing before him fully exposed. Naked. Flawless. She feels like she is on display. She's never been so exposed in front of a man. She feels her vulnerability. She feels like running, but she opts to stay and take the journey with him.

Damian removes his own clothes. Not hurriedly like a man about to devour her. No, he does it slowly so that she can watch his body be revealed piece by piece. Her eyes widened at the sight of him. All of him from head to toe. Chocolate, but not too dark. Lean and muscular. Hairy in the right places. Beautifully endowed. She covers her mouth like someone who has been caught with their hand in the cookie jar.

Damian lifts her and lays her on the bed. She hesitates. He looks at her questioningly.

"Damian…I… I have never made love in a bed," she says almost embarrassed. "I've only had sex from behind, fully clothed, no panties, hair in my face… I…"

He gently reassured her. "I will not allow you feel like just a piece of meat. I want to look at you while I make love to you. I want to see you. I want you to see me…"

With that, he lay next to her and caressed her skin. She shivered at his touch. He used his fingers and stroked her arms, her stomach, her breasts, her hips and thighs. He kissed her body softly. He kissed her breasts and nibbled her nipples. Her body responded. She was covered in goosebumps. She gasped with each touch, each kiss.

He kissed her passionately, but softly. He didn't want to rush, but she begged for him.

"Make love to me, Damian… I want to know you as the man you are…"

He kissed her again and lightly mounted her. She spread her legs to receive him. He touched her vagina and remembered how she felt those months ago. He looked at her as if to ask, "Let me taste you…" She closed her eyes and he took her in his mouth. Lovingly, he caressed her lips with his tongue as she grabbed his head and slowly moved her hips in response to the movement of his mouth.

"I want you, Damian… Please, Baby…" she said softly.

"You have a condom?" he asks.

"I don't want one with you. I want to feel the real you inside me..." she says longingly.

He crawls slowly up to meet her, looking at her tenderly in the eyes. Positioning his penis near her moist vagina, he takes his time and pushes himself inside. Tiny, slow strokes until he is fully emersed inside. She gasps with each stroke. She is almost beside herself, having never had a man take such good care of her, never having a man not treat her like a dumping station (although that's what she allowed as Skyy).

She moves her hips in rhythm with him, both moaning in response to what their bodies are feeling. No rushing. Nothing to prove. She wraps her legs around his waist, and he gives himself to her in a way that she is almost at a scream. He kisses her the whole time and talks to her lovingly. She is holding on to him like it is the last time she will see him. She is softly calling out his name as he gives her deep slow strokes that feel like he is writing his name inside her walls. He is whispering her name in her ear, and it drives her crazy.

She tries to speed things up and get wild with it, but he whispers, "You don't need Skyy with me. Take your time, Baby... take your time..." She adjusts her speed and enjoys the journey.

After almost an hour, she can feel him stiffening. She doesn't stop him. They both climax together. Ecstasy realized.

A grown woman.

A grown man.

An enrapturing experience.

A chosen love.

Both Zora and Damian lay in one another's arms in silence. No darkness in the room. A light illuminates the moisture clinging to their skin. Breathing slowing. Embrace tightened. Security. Trust realized.

Zora runs her fingers through the hair on Damian's chest as she nestles her head in the crook of his armpit. He kisses the top of her head. She speaks softly.

"Damian… I don't… I don't know what loving you will look like, but I know I'm done pretending that I don't."

He shifts a bit. "Look at me, Baby…" he says softly. She looks up at him.

"I have no rules or guidance at the moment. I just want to love you, Zee. That's all. We can work out the details as we go, if that's what you need."

She lifts up onto her elbow and cups his face. "I want to try… love that is… loving you, Damian. You were the last person I loved, and my heart has been pulled back into your sphere to complete the circle… close the gap. I don't want to run anymore."

"I feel the same. You were the last person I truly loved and I love you still… more so now than ever."

She playfully pokes him in the chest. "You keep making love to me like you just did, I may be convinced to keep you around long term," she says giggling.

He laughs back and pats her butt. "This is who you get. This is me, Zee. I'm patient." He lightly kisses her face.

"You keep letting me in, I'll be here to love you. Whenever you're ready, I'll be right here. I'm not going anywhere."

"How can you be so sure, Damian? How do you know we can really work?" she asks quietly.

He looks at her eye to eye. "Because sacred secrets can never separate sacred souls."

With that Zora crawls on top of him and they make love again and all through the night.

The Closing Message:

Sacred secrets do not isolate sacred souls. Silence does.

Epilogue

Sacred Secrets was never about the secret itself.

Secrets are ordinary. Everyone has them. They are not special, not rare, not even particularly dangerous on their own. What gives a secret its power is not what it contains, but what it protects. And what it protects is usually not pleasure, not rebellion, not even desire. What it protects is fear.

This story is about what happens when truth finally enters the room and refuses to ask permission.

Truth does not arrive gently. It does not knock. It does not wait until people are ready. It comes when the body can no longer carry the weight of what has been hidden. It comes when coping mechanisms collapse under the strain of proximity. It comes when survival tactics are mistakened for identity for so long that they begin to erode the very self they were built to save.

Zora's story is not erotic. It is psychological realism. It is what compulsion looks like once agency has been eroded by trauma. It is what addiction becomes when it mutates under emotional intimacy. It is what happens when a person finally feels something real and is terrified by how destabilizing that feeling is.

Because connection is not always comforting.

Sometimes it is catastrophic.

Addiction promises relief. Connection demands presence. Addiction numbs. Intimacy exposes. Addiction allows the illusion of control. Love threatens it. That is why trauma survivors often cling to the very behaviors that are destroying them. Not because they are reckless. Not because they are immoral. But because addiction offers a predictable sanctuary when emotions feel like an uncharted cave.

In Zora's world, sex was never about pleasure alone. It was a remedy for loss. A way to regulate the nervous system when nothing else felt safe. A language learned before language existed. A form of reassurance when reassurance was never given. Her addiction did not begin as defiance. It began as adaptation.

And adaptation, when it is no longer needed, becomes a prison.

Confession did not cure her.

Revelation did not free her.

Exposure did not heal her.

Truth does not heal by itself.

Truth destabilizes.

When Zora spoke, the trauma did not scream. It exhaled. Years of holding breath finally released through her body, and what followed was not peace, but collapse. That is what real truth does. It ruptures reality. It dismantles the scaffolding that once kept the pain contained. It removes the lie of safety the secret provided and leaves the survivor standing in open air, exposed and shaking.

This is why healing is so often mistakened for breaking.

Trauma survivors are not afraid of pain. They have lived with pain their entire lives. What they are afraid of is loss of control. Of being flooded. Of being seen without armor. Of having their carefully constructed coping systems taken away before something sturdier can be built in their place.

Addiction destroys safety first. It convinces the person that they are only safe inside the behavior. It reframes survival as identity. It whispers that without the ritual, without the compulsion, without the dissociation, there will be nothing left.

Love threatens that narrative.

Love does not negotiate with addiction. It does not argue. It does not shame. It simply stands close enough to be felt. And proximity is dangerous to trauma. Because closeness collapses distance. And distance is where survival lives.

Zora did not spiral because she was weak. She spiraled because something truer than her addiction entered her life and her system did not know how to hold it. Her body misattributed relief to sex for so long that it could not immediately recognize connection as nourishment. Her nervous system reached for the familiar when the unfamiliar felt like death.

This is what re-traumatization looks like. Not a return to the original wound, but the collision of past and present. Two timelines crashing into each other without warning. The child who survived and the adult who loves suddenly occupying the same space.

And Damian's presence did not erase that collision.

Love does not erase trauma.

It absorbs it.

Damian did not save Zora. He did not cure her. He did not redeem the past. What he did was far more difficult. He stayed. He accepted without minimizing. He bore witness without defense. He did not demand healing as proof of worthiness. He did not require progress as a condition for love.

This kind of acceptance is rare. Most trauma survivors never receive it. Most are tolerated, managed, fixed, corrected, or abandoned the moment their coping mechanisms become inconvenient.

But once someone accepts the worst thing about you, there is nothing left to hide behind.

That is where reckoning begins.

Not a dramatic reckoning. Not a cinematic one. A quiet one. The kind that forces a person to confront the interior truth of who they became in order to survive. The kind that demands dignity be restored not through forgetting, but through acknowledgment. The kind that says you are not broken for hurting like this.

Trauma does not disappear when love arrives.

Love does not rewrite history.

Love does not absolve harm.

Love simply says, you do not have to carry it alone anymore.

Zora's healing does not conclude neatly. Damian's guilt does not resolve cleanly. The family's reckoning does not close every wound. This is not that kind of story. Healing is not linear. Recovery is not guaranteed. Attachment is frightening. Abandonment echoes long after truth is spoken. Grief lingers even in safe spaces.

But something irreversible has occurred.

The secret no longer rules.

What once lived in silence now lives in daylight. And daylight changes the shape of things. It reveals the cost of deflection. It exposes the fragility of false safety. It invites courage where shame once reigned.

Trauma flinches.

Love stays.

And staying is an act of defiance against everything trauma taught the body to expect.

This is not a story about purity.

It is a story about permission.

Permission to feel.

Permission to grieve.

Permission to love without certainty.

Permission to exist without hiding.

Sacred secrets lose their power the moment they are faced in truth. Because what is faced in truth can no longer rule in silence.

For all inquiries write us at:
Prison Empire Publishing / Second Chance Publishing

PrisonEmpirePublishing@protonmail.com

PrisonEmpirePublishing.com

You can reach us 2ndChancePublishing@gmail.com, if you're an incarcerated individual looking to get your book published.

PRISON EMPIRE PUBLISHING

SECOND CHANCE PUBLISHING EST. 2021

CHECK OUT OUR OTHER BOOKS:

www.prisonempirepublishing.com
Amazon.com
Barnes & Noble
IngramSpark.com

CONNECT WITH US

PrisonEmpirePublishing@protonmail.com

www.ingramcontent.com/pod-product-compliance
Lightning Source LLC
LaVergne TN
LVHW052021200926
848481LV00005B/1546
* 9 7 9 8 2 9 5 6 3 2 0 9 9 *